Irishmen in the Great War
1914-1918

Irish Newspaper Stories

1914

Irishmen in the Great War
1914-1918

Irish Newspaper Stories
1914

Edited by
Tom Burnell

Pen & Sword
MILITARY

First published in Great Britain in 2014 by
PEN & SWORD MILITARY
an imprint of
Pen & Sword Books Ltd,
47 Church Street, Barnsley,
South Yorkshire.
S70 2AS

Copyright © Tom Burnell 2014

ISBN 978 1 47382 120 0

A CIP catalogue record for this book is available
from the British Library

Designed by Factionpress

Pen & Sword Books Ltd incorporates the imprints of
Pen & Sword Aviation, Pen & Sword Maritime,
Pen & Sword Military, Pen & Sword Select, Pen & Sword
Military Classics, Leo Cooper, Wharncliffe Local History

For a complete list of Pen & Sword titles please contact:
PEN & SWORD BOOKS LIMITED
47 Church Street, Barnsley, South Yorkshire, S70 2AS, England.
E-mail: enquiries@pen-and-sword.co.uk
Website: www.pen-and-sword.co.uk

CONTENTS

FOREWORD by *Kevin Myers*

What a sobering, saddening and enlightening thing it is, to read the breathless newspaper accounts of the early stages of a war that no-one, absolutely no-one, had the least idea would still be underway, but now ten times as savage, in four more years' time. All the naivety of everyone – the soldiers, the newspaper reporters and the readers – would soon be lost, never to be recovered by European civilisation, even to this day. Yet even as they stand, at the dawn of the worst war that the world had the known, these stories of death and bereavement are deeply moving. But such loss as these pages relate was not the prelude to wisdom and cessation, but simply to more of the same, with a fearsome, gathering intensity, until finally much of the globe was caught up in the Holocaust.

Journalism does more than relate what the writer wants to convey, but also – and usually, unintentionally but every bit as importantly – the culture, myths and the expectations of both his subject and his audience. In the early despatches of the war, Irish soldiers are routinely referred to as 'devil-may-care', as the caricature that was established in Wellington's armies continued into the imperial wars in India – pace Kipling – and had been reinforced during the Boer War, again reappeared. Caricature within groups is of course often self-replicating. Irish soldiers, especially of Catholic peasant stock, and certainly in the early period of the Great War, often tried to live up to the cliché-expectations made of them. Indeed, twenty-five years on, Sam McAughtry, a Belfast Presbyterian, found the Irish broth-of-a-boy expectation of him after he joined the RAF quite a challenge (if an enjoyable one) to live up to.

Irish soldiers in these early reports repeatedly re-employed the vocabulary born of imperial soldiering, in which the enemy were usually not a match for the their fighting spirit. 'They cannot stand the bayonet', declared one voice from the Front, as if that were the decisive weapon of the war, rather than being a largely irrelevant inheritance that would have little use in the coming years, save against the already-helpless and surrendering. Another staples of war, the 'spy', makes his early appearance here. An Irish soldier reports that a Belgian baker was often seen behaving strangely. Only after the Irish had moved on did they hear that the baker was found to have been sending carrier-pigeon messages to the Germans, and was shot. Yet another unfortunate local was said to be in possession of important Belgian military documents, and duly met the same fate. How either man got his pigeons or his documents, we do not hear; and I suspect both stories are part of the Apocrypha of War.

Yet, we see in these pages some reincarnations, within the popular imagination, of the kind of technological fantasising that H.G. Wells had made the staple of his fiction before the war. We read of a new explosive, 'melinite', perfected by a Mr Turpin, which, when exploded above a flock of 400 sheep, left no survivors. And when tried upon German trenches, it killed all those in its path. An American Red Cross man is quoted as saying: 'I saw the German trenches as the French guns left them. They were filled with dead in such posture as the world has never seen since the destroying angel passed above the Philistine camp in that avenging night of Scripture. It was as though some blight from heaven had fallen upon them. They stood in line, rifles to shoulder, a silent company of ghosts in the grey light of dawn. I approached them. There was no horror in their faces, no anger of surprise even. Only over them was a film of fine, greyish powder. You would have said that they had travelled a long and dusty road. I have seen men before who had died from asphyxiation, but here was no sign of the agonising struggle for breath. It was as if a deep and sudden sleep had overtaken them – only their eyes were open. They might have been there from all eternity thus, their rifles at rest. I felt that if I touched them they would crumble into dust. Never have I seen anything more terrible than these erect, silent figures in the chill dawn.'

As fantastic – quite literally – was the 'Secret War Plan' of the Early of Dundonald, which was expected, quite inexplicably, to bring the war to a hasty conclusion. The report declared its details to be 'well known', so much so that it gives none. A recent Italian experiment, we are similarly told, revealed that an electrical shock could kill all enemy soldiers over several square miles of battlefield. And a 'Mr Hudson Maxim', inventor of the 'silent rifle', had perfected a device for covering the enemy's share of the battlefield with sulphuric acid gas, thus immobilising him. Never mind, firstly, that the gentleman was actually named Hiram Maxim, and secondly that he had not invented such a weapon; we now know that poison gas, based on hydrochloric rather than sulphuric acid, was just seven months away from making its abominable appearance.

Nothing quite matches the shock of the new. 'When a few weeks ago news came through that duels had been fought in the air between aeroplanes, everybody was surprised,' declared one article. 'The actual fighting is done by the passenger.' Is it any wonder, with so much that was unexpected bursting upon the world, that we here read of a group of boatmen on the Irish Sea beholding and following 'a sea-monster'?

Amid all the deadly innocence and beguiling murderousness of the time, we can still hear the authentic voice of the Irish countryman, such as the lamentations of Private Smith of the Irish Guards.. 'There was a big herd of cattle on the farm, and it was as pretty a sight as one could see. During the night the Germans shelled the farmhouse and buildings, which caught fire. In the morning the soldiers went to the smouldering ruins, and in the cattle sheds they (stet) were horrified to discover that all the cattle – numbering in all 140 – had been burned to death. At some of the stalls it was clear that the animals had made desperate attempts to get their liberty.'

Private Smith, as the author reveals in one of his many sterling, scholarly interpolations, was himself to die of wounds in 1916. By that time, of course, he was a veteran of the front. The first Irish soldier killed on active service in the war didn't even make that far: Private James Ryan, of Stoneyford, County Kilkenny, was killed by an apparently blacked-out train while on sentry duty, guarding the bridge to Fota 19 August, 1914.

War, and rumours of war, abounded in the news pages of the time, as testified to by Private John O'Gorman, Royal Irish Regiment. 'Dear Brother,' he wrote, 'You must excuse me for not writing before now, but I was very busy marching day and night. We have been through very heavy fighting. The first fight we were in we lost 5 officers and over 500 men. At the battle of Mons there were the Royal Irish, the Gordon Highlanders, Royal Scots, and the Middlesex Regiment, 4,000 strong, against 42,000 Germans. Now our regiment is 302 strong out of 1,020. I am not allowed to mention what part of the country I am in. We are resting now for a day or two, after marching over 200 miles. I and the brother are all right and getting on well, thank God. We have escaped without a wound, although we have been in every battle the regiment was engaged in. I would be very thankful if you would send me a paper with news of the war in it.'

There you have it; a report from the front, professing to know even the size of the Germany army to the nearest thousand (not 40 or 45,000, but 42,000) and still asking for news. Happily, this veteran of the retreat from Mons appears to have survived the war – yet almost the only testimony from his generation of Irish soldiers was that recorded by such letters from the front, or interviews with them on leave or in hospitals in the UK, which then made their way into the local newspapers of Ireland. However hyperbolically presented they were in their original form, these now form an absolutely invaluable insight into both the facts and the myths of the time. They thereby constitute an extremely important resource which, if used properly, can give us a powerful understanding of how the war was both experienced and perceived. For many decades, the story of the Irish soldier in the Great War was largely a guilty secret, within the publicly unspoken memories of their families. The veil of ignorance is now being lifted and here, for the first time in nearly a century, we get a comprehensive depiction of how Irish newspapers reported on the lives of the Irish regular soldier at the Front, against a backdrop at home of almost semi-hysteria. For this quite monumental achievement, we owe the author a profound debt of gratitude.

ACKNOWLEDGEMENTS

I would like to thank the following good hearted and tolerant people, without who's help and patience this project would not have been possible:

Mr Kevin Myers, Journalist and Historian, Dublin; Mrs Ruth Burnell, Holycross, Tipperary; Mr Jimmy Taylor (Historian and Author); Miss Kathlene Burnell, Dublin; Mrs Margaret Gilbert, Knockbrandon, County Wexford. Mr Seamus Burnell, Tombreane, County Wicklow; Mr Paul Burnell, Maynooth, County Kildare; Mrs Michelle Malone-Burnell Maynooth, County Kildare. Mr Patrick Burnell, Maynooth, County Kildare.

Mr Greg Burnell, Dunshaughlin, County Meath; Ms Mary Guinan Darmody and Mr John O'Gorman, Thurles Library; Mr Peter Beirne, Ennis Local Studies, Ennis Library, County Clare; Carmel Flahavan, Carlow Central Library. Mr Peter Beirne, Clare County Library; Mr Michael Lynch, Kerry County Library. Aisling Kelly, Kilkenny Library; Marguerite Gibson and Amanda Hyland of the Local Studies Section of the Library in Portlaoise. Mr Mick Shanahan (Military Historian, Ardroe, Pallasgreen); Mr Paschal Sage (Royal British legion); Mr Philip Lecane (Author of *'Torpedoed! The RMS* Leinster *Disaster*); Miss Rosemary Edwards of the County Library in Tullamore; Ciarán Reilly, Edenderry Historical Society, Kildare; Jimmy Taylor, Wexford Town, Tipperary; Etta Coman and Sinéal O'Higgins of the Waterford City Library; Ger Croughan, Dungarvan Central Library; Gordon Power, Waterford; Eddie Sullivan, Waterford; Emmet Kennedy, Kilnagrange, Kilmac; Thomas and Terry Denham of the Commonwealth War Graves Commission. Athlone: Gearoid O'Brien, Senior Executive Librarian; Mae McLynn, Executive Librarian; Aine O'Regan, Senior Library Assistant; Anne McDermott, Library Assistant; Kathleen Cleary, Library Assistant; Elsie Prendergast, Library Assistant; Lorraine Dockery, Library Assistant (Aidan Heavey Library) Mullingar Library; James Elliffe Library Staff; Cailin Gallagher, Executive Librarian; Gretta Connell, Senior Library Assistant; Edel Olcese, Senior Library Assistant; Catherine Heaney, Library Assistant; Anne Byrne, Library Assistant; Breda Fallon, Branch Librarian; Hazel Percival, Wexford Town Library.

Tadhg Carey, Editor, *Westmeath Independent*; *Kings County Independent*; Mr Brian Keyes, Editor, *Kilkenny People*. Mr Brian O'Loughlin, *Westmeath Examiner*; Derek Fanning (Deputy Editor), *Midland Tribune*; Mr Johnny O'Connor, Editor, *The Munster Express*, Mr Michael Dundon, Editor, *The Tipperary Star*; Mr Conor O'Boyle, *Carlow Sentinel/Carlow Nationalist*.

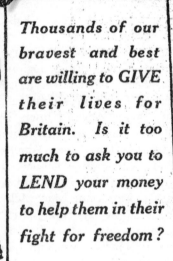

August to December

AUGUST

Bombarded from the Sky
Soldier Killed on Railway
Famous War Songs
Huge Guns of War
Irish Giant Soldiers
Kilkee Man's Letter from the Front
Looking For Gold
Prophetic Article
What Aeroplanes Will Do in the War
What the Galloping Kitchen Does
Why it Rains After a Battle

SEPTEMBER

An Awful Sight
Bullets in the Brain
Cost of the War
German Mines
Guns by the Inch and Pound
How Cossacks Fight
Learning to use the Bayonet
Letter from Waterfordman
Mines in the Open Sea
On Active Service
Piercing Steel a Yard Thick
Putting Armies to Sleep
Soldiers With Charmed Lives
The Brutality of War
The Submarine
What a Battlefield looks like
What's in an Aim?
Will Your Soldier Boy Return
Wounded on the field
Wounded Soldiers in Callan

OCTOBER

All about actions of the forward line and of the rear
A Tale from the Trenches
About a Rifle

An Old Campaigner Gives Useful Hints
Carrickman's Experience
Clonmel Man's Narrow Shave
Diabolical War Plans
Dodging the Shells
German Prisoners At Templemore
How Airmen Fight Duels
In the Trenches. (2)
Irish Rifleman's Adventures
Leinster Officers Letter
Methods of Advance That are Irresistible
Royal Irish at the front
Sky Pointing Cannon and Aircraft
Testing the Guns
The Awful Invention
The Enemy's Sugar
The Munster Fusiliers
The Post in War
The Torpedo
The War and Wild Game
This Ship for Sale
Those Silent Orders
Up-to-date War Dodges
Watching a Battle from the Air
Waterford Soldier's Story
With a Routed Army
Wounded Irish Guardsman Returns to Birr

NOVEMBER

A Gurkha Charge
Are big guns tested before being used in battle- and if so, how?
A Waterford Merry with the French Army
Are Sheds for Zeppelins Easily Constructed?
Back From Douai
Ballyhale Soldier's Experience
Boy Labour
Carrick-on-Suir Lady's Thrilling Experience at Liege
Clara Rangers Story
Clareman's Letter from the Front
Elephants as Work-Horses
From Catapult to Cordite
German Dead, Furnaces Kept burning
Getting Food to the Trenches
Giant Gun's That Shatter Steel like Tin Cans

December

August, 1914

Bombarded from the Sky
A Night of Horrors – Antwerp, 25 August 1914

I have just lived through the most tragic night of the war. For the first time in history a great civilised community has been bombarded from the sky in the darkness of night. Count Zeppelin, whom the Kaiser called the greatest genius of the century, has performed the greatest exploit of his life. He may well be proud of his achievement. 1 he has mangled and slaughtered non-belligerent men, women, and children. He has thrown bombs on hospitals where the Belgians were tending German wounded; he has staggered humanity. On August 5 the German commander warned General Leman at Liege that if the forts did not surrender the Zeppelin fleet would not move at once. The forts of Liege did not surrender, and the Germans have been as good as their word. They have surpassed themselves in the art of striking terror, and they have placed themselves outside the pale of humanity.

I was awakened at one o'clock this morning by a frightful cannonade. A Zeppelin had been sighted about 700 feet above the town. I at once went out into the streets. I have scarcely left the scene of the catastrophe. I my calculation there are about 900 houses slightly damaged and about 60 houses nearly destroyed. The number of victims is unknown. In a single house I found four dead; one room was a chamber of horrors, the remains of the mangled bodies being scattered in every direction. In the house opposite a husband and wife, whose only son had just died in battle, were killed--a whole family wiped out. It is significant that the Zeppelin bombs were well aimed at public buildings, at the barracks, at the Government offices, and especially at the Royal Palace.

I was given by the King's Secretary two fragments of a bomb that had been found afterwards, from the Palace. In order that all the Governments of Europe ad America should be informed from ocular evidence about this great German crime, in order that the whole diplomatic corps might issue a joint protest against this outrage to the law of the nations, I prevailed on the following to accompany me through the town; The Under-Secretary of Foreign Affairs, baron von der Elswtoq, the Papal Nuncio, the Russian Ambassador, Prince Pougatchef; the Ministers of State, Vandervelde, the

King's Secretary, they were all terror-stricken. Prince Pougatchef was so horrified that he refused to follow me into the chamber of horrors. The population is in gloom.

The Zeppelin tragedy eclipses for the moment even the great battle which is being fought in Brahant and Hainau. Dr Sarolea. TS, 08-1914

Soldier Killed on Railway

On the Great Southern and Western Railway at Fota Bridge, not far from Queenstown, a private of the Royal Irish regiment, names James Ryan, aged 20, a native of Kilkenny, was killed on the permanent way whilst on protection duty. An engine struck him, tearing away the back portion of his head, and knocking him close to the rails, where he died. At the inquest on Thursday a verdict of accidental death was returned, and the jury recommended the next of kin to the kind consideration of the military authorities and the railway company.   LC, 08-1914

The soldier who was Private James Ryan, Royal Irish Regiment, born in Kilkenny. See 'Soldier Killed on Railway'(WN, 01-1915) for more information on a court case regarding his death.

Famous War Songs

Where there is song there is victory. We read that English troops on arrival in France sang that idiotic music hall ditty with its smutty references 'A Long Way to Tipperary'. Have we any Irish song of vigorous patriotic sentiment set to music to sweep one away, to carry men along with new hope, putting new spring into their tired limbs, and lift with exultation the heart that is beginning to droop? Certainly 'A Nation Once Again' is not a rousing song. It is a dirge. Happy is the army which goes oj singing longest for where there is song there is victory. 'Let no one think that a great war hymn is a mere literary exercise. It is far more than that. It is a living thing. When nations are stirred to their depths they may be more moved to frenzy by the song or the hymn which suddenly is found to be what for fault pf a better word, we call inspired. Think of some of the songs which have stirred nations to their very soul. Can anyone compute to what extent the 'Marseillaise' has helped to shape the course of the world's history? Its author was no great musician. Rouget de Lisle hardly knew enough music to be able to put down the notes on paper. But the miracle of inspiration was accomplished in an hour or two, and the strains, which breathe the very soul of revolutionary longing are now the National Anthem of France. The famous deputation from Marseillas sang it as they entered Paris in 1792; the Army of the Revolution sang it at Valmy and Jemappes; and their great grandsons are singing it this very day on the battlefields of Belgium. As little can one imagine French soldiers without the 'Marseillaise' as the Italian army singing other war-hymn when it moves to battle than the

Hymn to Garibaldi, 'Si scopron le tombe,' to the strains of which the immortal Thousand overthrew the throne of King Bomba. It is the great patriotic song of the Italian nation, and their whole soul rushes to their lips as they sing So with the two superb national songs of Germany, Schneckenburger's 'Die Wacht am Rhein,' and Fallersleben's 'Deutschland, Deutschland uber alles' – that the legions of the Kaiser have marched at his call. Both date from about 1840; both were inspired by the passionate desire to keep German the left bank of the Rhine.   TS, 08-1914

Huge Guns of War
Siege Guns Which Fire One-Ton-Shells

The extraordinary advance made in the science of warfare in recent years is in no way better illustrated than the matter of siege guns, such as were used by the Germans to subdue the Liege and Namur Fortresses. The mediaeval cannon was clumsy, made of iron bars looped together with iron rings and projecting stones; this ineffective engine was discarded in favour of bronze 'bombards' and cast iron connonades. To-day, however, the siege gun is a cumbrous mass of steel or wrought-iron, weighing anything from 40 tons to 150 tons. The largest are capable of firing a shell weighing practically 1 ton, and with sufficient force to penetrate wrought iron at a distance of 1, 000 yards to a depth of nearly 2 feet. While some are sighted for a range of five miles, and at that distance may be relied upon to strike an object 10ft high, in actual battle, fire would rarely be opened at a greater range than about two miles owing to atmospheric and other difficulties. Even under the most favourable conditions the bringing up of siege guns and the placing of them in position is a Herculean task of transport and engineering.

A Herculean Task
The enormous engines of war have to be hauled up steep mountains and placed on a solid bed of concrete. The labour such a step requires is about equal to that of erecting a large machinery plant. When in position, the gun is hidden by earth-works thrown up around it and screened by brush-wood. Adapted for high angle-rife, its heavy shells can be thrown over any outworks and directly upon the place intended to be attacked. All these preparations involve immense trouble and often much loss of life from the enemy's fire, but one a siege gun is in position, even the strongest fortified place is bound to suffer severely.   TS, 08-1914

Irish Giant Soldiers

Three giant sons of Mr William A Jones, Clerk of Hacketstown Petty Sessions, have joined the Army since the outbreak of the war. They are: Lieutenant Robert, R. E., height 6 ft 3 ? inches; Corporal W. J., North Irish

Horse, height 6 ft 2 ? inches; Private Richard, Canadian Volunteers, 6 ft 0 ? inches. Their grandfather was 6 ft 5 inches.   KCC, 1915

Robert and William survived the war, Richard was killed in action in May-1915.

The following is taken from *The Scotsman* in its issue of 22 November 1914. Private Smith came from Seskinrea, Leighlinbridge.

Irish Guardsman's Battle Stories
The Fighting around Mons

Private John Smith, 1st Battalion, Irish Guards, who is at present recovering from a shrapnel wound received in the recent fighting at Ypres, tells an interesting story. Private Smith arrived at Deaconess Hospital, Edinburgh, on Saturday. He has been at the front since the beginning of the war.

He took part in the trying times at Mons, the retreat, the recovery, the fierce battles of the Marne. He was at the 'siege' of the Aisne, and latterly he was in the fighting at Ypres, and Ypres, according to Private Smith and several other soldiers who took part in the operations at that place, was the worst of the lot. For 15 days Private Smith was in the trenches. He described a particularly fierce German attack, the issue, which for some time hung in the balance, being decided, as frequently happens, by 'cold steel'.

'On the 8th November,' said Private Smith, 'the Germans started shelling our trenches about eight o'clock in the morning. They kept hard at it for hours, and then the infantry came forward to the attack in great masses. It was terrific. The French were in the trenches next our regiment, and the Germans broke through their lines at several points. This made it necessary for us to retire to a new position, and in doing so we lost a lot of our men. We formed up, however, and went at them with the bayonet. But it was no use; there were far too many of them. We fell back again, and just then the 2nd Life Guards came on the scene. That decided it. They put in their bayonets and made a tremendous charge, driving the Germans back, and taking 200 prisoners. Our losses were heavy, but for every one we lost it is certain the Germans lost twenty.'

The Prussian Guards.

On two occasions Private Smith came up against the German 'crack' corps, the Prussian Guard. There is no doubt, he says, that the Prussian Guard is a superior soldier to any other corp in the German Army. They are picked men, many of them, if not the majority, six feet high, and strongly built. 'A finer body of men,' said Private Smith, 'it would be hard to find. They are very plucky, and they seem to be a better class of men altogether, intellectually and physically. When they come to the attack they give tremendous shouts, and they come forward in oped order, and not in masses, as is generally the case.'

One case of treachery came under Private Smith's notice. While his regiment was at Soupier, the bread was supplied to the troops by a local baker. This man came under suspicion, and he was subsequently arrested. Nothing could be proved against him, however, and he was liberated. When the British left, the place was occupied by French troops, who were warned to keep the baker under observation. On the first day that the French arrived the baker was discovered endeavouring to send information to the enemy by means of pigeons. He was shot.

An Exciting Encounter

It was at Soupier that Private Smith and a 'chum' had a narrow escape. 'We were fighting at the edge of a wood,' said Private Smith. 'The Germans were some distance in front. Presently some Germans showed themselves carrying a white flag. But we had been so often 'had' with that dodge that the officer told us to keep on firing, which we did. Shortly afterwards we got the order to advance, and crossing a field we came upon a crowd of Germans, Some of us fixed bayonets and charged, and a number of the Germans put up their hands. We disarmed them and sent them into a wood. We then crossed over a small hollow, and climbed a slope, and at the other side we ran into another crowd of Germans. My chum and I were somewhat detached, and three Germans came straight at us. One was an officer with a revolver, and the other two had fixed their bayonets. One of the soldiers made a lunge at me, but I caught his bayonet and put him out with a knock on the head. When I was engaged with this fellow the second German came at me with his bayonet, but before he got close my chum ran his bayonet through him. The officer fired on us with his revolver; missed us, but one of the bullets hit one of several Grenadier Guards who were coming to our aid. We captured the officer. Some time after this we had to lie five hours in a turnip field. We got between the enemy and our own men, and there was a hot rifle fire from both sides. We lay there till dusk, when the Grenadiers advanced. One of our men was shot while we were lying in the field.'

Cattle Roasted to Death

One of the most affecting sights which Private Smith saw was at a farm near Soupier. There was a big herd of cattle on the farm, and it was as pretty a sight as one could see. During the night the Germans shelled the farmhouse and buildings, which caught fire. In the morning the soldiers went to the smouldering ruins, and in the cattle sheds they were horrified to discover that all the cattle – numbering in all 140 – had been burned to death. At some of the stalls it was clear that the animals had made desperate attempts to get their liberty.

Private Smith said that the health of the men in the trenches was very good notwithstanding their privations. This was entirely owing to the precautions that were taken. There was practically no fever, which we believed was very prevalent in the German trenches.   NLT, 08-1914

John Smith died of wounds in May-1916 and is buried in Lincolnshire.

Kilkee Man's Letter from the Front
'Stood our Ground to the Last'

Lance Corporal Edward Twomey, a Kilkee man, to his mother.

'We have had some very hot fighting. We were in the thick of it all the time. Our regiment was posted to cover the retreat for five days, and the Germans were as thick as bees around us all the time. When you are put on duty of that kind there's no question of giving way until your task has been completed, and we stood our ground until the last. That meant in some cases that we had to be cut up, but we were selected because we could be relied on to make the best possible show and delay the enemy as long as possible. '

'Some of our detachments had rough luck in every way, but they carried themselves with a steadiness that won them praise from everybody, and they made the Germans realise that they weren't going to have it all their own way.

'The Germans were furious over the stand our chaps made. They had never expected anything of the sort, and though they kept out of the way when we were anything approaching their strength, they were very brave about rushing us when our ammunition ran out and our weakness in numbers was obvious.

'They didn't reckon on the bayonets, and when we received them that way you may guess there was a nice howl all round.

'General French has thanked us for the way we behaved, and praise from him is worth a great deal more than from any other men. He is not in a hurry to say nice things about us, but when he does speak, we know he means every word of it, and maybe more. That's the way to get round the soldiers.'   (CJ, 08-1914)

Looking For Gold

There is a good story going the rounds and there is some foundation for it. The story runs that a lunatic in a certain Munster asylum kept continually telling the attendants that 'long ago when he was mad' (before he came to the asylum) he had hidden 200 sovereigns near a bridge in a locality well-known to may of our readers. The story continues that last week two attendants and two police, accompanied by the lunatic as director of operations, went in quest of the gold. When they reached the spot the lunatic calmly said, 'Tis you who must be mad – not me. ' The golden tale was a myth.   (TS, 08-1914)

Prophetic Article

An article published two years ago from the pen of Mr Hilaire Belloc, a famous Catholic writer, has been quoted in the English *Times* as one of the most astonishingly accurate forecasts of a great war, in the history of journalism. The keynote of the article is contained in a sentence which foretold that 'a siege of Liege would be the first imperative necessity imposed upon the Germans at the outset of the campaign. When Mr Belloc wrote his remarkable article Germany was on the brink of war with France and Great Britain and he endeavoured first to show that, as Liege could neither be neglected nor carried, it would have to be reduced; and to prevent this reduction would be the whole business of Anglo-French forces advancing from the direction of the sea towards the lower line of the Marne. The article went on to show how the Germans were likely to be beaten.   (TS, 08-1914)

What Aeroplanes Will Do in the War

By B. C. Hucks, the Famous looping-the-loop Airman who has just joined the Royal Flying Corps as a second lieutenant.

There is little doubt that the big European war which is now in progress will prove in no uncertain fashion the value of the aeroplane as a dangerous factor on warfare. For it happens that each big Power involved in the struggle is in a position to place in the field a number of the latest type of military machines, piloted by trained airmen and carrying observers. Germany, if anything, are ahead of France in aeronautical matters. They have perhaps a round dozen of big dirigible balloons which can manoeuvre for long periods at night time, and thus have an advantage over aeroplanes, which can in the ordinary way be safely used only during daylight. On the other hand, these dirigibles have many disadvantages. They have to be given their daily feed of hydrogen, an expensive item; they need a large landing party to assist them when starting and alighting. They are almost unmanageable in bad weather, and they present an easy target to hostile artillery unless they are flying at a great altitude. Being covered by light coloured fabric they can be detected easily during night time by search-lights. But Germany has also a tremendously strong fleet of aeroplanes, which will probably be of more use to her than her airships. One estimate places her fleet of heavier than air machines at over seven hundred strong. Neither France nor any other nation can muster this number.

They Won't do Big Things

With regard to what aeroplanes will actually do during the war, I do not anticipate that they will achieve any big coup. We must not overlook the fact that aeroplanes are still in the experimental stage for general flying did not commence until five years ago. The effect this war will have on aircraft, however, will be to provide much invaluable data concerning the value of aeroplanes in warfare. I think aeroplanes will prove most useful for scouting purposes. The moral effect of a fleet of aeroplanes hovering over the enemy's camp is an aspect which should not be overlooked. The enemy harassed in this manner know that their exact position is revealed to the other side and they know that at any moment they may be surrounded unawares. Then, again, they expect bombs to be dropped on to them at any moment, and both these demoralising factors are. I think sufficient to throw a military squad into a state approaching panic.   (TS, 08-1914).

What the Galloping Kitchen Does

Since the army marches on its stomach, the greatest battle of all involves the greatest catering feat of all times. Two millions of men along the frontiers of France must be fed, or they cannot fight. They must be fed with bread and meat ad vegetables, and kept supplied with water. Every German and every Frenchman among them is, besides, entitled daily to over an ounce of coffee and to a share of sugar and salt.

5, 000 Cattle a Day

The scale of rations in the different armies varies, but on the rough military assumption that one ox feeds 400 men these will consume 5, 000 head of cattle every day. They will consume something approaching four million gallons of water. These are the barest necessities. Then for each horse the allowance is twelve pounds of corn or its equivalent, and from five to ten gallons of water. And the cattle and sheep for slaughter must be considered, for unless they are kept in condition the yield of meat will suffer. For a time, of course, the troops will live on the country through which they are passing. When that is eaten bare each army will depend on its own base. Then will come the test of the commissariat with its effect on the fortune and duration of the war.

The military base may be described as the heart of the supplies system – it radiates energy through a network of channels to the body and limbs of the army in front. We may see the manner in which it works by considering what would happen in the case of a British Expeditionary Force being sent to the Continent. The base then would be established at the port of landing. It would be formed before the arrival of troops and would be stocked with several months supplies. As far as possible stores would be sent by railway.

From the railway they would be taken on to depots along the line of communication by motor lorry. Every depot would gather in supplies from the surrounding country as long as they lasted – cattle, corn and hay would be purchased and baker's and butcher's portable places set up. The transport would be done by stages, at a sufficiently fast pace to keep several day's supplies immediately accessible at the temporary field depots in the area of actual fighting.

The defence of the line of communication is, of course, the first consideration. Great Britain is not without experience in this matter, for in many of her campaigns the line of communications has had to be maintained across great wastes of country where no food was available. In the Afghan campaign in the early eighties, between Kabul and Peshawar, a distance of 160 miles, 15, 000 men were guarding the communications, while 12, 000 were engaged in fighting.

Now if the German commissariat proves unequal to the huge strain imposed upon it, it may be that the German war lords will have to deal not only with France and Belgium on the west, and Russia on the east, but that a new trouble will arise midway between the two.   (TS, 08-1914)

Why it Rains After a Battle

These heavy downpours have more than once helped to make history. It is one of the extraordinary things of warfare that a big battle invariably produces torrents of rain. History contains innumerable instances, both on land and sea, and on more than one occasion the storm or showers that followed an engagement had no small influence upon the life of nations. We can hardly have a better example that that recorded in 1588, when England was threatened by the great Spanish Armada. After its encounter with our own fleet, it was, as we all know, struck by a heavy storm, which completed the work of our own gallant seamen.

The soldiers who fought so bravely under the leadership of Marlborough at Blenheim in the year of 1704 had to suffer the misery of successive downpours after their brilliant victory. Marlborough was anxious to follow up his victory without delay, but his men were so worn by the fatigue of the battle and the discomfort caused by heavy rains that he was unable to push on for several days.

On June,. 1815, the British defeated the French at Quatre Bras, and Napoleon worsted the wily Blucher at Ligny, both within measurable distance of Waterloo. The heavy rains which followed made the clayey soil almost impossible for cavalry manoeuvres at Waterloo (fought on June 18th), and so crippled the tactics of Napoleon. During the early weeks of the siege of Sebastopol in 1854, the roar of cannon and explosion of bombs was followed, day by day by heavy downpours of rain, until, as we read, men stood in the trenches knee-deep in mud. A terrible gale broke over the Black Sea and caused great disaster to transports, and on the heels of this tempest came a heavy, steady downfall of rain that brought death to hundreds of gallant fellows.

In yet another instance the heavy cannonading of a siege brought in its train a disturbance of the elements. This was just prior to the fall of Plevna, in 1877, when the moisture of the clouds was turned to snow as it fell, and, by increasing the sufferings of the besieged helped to make Osman come to the determination to try a last chance for freedom.

The explanation of the rain is simple, and has been made use of for the benefit of agriculture in various parts of the world. The atmosphere is laden with moisture, a concussion caused by loud reports or noises will often burst the clouds, with the natural result that the drops of water fall to the earth. This has been tested when farmers have been groaning over the drought, and scientists have induced the desired rainfall by causing cannon to be discharged at altitudes varying with the locality. When, however, the discharge is continuous, as in battle, it is obviously more effective.   (TS, 08-1914)

September, 1914

Some Officer Casualties

Major Pack-Beresford, Kents, who was killed, was a Carlowman. The late Major Brooke, Temporary Lieutenant Colonel since 1907 in India, was a son of the late Sir V. Brooke, Colebrooke, Fermanagh. Captain Creswell, reported killed, an all-round sportsman, and well-known at Belfast, as were also Lieutenants Leishman, Openshaw, Oakes, Margetts, and Paget. Captan Lutherm killed, was prominent in Irish cricket this year, having assisted the Garrison and Leinster teams. He was aSussex County man, Lieutenants Oliphant and Earle played for Monkstown last year. Lieutenant Colonel M'Micking(sic), commanding the Royal Scots, was only slightly wounded, and he resumed. M. M'Micking, daughter of Duke de Stacpoole, has four brothers at the front, three in Irish regiments, and one in the Royal Artilery. The family of the late Major Stafford, of the Wellingtons, stationed in Dublin before the war, reside in Palmerstown Road. Captain Acroyf (killed) and Captain McDonald (missing) also resided in that district. Lieutenant Teeling, of the K.O.S.B. (missing), a son of Mr Teeling, Accountant General of the Irish High Court, is a Barrister who gave up law for military life. He was a member of the Dublin Repertoire Theatre Co., and appeared in several parts. The Army Medical Corps, non-combatants. Of course, has one doctor wounded and twelve missing. Captain Egan, one of the corps, is a Dungarvan man. Colonel Bond, D.S.O., reported as killed, got promotion while serving in Dublin with the Yorkshire Light Infantry.

Lieutenant Joynson, who is missing, was the owner of the horse who won the race at the last Curragh meeting, and was a constant rider to hounds with the Wards and Meaths. Mrs Joynson was presented at Dublin Castle the season before that. Major Chandon Leigh, also missing, was also known in Dublin society. (LC, 09-1914)

The Royal Irish Regiment
Casualties to Officers

Colonel St. John Cox, commanding the 2nd Royal Irish Regiment, who was in a London Hospital wounded, in a letter to a friend (published in the *Morning Post.*) says: 'The poor battalion suffered dreadfully. Our medical officer is a prisoner, and Mr Tandy has been wounded in the head, but is still doing duty. At Mons, we lost Captain Mellor, killed by a shell; Mr Gibbons, killed by machine-gun fire; Captain George, severely wounded in both legs; Captain Fitzgerald, wounded (these two had to be left of the field).

'Captain Forbes is missing, and no one knows what happened to him. Mr French is badly wounded in the shoulder. Mr Phillips, wounded; bullet remains in, Mr Shine, bullet wound in groin. Mr Guinness, several superficial wounds (these last four got into hospital at Mons, and are probably prisoners).

'Caudry casualties – Major St. Leger, missing, Major Panter-Downes, badly wounded, stomach; missing; Mr Anderson, missing; and Mr Magrath, missing, are prisoners.' This is the first news of the officers missing.   LC, 09-1914

Colonel St John Cox survived the war. 40 year old Brevet Major Panter-Downes, died of wounds at the Marne, September, 1914. He has no known grave and is listed on La Ferte-Sous-Jouarre Memorial in France. 23 year old Lieutenant Archdale Maurice Stratford Tandy, was killed in action a month after this article was published. He has no known grave but is listed on the Le Touret Memorial in France. His father was a Colonel in the Indian Army. 36 year old Captain Walton Mellor was killed in action a few weeks after the war began. He is buried in St Symphorien Military Cemetery in Belgium. 22 year old Second Lieutenant Charles Barry Gibbons died with Captain Mellor and is also buried in St Symphorien Military Cemetery in Belgium. 36 year old Major Ion Barry George, died in May-1918. He was a prisoner of war in Germany and is buried in Brookwood Military Cemetery, UK. No officers named Fitzgerald died with the Royal Irish Regiment. 32 year old Captain Fergus George Arthur Forbes (The Earl of Longford) died in the first month of the war and is buried in St Symphorien Military Cemetery in Belgium. 19 year old Dungarvan Officer Second Lieutenant John Denys Shine, died in the first month of the war. He is buried in Mons (Bergen) Communal Cemetery in Belgium. Second Lieutenant Eric Cecil Guinness, D.S.O. died in September-1920.

There were two officers named Phillips with the Royal Irish regiment who died in the war-Captain Edward George Dunscombe Phillips, died November, 1916 and Lieutenant Charles Ernest Phillips, died October, 1918).

From the Front
Tipperary Lady's Experience

The Battle of Liege

Big German Casualties

How Spies Are Treated

Interesting Account

Some interesting facts regarding the recent happenings in gallant Belgium were given to a Tipperary Press man on Friday by Miss M. J. Fitzgibbon, daughter of the Mayor of Clonmel (Alderman T. Fitzgibbon), who has recently returned from the south of Belgium. Miss Fitzgibbon says that the country is quite calm despite the awful crisis; that Business goes on at almost a normal condition, and that the army are grimly determined to defend the honour and independence of their country. She tells of acts of barbarity on the part of the Germans, who have fired on the Red Cross and the wounded. After hoisting a white flag they fired on the Belgian patrol, who went out from Liege to inquire the meaning of the flag of truce. She says the number of German casualties in the big battle at Liege was 43,000, 8,000 killed, and 37,000 wounded and prisoners, while the losses of the defenders were 3,000, and a proportionately small number killed. Miss Fitzgibbon says that the war has brought out a marked manner of religious fervour of the Belgians, who are a Catholic people. In all the churches where are special devotions with daily Mass offered up for the success of their cause. She says it is a most edifying sight to see both in the busy cities, and in the quiet little hamlets all the inhabitants, young and old, men and women, going to morning Mass and praying to the Saviour and his Blessed Mother to protect their beloved country, and she says with such a fervent, trustful appeal from a devout action to the Throne of God, the people are confident that God is with them, and strengthening the arms of their brave defenders, and they have implicit confidence that their just claim will prevail. The Belgians have taken every precaution to guard against their enemies getting information of their secrets or movements.

There is absolute censorship on all communications. All men employed on or about the railways are sworn to absolute secrecy as to the movements of troops. There are numerous German spies scattered through the country, but they are marked men, and are being quickly secured. No one is allowed at large without passports from the authorities. One German spy was caught concealed in a corn field with a fully equipped wireless telegraph apparatus. On being searched he was found to have a large quantity of gold and documents. He was tried and executed. Another, a workman, who had been in the employment of a Belgian gentleman for about fifteen years, was visited by the police. His employer was rather indignant that the man should be suspected, declaring he was most trustworthy. The police, however, insisted, and did so. On search and investigation being made, the man was found to be possessed of important secret papers belonging to the Belgian Government. The spy, for such they proved him, was shot.

LL, 09-1914

Mons and Cambrai
Mullingar Man's Vivid Description of Fighting at the Front

How He Was Wounded

A Fight Against the Odds

The 'Haunting Roar of the Cannon'

The first wounded soldier from the front from Mullingar district arrived here on Wednesday, in the person on Private Thomas Whelehan, Royal Inniskilling Fusiliers. Whelehan, who is only 27 years, and has a young wife and child, resides in Mullingar, and appeared on his arrival in excellent spirits. Interviewed, he gave some vivid and interesting details of the fighting at the front, in particular about the great battle of Mons:

'It was at Cambrai, exactly,' he said, 'that I received the wound which put me out of action. We started from Mons on the Sunday afternoon. We knew the enemy were in full strength, very much greater strength than our men. Myself and my comrades were on outpost duty, and about 2,30 were severely attacked by the Germans, who were immensely superior to us in point of numbers. Still, by desperate fighting we held the position in good style against the undoubted great odds of numbers till 6 p.m., when we were ordered to retire, fighting however, every inch was we went for a considerable distance. Then the enemy got through us, but it was a short-lived success, as reinforcements came up to us and beat them back. At Cambrai I was first personally acquainted to the enemy's attentions.

It was when my cap was just clipped off my head by a shot, and the next thing was two fingers of my right hand were badly mauled at the tips by a rifle shot. But it was later, when a dose of shrapnel came along and tore an ugly big wound in my right hip that I temporarily got out of touch with the dreadful doings around me. I had seen many of my comrades fall and now I got my own souvenir of the War. When I came to I dragged myself away with much pain as best I could, but after a little time one of our officers came up and had me attended to with other wounded and we were eventually taken to a Belgian war hospital by Red Cross Nuns and Christian Brothers. We weren't long in that place till it was shelled by the Germans, and we had to leave for another hospital. But the enemy shelled it, too. Later we were taken to Rouen, and thence to Brighton, where we arrived on 1 September.

Asked as to the character of the weather during his time at the front, Whelehan said it was mostly fine in the daytime, but rained in torrents at night. 'There was no such thing,' he said, in reply to a question, 'as continuous resting at night. We might get an odd rest for half an hour at a time, but no more.

'You asked,' he continued, 'whether the enemy were usually far from or near to us during the nights. Well, we could not know, but we were nearly always informed by a reminder of his whereabouts early after daybreak, the notice being in the form of shells. Yes,' he added, 'our men were fighting against terrible odds in numbers; there is no doubt of it.

The scenes were terrible on the field of battle and the actions fierce, but what most pressed me was the appalling, the haunting sound of the cannon. For a long time after, and even now at times, the indescribable roar and shaking of the extraordinary sound comes into my ears, and it was so, I believe, with others of us also.'

Private Whelehan, is a member of a respectable Mullingar family, and since his return has been visited by sympathetic friends of all classes.

WE, 09-1914

Private Thomas Whelehan later transferred to the Labour Corps and survived the war. His brother, Christopher of the Royal Irish Fusiliers was killed in action in April, 1915. He has no known grave but is listed on the Ploegsteert Memorial in Belgium. See also the following account, Mullingar Man Home from the Front.

Mullingar Man Home from the Front
The Battle of Mons

Graphic Description

Mr Thomas Whelehan, of the Royal Inniskilling Fusiliers, who was wounded at the battle of Mons, has just arrived home in Mullingar. Our representative had an interview with Mr Whelehan on Wednesday morning, and found him in excellent spirits. He was suffering from a shrapnel wound in the right hip and from bullet wounds in the hand. After inquiring as to the patients condition our representative said he would like to hear something more about the fighting at Mons, which had been described in the Press as terrific.

Mr Whelehan, cheerfully consenting, commenced by stating that they started from Mons on Sunday afternoon. They knew the enemy were in full strength. 'We were on out-post duty,' he continued, and about 2, 30 p.,., we were severely attacked by the Germans, who were immensely superior to us in numbers. We held the position against desperate fighting until ordered to retire at 6 p.m. we kept retiring and fighting for a considerable distance. The enemy got through us, but were beaten back again by reinforcements.

Mr Whelehan stated it was at Cambrai he got wounded, by shrapnel and was struck by bullets on the fingers. He and the other wounded were then taken to a Belgian hospital by Red Cross Nuns, and Christian Brothers. Thedy were not long there until the hospital, a temporary structure, was shelled. They had to leave, and the next hospital was also shelled. They were then brought to Rueon, and thence to Brighton, arriving in the latter place on 1st September.

Asked as to the nature of the weather, he said the days were fine, but it was almost constantly raining at night.

'Were you allowed to rest at night?' asked our representative.

'No,' he said, 'there is no such thing there as resting at night. We might get a rest for half an hour, but that is all.'

'Were the enemy far from you at night?' queried our representative.

'We could not know,' he said, 'but we always got a reminder of their presence early in the morning by shells. We were fighting against terrible odds.'

Mr Whelehan is son of the late Mr Thomas Whelehan, who for upwards of 30 years was in the employment of Dr J Dillon Kelly. He informed our representative he was progressing very favourably, but is still under medical treatment.

MR, WN, 09-1914

Private Thomas Whelehan later transferred to the Labour Corps survived the war. His brother, Christopher of the Royal Irish Fusiliers was killed in action in April, 1915. He has no known grave but is listed on the Ploegsteert Memorial in Belgium. See also Mons and Cambrai).

Irish Soldiers in the English Hospitals
Their Kind Treatment
Letter from old Athlonian

To the Editor. Dear Sir,

I think it might interest some of your readers to hear from an old inhabitant of Athlone something about the war our soldiers are treated in the hospitals prepared hurriedly for them in the South of England. I have been kindly allowed to visit some of these hospitals, my reason for gaining admission being that I have a son at the war. The hospital where I am at present visiting was, a few weeks ago a large school, three stories high, but it has been transformed into a most cheerful and delightful, all cheerful and bright with plants and flowers in profusion, rows of snowy-quilted beds hung with many trophies, as well as the flags of the Allies and Lord Kitchener's picture at the head.

The kindly nurses whole thought seems to be to make the patients happy and give them as good a time as possible. It is good to see how cheerful and happy these wounded heroes are. The great number of the patients are not suffering much, and the Wounds are nit of a serious nature—many being foot and leg wounds from shrapnel. A great proportion of the men can be up, and many can be about in the open space in the front of the hospital, where motor drives are arranged daily for those who can avail of them, and crowds are always outside waiting to see them off. We brought daily a great supply of illustrated dailies and magazines, all of which were eagerly seized on. We also brought pouches of tobacco and cigarettes, and they also seemed very welcome. The wounded chiefly came from Mons, and that locally, and thy stated that there was great difficulty in getting food there to eat. It was good to see the great dishes of roast chicken and custard puddings coming into the wards, fruit of all sorts, great baskets of peaches, fine grapes and apples, all sent in by neighbours to those brave men. When the men who were not much injured were able to be up selections from gramophones were played for them. I asked in each ward if there were many Irish there, and I found a great many from Munster, Dublin, the West and the North, all glad to shake hands with an Irishwoman, and did they not warm up when I was told them I was the mother of a soldier at the front, and 'God send him safe home' was the prayer that came from all their hearts. One fine looking guardsman, who was badly wounded in the leg, gave me some information as to the special service in which my son was engaged. I saw him reaching for something at the head of his bed, and at last he produced his service cap. Such a cap has rarely been seen, but it saved his life, for a bullet had glanced off the wire, while small was doubled up like a corkscrew. The head was slightly wounded, but the wire saved him from instant death, though these were six holes in other parts of it, and half the badge was shot away, and a piece of the peak was missing. How the man escaped is nothing short of a miracle. However, the poor fellow is cheery and bright, and longing to return again to the front. In the next bed was a man of the Munsters, who was vastly pleased to get a packet of tobacco, and showed us his little metal ration box full of Belgian tobacco, which did not look as good as good as ours. He explained how the ration box had three divisions in it, one for tea, one for sugar, and one for cocoa. We had brought this man a little gift last week, and I was much touched at his gratitude when he insisted on one of us taking his little ration box as a token of remembrance, as well as the tobacco that was in it. I could write much more about these brave men, but it would take up too much space. It would be a pleasure if the people saw for themselves the arrangements made for sending the sick and wounded soldiers to whom we owe so much, and to learn from one who lived for years in Athlone of the loving care bestowed on them during the weary hours they have to wait until they are fully recovered. No-one could go through the hospitals without being impressed with the fine courage and cheerful willingness to bear suffering and discomfort shown by all the patients—some of whom are very young, some the fathers of families, and all proud that the country recognises its soldiers, and so much it owes them. Notwithstanding the hardships the men suffered they seem to be in the best of health.

They say the kindness of the French was wonderful, that many flying from their burned homes, with very little food, insisting on giving all they had to the soldiers. They gave the soldiers all the fruit they possessed, and indeed it was on fruit they mostly lived before and after the terrible Battle of Mons. I felt the verse of Kipling's was very applicable to these men—for these men recking(sic) little of what they had to face, and only eager to go back to the same risks, needed no 'if' – for our troops have finely carried out his ideal:

> If you can force your heart and nerve and sinew
> To serve your town look after they are gone,
> And so hold on when there is nothing in you
> Except the will which says to them, 'Hold on.'
> As they have gone may they continue to go further
> From East to West, from South and North,
> Under the great God-speed of Heaven.'
> Yours, etc.,
> Old Athlonian.

WI, 09-1914

Kilkenny Soldier's Death
Sad Affair in County Cork
Interesting Evidence
Killed by a Passing Train

Coroner Mr Rice arrived at Fota by motor from Fermoy at 1.30 pm on Thursday of last week to hold an inquest on the death of James Ryan, Annamult, Stoneyford, County Kilkenny, private of the 4th Royal Irish Regiment, at Belvelly. The inquest opened at 3.30 at Fota.

District Inspector Murphy represented the constabulary, and Major John J E Poe appeared on behalf of the battalion. A jury, of which Mr James Wise was foreman, having been sworn.

Sergeant Michael Lawlor, of the RIR, in reply to the Coroner, said he knew the deceased, who was placed on sentry duty at No 1 bridge, Fota railway line at 12 midnight on the night of the 19th. There were four men there. Sentry Doyle informed him of the accident and he went there and found a man lying at his post with a rifle by his side. Witness did not examine the rifle. It was then 25 minutes to 2 o'clock.

Private Daniel Sullivan stated he was on duty with deceased. About 1.30 he left deceased standing at the bridge on the water side. The train was going so quick from Queenstown it must have drawn deceased in. The train was on military service. Witness walked back and found deceased lying on his back, unconscious, and witness shouted to Corporal Doyle. There was no light. Witness was nearly run over and he had to jump clean out of the way.

Engine driver, Cornelius Spillane, Lower Road, Cork, deposed that he was in the employment of the GS and WR Co. On the morning of the 20th inst, he left Queenstown at 1.5 with a single engine. He had been in Queenstown the night before with a breakdown gang, to put a waggon on the lines off which it had got. He was accustomed to this duty. There were no trains after 11.45 pm down. The management of the engine was at his own discretion, and he did not expect to meet any obstacle on the line in the usual way. He knew the line was occupied by the military and had seen military among the bridges, and at Fota bridge, on other occasions. It was a dark night. There are no particular orders for the use of single engines under these circumstances, except to whistle on approaching stations. He was not aware of the occurrence until about 1 o'clock that day. He received no special orders as to his conduct on the occasion. He had white lights in front of the engine and red lights on the rear. The fireman put them on, and witness examined them and had the lights re-arranged in Cork and also in Queenstown.

Fireman Meany concurred with the driver's evidence.

Private Thomas Delany stated that at about 1.20 am on the 20th inst, he saw an engine from Queenstown with a red light behind, but it had no light in front. It gave no alarm. Witness ran across to the other side of the bridge when he saw the fire of the engine.

Private Barlow stated that he also was a sentry, and agreed with the evidence on Private Delany.

Private Corcoran stated that he was also on the bridge with Barlow. There was no light on front of the engine, but a red one at the rear.

Dr Cecil Orpen, Youghal, deposed that he was on temporary duty attached to the military at Haulbowline. He examined the body of deceased. The injuries were of such a nature as would be caused by a passing engine and he was certain death was not caused otherwise.

Major John Julius Evans Poe deposed that he was called about 2.30 am owing to the death of deceased, and found that he was killed by a passing train. There were naturally risks, great risks, on the bridge attached to sentry duty, especially at night, and the men had not full experience on them in this time of warfare. The strictest cautions are given and observed. The engine was not on military duty, as far as he knew, but it was, he heard, in the charge and control solely of servants of the company. He would strongly suggest that bells or some such means of warning be attached to engine to tell of their approach in addition to the ordinary ones employed. He had daily experience abroad of such practice, being observed by railway companies. The deceased was a neighbour of his, and belonged to a very respectable family. He was a soldier of two years, had a good character, never drabk and was all round a splendid character. He had a father, mother, and sister dependent on him. Witness sent 10s for him to his parents last Saturday.

The Coroner, in addressing the jury, observed that on the telegraphic report he felt some delicacy, if not difficulty, in deciding as to the exercise of his jurisdiction. A similar difficulty, and that he experienced, though not expressed by him at the Aghada inquiry a few days ago. For although the military were not in actual combat in this country, it was sincerely hoped they would not be, yet he appreciated the fact that war was declared and casualties occurring in the performance of military duties belonged rather to the domain of military or martial law to be dealt with as matters of military discipline, into which it was neither his desire nor province to intrude. However, it now transpired from the evidence given that although the military had very properly assumed control of the railways, yet the duties were still performed by the civil servants of the company, and in that respect he was glad he held that inquiry in the interests alike of the military and of the public.

As to the disposition of the deceased and his comrades in the places where their duties called them, though involving inevitable risks, especially by those hitherto unaccustomed to such, or acquainted with the places, he felt that it was no more his duty or that of the jury to enter upon consideration of those matters, no more than of the disposition of the troops now placed in foreign lands and therefore, whilst they would extend to this gallant regiment and their distinguished officers every encouragement and sympathy, they were entitled to, in the defence of the country's common interests, yet he would confine the inquiry altogether to the aspect presented by the responsibility of the engine driver on the occasion.

In that respect he wished to point out for their attention the common law obligation on the part of the company's servants. The use of the engine occurred under very exceptional circumstances, both to time and risks it was exposed to, In the darkness of the early morning it proceeded from Queenstown, save what may be given in ordinary times by a whistle or the use of two lights. In his [Coroner's] opinion, considering that the line was patrolled, in fact protected by military troops at every bridge and points of danger, of which fact the driver had knowledge, he thought that prudence would suggest the stoppage during the night of this engine at Queenstown, or if compelled to return, they might have those signals of warning suggested by the gallant Major.

As there was a conflict of evidence between the military and civilians, in respect of the lights used on the engine, he would not, in justice to the driver and his companion, ask the jury to decide this question. He felt that both parties gave their evidence with candour and truth, and it was easy to conceive how the military witnesses, in the excitement of the moment, may be deceived. He, however, felt strongly that it was a most commendable case to present to the consideration of the military authorities and the trustees of the public funds now being raised to meet such cases, as also to that of the Railway Company, who, he felt assured, would contribute to the assistance of the next-of-kin dependent on deceased. He asked the jury to find the facts simply, and with himself, to convey their sincere sympathy with the next-of-kin and the comrades of deceased, as well as to the distinguished officer who seemed to feel the case very deeply.

The jury found that deceased died at Fota on the 20 August, from injuries received from a passing engine. He was unmarried, aged 20 years, and we strongly recommend the next-of-kin of deceased to the consideration of the military authorities and the public bodies entrusted with the relied of dependents of soldiers on military service, and also to the Great Southern and Western Railway Company.

Major Poe, on behalf of the military, wished to convey his appreciation of the very nice manner in which the Coroner conducted the inquiry.

District Inspector Murphy wished to entirely concur.

KP,09-1914

Private James Ryan, born St Mary's, Kilkenny was buried in Cobh Old Church Cemetery, County Cork. A case against the Great Southern and Western Railway was dismissed in January, 1915.

Letter from Munster Fusilier
German Brutality

The following has been received in Cork from Private N. Crowley, in the Munster Fusiliers, who was wounded at the front and is at present in one of the English hospitals.

'Dear Loving Mother,

Just another letter. I am writing to you hoping to find you in the best of health. I am going on fairly well myself, thank God for it. I am very glad to tell you I am going back to Ireland once again. But there is one thing I have to say. I would like to go back to the front again, and gett my revenge off those cruel-hearted Germans, for what I have seen them doing was something desperate. They shelled all the houses in Belgium, and cut up the poor women and children. I am getting sent to the depot at Tralee, for all my regiment are strayed about and more of them cut up. You would not believe the name we got for saving the artillery guns. The Germans came at close quarters to the battery of the Field Artillery. When we were right behind in the breeches we heard the horses roaring, and after that we saw them fall to the ground with wounds all over them. We came up and took their places and pulled the guns, and did all the work ourselves. We got right through the Germans, firing and sniping all round us. I am sending you on a piece of newspaper to let you know it is true. The wound in my leg is healing up, thank God. I don't think this war will last long. You can show this piece of newspaper to some of the neighbours, and tell them they should be proud of the brave old Munster Fusiliers.   LC, 09-1914

Private Crowley survived the war.

An Awful Sight
The Effect of Melinite

There have been rumours of it before, of this terrible explosive which M. Turpin, the inventor of melinite, had placed at the service of France. It has been tried once near Chalons, so it was said, on a flock of sheep. A shell charged with the new explosive burst above them. The smoke cleared away. Of the four hundred, four hundred were dead. It has been used now, I learn, in the bitter earnest of war. A friend of mine, a member of the American branch of the Croix Rouge, [Red Cross] returned to Paris a few days ago from a visit to the trenches around Meaux, whither he had gone with his ambulance to bring in the wounded. The strange horror of what he had seen there was still in his eyes, 'I saw,' he said, 'the German trenches as the French guns left them. They were filled with dead in such posture as the world has never seen since the destroying angel passed above the Philistine camp in that avenging night of Scripture. It was as though some blight from heaven had fallen upon them. They stood in line, rifles to shoulder, a silent company of ghosts in the grey light of dawn. I approached them. There was no horror in their faces, no anger of surprise even. Only over them was a film of fine, greyish powder. You would have said that they had travelled a long and dusty road. I have seen men before who had died from asphyxiation, but here was no sign of the agonising struggle for breath. It was as if a deep and sudden sleep had overtaken them – only their eyes were open. They might have been there from all eternity thus, their rifles at rest. I felt that if I touched them they would crumble into dust. Never have I seen anything more terrible than these erect, silent figures in the chill dawn.'   TS, 09-1914

Bullets in the Brain
All About the Army Surgeons Miraculous Cures

Many a man is walking about to-day who was shot through the brain in South Africa. Many a lover, brother, or husband, is lying stricken on the field with a bullet wound in his heart or his head. A few years ago sweetheart, sister, or wife would have given him up for dead, and wept bitter tears over the loved one who would never return. But no so now. The modern surgeon – a miracle-worker if ever there was one – has changed all this. His X-ray and his lancet are a few of the magic means of bringing the apparently dead to life, and filling the heart of the home with joy near to bursting. It is certainly a crumb of comfort to a man about to fight for his country to know that in battle not one in every 1,000 projectiles of all descriptions and weight take effect, but it is better to know that many of those which hit him in the head or body are, comparatively speaking, harmless.

A remarkable case of this kind occurred during the South African campaign. Corporal Thomas, of the Worcester Mounted Infantry, was leading his pony up a hill at Arundel when a Boer, about 400 yards away, fired at him and hit him four times. One bullet went through him in immediate proximity to the heart, and another passed through the upper part of the abdomen. Had this happened at Waterloo, Mrs Corporal Thomas would have been bereft of her husband, and the Thomas children would have been orphans. But it was in South Africa, and Sir William MacCormac was in attendance on the corporal. He examined the patient and found there no symptoms of internal injury to either the chest or the abdomen. The corporal had a slight rise in temperature for three days, and a week later he was sitting in a train condemning the fate which transferred him down country 'all on account of a little stiffness in my finger-joint.'

Every surgeon who knows anything about his business can recall instances of recovery after the heart has been injured, and the army surgeon, most of all, knows that even a bullet, lacerating and destructive though it may be, is not always fatal. Men alive to-day who carry in their hearts bullets which have made their homes there. In the past campaign in Morocco a French soldier was wounded by a pistol ball which lodged in the left upper chamber, or auricle, of the heart. For a week or two he walked about as if nothing had happened; then he began to feel a little pain, and his breathing became difficult. The X-rays were applied to his chest, and the bullet was seen lying embedded in the soft flesh of his heart and wagging like a pendulum at every heart-beat. It was the work of an hour to get him in hospital, open his chest, and extract the bullet, and long before the fighting ended the gallant trooper was out with his rifle again.

Dr Chafer, a German surgeon who went through the Russo-Japanese War, personally examined 500 soldiers of one Russian regiment, all of whom had fully recovered from their wounds. Three months after the battle of Mukden, he said, half of the soldiers wounded there were again at the front performing full duty. In some regiments no less than 70 per cent of those wounded at Mukden recovered and resumed active service within three months. 'Never despair' is the motto for the soldier stricken in the field, and the ray of comfort for the beloved ones waiting for his return.

Here is a remarkable case of recovery. A major was shot at Maritsam while engaged with the Mafeking Relief Force. A Mauser bullet struck him in the back, and he fell to the ground paralysed in both legs. For two months he lay at a farmhouse, and then he was brought into the Imperial Yeomanry Hospital, by which time he had recovered the use of one leg. On examination, the bullet was found to be two inches below the skin, and a piece of broken bone was pressing on the spinal cord. Sir Alfred Fripp brought his miracle working skill to bear on the patient, extracted the bullet, and relieved the pressure on the spinal cord and in course of time the gallant major was on his feet again, walking with the aid of two sticks. The bullet travelled through his skull and out the back of the jaw on the left side. He was not pretty to look upon, but he made a marvellous recovery, which was the main consideration.

While he was in South Africa, Sir Frederick Treves came across many instances of what he called 'marvellous anatomical feats' performed by the Mauser bullet, perhaps the most remarkable being those in which the bullet passed through the brain without causing more than 'trifling symptoms'. The modern surgeon cures these wounds, and at the same time heals the broken hearts at home.   TS, 09-1914

Cost of the War

How enormous is the expenditure connected with the war is shown by the nation's weekly balance sheet. During the seven days to Saturday the expenses reached £8,443,790. Of this £8,405,990 was spent on supply services. In the previous week the sum of £12,182,531 was spent, of which £12,179,151 was on supply services, and Ireland must pay its share – the blessings of Empire.   TS, 09-1914

German Mines
A Diabolical Device

A Hull trawler has reported that a British gunboat has captured a trawler, purporting to belong to Grimsby, which has been mine laying. There were 200 mines aboard her. The German plan appears to be to capture British trawlers, man them with German crews, and then start mine-laying. A cunning German ruse to destroy shipping has been discovered by the Grimsby steam trawler *Agatha* – her master states that a ship's boat was sighted, and the trawler went towards it. A boat was put out, and the derelict found to be a ship's lifeboat. A line was secured to it, and passed to the trawler which intended to tow it home. When towing was begun a terrific explosion occurred, too far off from the trawler to do damage.

A mine had been attached to the lifeboat by wire in such a manner as to blow up and also the ship which steamed alongside the lifeboat to pick it up.   TS, 09-1914

Guns by the Inch and Pound
Artillery terms simply Explained

To the average man, such phrases as '3-pounders' and ' 6-inch' guns are familiar – but he nearly always reads them without fully understanding their meaning. A pound gun, is a cannon which receives its name from the weight of the shell it fires. Thus a gun known as a '3-pounder' is so called because it fires a shell which weighs three pounds, an a gun firing a 5-pound shell would be called a 5-pounder. ' The size of most small guns is still described by the 'pound,' but the majority of large guns made today are 'inch' weapons. In this case the size of the gun is obtained from the size of its bore – a 10-inch gun having a bore of 10 inches diameter, and a 12-inch weapon a 12-inch bore. The largest naval guns in use in the Navy at the present day are the 15-inch weapons, which fire a projectile weighing almost a ton. Next to these comes the 13.5-inch gun, and then the most popular weapon of all – the 12-inch, which fires an 850 pound shell.

                                                                                    TS, 09-1914

How Cossacks Fight

The Half Moon of Death
Everybody knows the word 'lava' applied to the liquid products of volcanic activity, but I am almost sure that it is not known that the same word was been applied for centuries to a special form of attack which the Russian Cossacks use ti destroy their enemies, says Lieutenant-Colonel Roustam Bek in and article in the London *Daily Express*. 'At the present time we have news from the Austro-Hungarian frontier that the Cossacks have annihilated a certain number of squadrons of Austrian cavalry. How did they do it? Of course with their traditional 'lava. ' Germans and Austrians know this attack, and have many times tried to introduce it in their army, but without success. Their men and horses lacked the smartness which always distinguishes the Cossacks. Cossack horses are specially trained for this attack, and do not need to be guided by hand or knee; they know what they have to do after the leader has cried 'Lava!' So both hands of the Cossack are free for fighting. When news is received that a detachment of cavalry is approaching or ready to attack an order to be ready for a lava is given at once by the commander. The leading sotnia (squadron) spreads out to right and left, and the others at full speed form up on either side of it in a semi-circle or a half-moon. Every man with a

lance is attended by a man wearing a shashka, a Cossack's sword, and all the officers, with the colonel at the head are in front of the men of each sotnia. The other sotnias in the neighbourhood do not wait for a special order, and at once take up the same formation, endeavouring to surround the attacking force from another side. With loud shouts and calls the Cossacks rush down on their enemies, and even if this first assault is repulsed, another 'lava' pours down on the shaken enemy, and very often another surprises them in the rear. In the present day the Cossacks besides lances and swords, also use hand grenades, which, if they do not cause very serious injuries, serve to demoralize both horses and men. A special reserve of 'lavas' follows an attacking force of *sotnias*, and picks up the wounded, and usually collects the ammunition and horses of the beaten enemy. Of course, in mountainous country and especially in narrow passes, the 'lava' cannot be used, but in such cases the Cossacks use the so-called 'living entrenchment'. They make their horses lie down, and fire on the enemy under cover of the animals. In the present war, when hostilities will usually be carried on in the plains, the Cossack 'lava' must play a very important part and terrorise the Germans and Austrians. It was 31 May, 1905, near the station of Vafangon, in South Manchuria, that three squadrons of Japanese were annihilated by the 'lava' of the 8th Siberian Cossacks. No single Japanese escaped, and not one was taken prisoner. I took part in this attack, and was wounded for the first time in the campaign.   TS, 09-1914

Learning to use the Bayonet
'They can't stand the bayonet!'

That has been said of the Germans after every engagement. To their credit it may be added that they face the most withering rifle and machine-gun fire, but when Tommy Briton and his French comrades get the order to charge with fixed bayonets the German soldiers break and fly. Despite the great increase both in range and deadliness of guns and rifles the bayonet is still the final factor in deciding a big battle. English army authorities have always recognised that, and instruction in how to use the bayonet has always been an important part in the training of our soldiers. So important is bayonet fighting regarded in fact that French soldiers are taught it practically individually instead of in numbers as in other parts of their training. Each bayonet instructor, in fact, only trains four pupils at a time, so that he can clearly see and point out the weaknesses of each man. When 'Tommy' begins to learn the various parries against an imaginary foe, dummy rifles with ordinary bayonets are used, but when he 'takes on' his instructor a spring bayonet is fixed on to his rifle. These bayonets have broad buttons on the end of them and recoil at once when they hit. The instructor and his pupils are, of course, well protected with masks, padded jackets, and gloves in case of accidents. When Tommy undergoes preliminary instruction, the first thing he learns to do is to attack a padded jacket hung on a wall, and the movement learnt from it is what is officially known as the 'Engage' or 'On Guard. ' This position is one in which the soldier is ready for any emergency, to thrust or parry, to jump forward or back. By it, too, he is taught always to keep his bayonet directed at the chest of his foe.

With this first instruction Tommy is also taught another absolutely vital point in bayonet fighting, that is, that his whole safety depends on keeping his opponent outside his bayonet point, for once the enemy gets 'inside' the bayonet, the soldier is more or less helpless. In bayonet fighting, in fact, the whole of the rifle is kept in front of the body, and Tommy never draws his rifle back before making a thrust. The 'throw point' is made at a man's chest, and is parried from the 'engage' position by moving the rifle to the right or left, thus pushing the attacker's bayonet away to one side or the other. By far the most effective form of attack is the 'low point, ' as it is called. To deliver this attack the solder drops down on his left hand, or on his left knee, and delivers the 'thrown point' in an upward direction. This attack is parried by a side stroke.

In addition to learning the above ways of attack and defence, the solder is also taught the 'beat,' that is to say the way of knocking down an enemy's guard by giving his rifle a smart hit with his own weapon. It requires considerable practice, however, to train recruits to use their bayonet quickly. A square frame of wood about ten feet high has running down its centre a wire on which is threaded a number of balls of thickly woven straw. A mechanical device releases these straw balls in succession from the top of the wire, and as they pass the recruit has to stab each one with a quick movement, withdrawing the bayonet in time to stab the one following closely behind. The advantage of this machine is that it not only teaches Tommy quick and accurate bayonet work, but it develops the wrist muscles necessary to withdraw the bayonet after it has accomplished its deadly work.   TS, 09-1914

Letter from Waterfordman

Mr Michael O'Gorman, 40 St. Alphonsus Road, Waterford, has received the following letter from a brother of his who is serving at the front in the 2nd Battalion, Royal Irish Regiment.

5 September, 1914

Dear Brother – You must excuse me for not writing before now, but I was very busy marching day and night. We have been through very heavy fighting. The first fight we were in we lost 5 officers and over 500 men. At the battle of Mons there were the Royal Irish, the Gordon Highlanders,

Royal Scots, and the Middlesex Regiment, 4,000 strong, against 42,000 Germans. Now our regiment is 302 strong out of 1, 020. I am not allowed to mention what part of the country I am in. We are resting now for a day or two, after marching over 200 miles. I and the brother are all right and getting on well, thank God. We have escaped without a wound, although we have been in every battle the regiment was engaged in. I would be very thankful if you would send me a paper with news of the war in it, as we can get no papers here but French papers, and we can't read them. – Yours, etc. John O'Gorman. WN, 09-1914

Private John O'Gorman later transferred to the Royal Irish Fusiliers and survived the war.

Mines in the Open Sea

A mechanical mine, such as the Germans have probably scattered in hundreds in the North Sea, is filled with gun cotton and dynamite, the charge varying from 30lb to 500lb. The latter is contained in a spherical steel case some 39 inch in diameter, and is rendered buoyant by containing air spaces. It is constructed so that it will float from ten to twenty feet below the surface of the sea, according to the strength of the charge. A 'contact' mine of this kind is fired either by a small electric battery, a pistol, a spring, or a suspended weight. The impulse which actuates the firing gear is given by the contact of the vessel or other object against which it bumps. After it has been placed in the desired position by the mine-layer a safety pin can be withdrawn and the mine, which may or may not be moored, is ready for its deadly work.

'Sweeping' the Seas.

The only possible way which may be taken by a country desirous of clearing its seas of fixed mines laid by the enemy consists of towing a wire sweep between two vessels. The middle of the sweep is weighted so that iot will drag along the bottom, and the two towing ships steam along about 300 yards apart. Anything that is caught in the trawl will either be carried away from its moorings and come to the surface, or will be dragged along or exploded by the trawl. The unanchored must be suffered to float round the seas until they come in contact with stone or ship. TS, 09-1914

On Active Service

The soldier when he is on active service has to carry a heavy load. At the front he is now carrying something like the following:

Clothing and boots 14lbs; Arms 11 lbs; Ammunition (200 rounds) 12 lbs; Entrenchment tool 3 lbs; Accoutrements 8 lbs; Articles in pack 10 lbs; Rations and water 6 lbs.

Total 64 lbs. TS, 09-1914

Piercing Steel a Yard Thick

Deadly explosives used nowadays and what they can do.

The majority of us now very little about the high explosives which are used in the mightiest engine of war – the modern battleship. Gunpowder, which we were told at school was made of sulphur, carbon and saltpetre, we have probably heard of, but this is the most primitive of all explosives, and is used very little to-day. Gunpowder was invented and first used by the Chinese in battle six hundred years ago, and from that far off day to this it has varied very little in its composition. Gunpowder, however, would be about as feeble in present day warfare as a Crystal Palace roman candle would if it were fired against a 11-inch armour plate. A few of the deadliest explosives which have superseded the use of gunpowder are nitro-cellulose, more familiarly known as gun-cotton, dynamite, lyddite and trinitrotolul, which is always abbreviated as TNT.

TNT is in greater use in up-to-date warfare than any other explosive, as it has many advantages, the chief of which is that it will not absorb water, and it can therefore be used as effectively under the sea as it can above. T NT and gun-cotton are both used for filling shells, and a considerable advantage these explosives have over primitive gunpowder is that they give off invisible gases instead of smoke. As an example of the destroying power of gun-cotton, it may be recalled that it was a quantity of this explosive which blew up the monster French battleship *La Liberté* and left it a mangled and shapeless heap of iron and fragments. The gun-cotton bent and ripped the armour plates, almost a foot in thickness, as though they were mere bits of cardboard. It seems difficult to believe that ordinary glycerine is one of the chief constituents of a most powerful modern explosive, but nevertheless this is the case. Glycerine when treated with nitro-acid and mixed with a special sandy material becomes the deadly nitro-glycerine. In addition to their value as dealers of destruction, the modern explosives act with far more rapidity than gunpowder. Gun-cotton, for instance, will explode many hundreds of times more quick than its predecessor, and this is a very valuable consideration in war.

The science of manufacturing big guns and explosives has been so enormously developed of late years that from 1906, when the first of the dreadnoughts was built, up to the present time, the weight of the shells which can be fired has been more than doubled. In plain words, this means that a twelve-inch guns of HMS *Dreadnaught* can fire shells weighing 850 lb, while the latest type of super-dreadnaught launched this year can fire 2,000 lb shells, or nearly seven tons of solid metal at every broadside. The penetrative power of the shells, due to the higher explosives, have also undergone immense changes, and whereas, those of the 1906 boat can penetrate one foot of armour plate, those of the 1904 pattern will bore their way through three times as much.   TS, 09-1914

Putting Armies to Sleep
Death-Dealing inventions that might be used in the War

A rumour has gone round to the effect that the Germans are in the possession of bombs and shrapnel which, on exploding, will emit fumes capable of rendering hundreds of men unconscious for a considerable time. There may be good grounds for the rumour, for 'sleep explosives' do exist. It was not many months back since a Saxon woman, named Frau Ida Bohne, invented a powder for shrapnel which has the power of producing a gas of such a deadly nature that anyone inhaling it is rendered insensible. It is said that the explosion of one shell containing this powder would be sufficient to send a whole regiment to sleep.

A chemist of St Petersburg discovered an anaesthetic which he claimed to be some thousand times stronger than chloroform. He appealed to his Government to enclose it in bombs an shells and fire them at the Japanese during the war between Russia and Japan. The Russian Government did not then trouble itself about the scheme, but when the war was over, experiments were made with the anaesthetic, and it was proved that a shell containing it bursting on the deck of an ironclad would render all those on board unconscious.

The Japanese are evidently possessed of a shell which is more destructive than those used by one or two other Powers. This shell, which Japan used in her war with Russia, and also in her war with China, generates such sickening, stupefying vapours when it explodes that those in the vicinity are forced to take to their heels.

Edison has told us that he could manufacture an appliance which would have the power of vomiting forth powerful streams of water charged with electricity. Whole armies, on coming in contact with it, would be thrown out of action, each man being paralysed by the electric current.

Herr Hartmann, a German scientist, assured the Army and Navy authorities of the Fatherland that he could charge rays of searchlight with electricity and that those upon whom the light might fall would be instantly killed. In order to prove this he annihilated a flock of two hundred sheep by throwing upon them an electric current of 25,000 volts by searchlight from a distance of six miles.

It is interesting to note that both Edison's and Hartmann's inventions have been fore-shadowed in fiction. The latter's deadly rays, for instance, have their prototype in Lord Lytton's *The Coming Race* and Mr H. G. Well's *The War of the Worlds*.

A very useful invention is a calcium bomb which was thought out by Edison. When fired from a specially-designed gun the bomb explodes and emits a light as clear as day. It is said that one bomb will light up the ocean for a mile or two around, and enable craft to be plainly seen. The American Navy department some years back acquired a remarkable chemical fire which can be directed into a town or on a ship at sea by means of a peculiar projectile fired from a gun. The chemical fire has the tenacity of ignited sealing wax, and will start a blaze upon which neither water nor sand has any effect.

At least one big Power has a large supply of smoke bombs. These bombs are thrown like a hand-grenade and also fired from a gun, and when they explode they thicken the atmosphere with a smoke that no searchlight can penetrate. These bombs would probably be of great use if a regiment of infantry desired to advance upon an enemy unseen.

A year or two ago a French scientist produced an invisible paint which he declared would prevent any war vessel being seen at night. A French torpedo craft was covered with paint and told off to assume the role of a hostile vessel endeavouring to force its way into harbour after dark. Three or four ironclads, equipped with searchlights, were placed in various positions to prevent the torpedo boat's entry into the harbour. Notwithstanding the fact that the little craft ran several times into the glaring rays given off by the searchlights she succeeded in reaching the harbour without being detected.

TS, 09-1914

Soldiers With Charmed Lives

It is one of the ironies of battle that while one man may be killed by the firsr bullet that comes his way his fellow may be hit a score of times and yet survive to fight again and to died peacefully in bed. Already the story of the present war has furnished several illustrations of this strange diversity of luck, notably that of Kruitchoff, the valiant Cossack, whose brother was the first man slain in his first action, while he, after receiving sixteen wounds, and killing eleven Germans single-handed, is reported to be on the highway to recovery. Even more amazing was the experience of Lieutenant J. Evans, of the Inniskilling Fusiliers, in the South African War. In the first attack of Pieter's Hill, Lieutenant Evans fell shot through the right shoulder by a Mauser bullet. For two entire days he lay on the hillside exposed to the fire of the enemy. When at last he was discovered, it was found that he had received no fewer than twenty six wounds. Such, however, was the Lieutenant's vitality, that within a few months he was a hale and hearty man and fighting as valiantly as ever. Among the men who survived to describe the inferna(sic) of Spion Kop, every square foot of it swept by the blizzard of Boer bullets and shells none had a more miraculous escape than Murray of the Scottish Rifles, who was struck by bullet after bullet. Dripping from half-a-dozen wounds, his uniform hanging around him in shreds, he staggered among his men cheering them as gaily as when the fight began.

In the sanguinary battle of the Atbara, G. W. Steevens, says, 'one piper had seven bullets in his body; a corporal in another regiment received seven in his clothing, one switchbacking in and out of the front of his tunic, and not one pierced the skin. Another man picked up a brass-box inside the zareba and put it in his breast pocket, thinking it might come in useful for tobacco. The next instant a bullet hit it and glanced away. ' It was in this battle that a colour-sergeant was discovered with fifteen wounds – a veritable 'lead mine,' as a surgeon declared; but so amazing was his vitality that within two months he was sound as ever again. Many a man carried a charmed life through that terrible fight on the banks of the Alma in the Crimean war; but none miracu;ously that Colour-Sergeant Luke O'Connor, the brave Irishman known today as Major-General O'Connor VC. When Ensign Anstruther fell at the very moment of reaching the parapet of a Russian redoubt, O'Connor severely wounded though he was in the breast, took the colours from the lifeless hand and proudly planted them on the redoubt. Through the whole of that day of carnage he carried them, refusing point-blank to go to the rear although scarcely able to stand for loss of blood. Through what perils he carried his flag and his life may be imagined from the fact that the banner he so bravely bore was found to have been hit in seventy-five places.

TS, 09-1914

The Brutality of War
What a Field Attack is Like

Odd as it may seem, battles are the exception and not the rule on active service in the ordinary way, unless you happen to be shut up in one of the fighting forts or in some similar corner. Day after day, wondering what he is up to, the ordinary soldier is marched about the country, sometimes in one direction, and sometimes in another, and he often gets 'to Birmingham by way of Beachy Head,' so to speak. Then one bright morning it is whispered that the cavalry has been standing ready pretty well all night, and, somewhere behind the skyline, there is a noise going on like fireworks. Hearing that, is he is wise, he has just as big a breakfast as he can stow away, and he fills his waterbottle with cold tea, as much as he possibly can, because it will not be at all certain that day if he will have any time at all for dinner. Cold tea is an excellent thirst-quencher, and he will be thirsty enough before he has got the enemy on the run.

From the Firing Line
He may or may not see men being carried back from the firing line away in the distance. If he does not, then there will be nothing to tell him anything about anything except the far-off noise of the guns and the rifles.

By-and-by, at the best moment to fit in with the General's plan, his battalion will move out. If it moves in fours, tight-packed, he will gather that he need not make his will for at least an hour. If, on the other hand, it is strung out across the country in one attenuated khaki line, with about ten paces between each man, then he may reasonably surmise that it will not be very long until quite a lot of sudden death is dealt out. It is not very likely that Tommy will see much of the enemy at first, though his ears will tell him that he is making the deuce of a noise with big guns, pom-poms, maxims, and rifle fire. In due course a fair share of the projectiles will come his way, and then his pals will begin to get hurt, first a mane here and there, and then quite a number, possibly.

Behind Cover
About this time quiet-voiced officers will tell him to lie down behind any sort of cover he can get, whilst the field guns behind him are trying to pound the enemy into a less than truculent frame of mind. As soon as the General in command thinks he ought to he will be moved on, too, and his officers will probably warn him to take advantage of all the cover he can find reminding him that he is no use to the King dead. When he has gone far enough forward he will be told to lie down, and an officer will show him the place at which he is to fire, and will tell him the range. Even now he probably will catch sight of little more than the head of an enemy occasionally, but as soon as that happens he will feel that he is doing something in the world after all. He will not fire in volleys, blending the report of his rifle simultaneously with the reports of his comrades' rifle, but he will go on the old Irish adage: 'If you see a head, hit it!' Tommy by now will be nicely strung up, he will be feeling as tense as he knows how to feel, and he may have a bad headache from lying on his tummy in the sun and from the infernal noise of which he seems to be the centre. The pivotal fact of the universe will appear to him to be that people are trying to kill him, and that it is high time that he had a smack at them, for he will not have seen what harm himself has been doing. After giving up all hope of ever moving again he will get the word to go, the line will rise up, and it will hurry forward to keep the appointment with the enemy.

With the Bayonet
Now this will reveal its exact position, its strength, and its intentions, and the enemy will try to change all three by means pf as heavy and well-directed a fire as he can pour in. Men will drop with a vengeance now. If the fire gets too hot, then the line will halt again, and try once more with rifle-bullets to take the edge pff the enemy's stomach for fighting. Or it may go straight on and try and settle the matter there and then with the bayonet. Tommy will have been led into all of this, so to say, gently—as a man takes his first bathe of the season, going in inch by inch, until the final plunge shows him exactly how cold the water really is. There was, the first far-off firing at other men, the comparatively safe advance, the zone where

a few men were dropped, and then the final rush in when those unwounded were entitled to think that miracles happen. After that comes the mouth of hell, when the guns are shooting at point-blank range, and it is only a matter of seconds before some old-fashioned work with the bayonet begins.

The Lust for Blood

If at this moment you could take Tommy outside himself, and tell him to listen to the noise he himself is making, he would ask you who the fellow was that was shouting like that, and why he was kicking up such a din. That sort of thing, however, cannot be done, so Tommy, mad with excitement, and worked up to the desire to spill large quantities of blood, goes on with a roar, until, in what can only be called a kind of dream, he find himself stabbing with the cold steel, and smashing at heads with the butt of his rifle. In the ordinary way he may be a kind enough soul; if you saw him now he would seem like a homicidal maniac consumed with blood lust. Yet made as he looks, you would see, if you could watch him coldly, that all the time he is fighting with his head, he is applying the bayonet-point or the rifle-butt with judiciousness. It is when the bayonet charge is over, and Tommy stands leaning, panting, upon his blood-stained rifle, that he will thank whatever gods he has, that he had the forethought to fill his water bottle with cold tea. TS, 09-1914

The Submarine
One of the newest terrors of naval warfare

The newest submarine carries one or more, quick-firing guns, which sink into her hull when she dives, being shut in by watertight doors. Such guns are intended for use against the conning-towers of hostile submersibles, and also against pursuing destroyers. Besides guns, these craft possess three, and sometimes four, torpedo-tubes, and it is, of course, upon their torpedoes that they rely for working the most deadly damage upon their enemy.

One of the reasons why such great faith is placed in the submarine as an effective sea-fighter is that the modern submarine possesses a periscope. This periscope is an arrangement of prisms, contained in a tube, which can be revolved from inside the submarine, so that the commander, looking in at the lower end of the tube, obtains a view of objects on the water around – and, of course, above – his own craft. Now considering that the 'eye' of the periscope is only about six inches in diameter, and considering that it only rises one foot and a half above the waves, you can realise how difficult it is for the look-out aboard a Dreadnought to spot his submarine foe. Even when he does so, his gunners must be first-class marksmen to hit so small a target, although this is possible, as was shown us the other day. Otherwise, the submarine creeps, creeps within range of the larger ship, which she presently blows into eternity with one or more torpedoes. In appearance the submarine is not unlike the rough outline of a cigar. It boasts a platform near the conning-tower, where the crew can stand when she is on the surface. When she is going to dive her ballast-tanks are loaded with water, and then her rudder is manipulated so that she passes under water in the desired direction, driven by electricity. She is also lighted inside by the same means. Naturally there is not much room in a submarine. At its deepest point it is just over six feet from floor to floor; and from here in either direction it quickly slopes away, so that a man must crawl on hands and knees aft or forward. There are also no portholes in these craft.   TS, 09-1914

What a Battlefield looks like
A War Correspondent Describes The Scene After The Fight

I am not asked to describe a battlefield while the conflict rages, and it is as well. To do so would be almost impossible, for the conduct of any fight varies with the combatants, the weapons employed, and the nature of the country. But when one comes to the aftermath of battle, when the tide of victorious or defeated humanity has surged ahead or ebbed away, then one is on surer ground. Always, whether the struggle has been big or little, there falls upon the new, almost deserted battle-ground and great silence, and a most deep and abiding sense of peace. I know this is contrary to what has been written in fiction, to what has been painted in pictures of great battlefields. I speak, however, from what I have seen, not from my imagination. Those pen or paint-brush pictures of death in every hideous form of distortion, of wounded men rending the skies with their cries and lamentations, of blood dyeing the earth until the very heavens are reddened as if by the reflection of a great fire, do not ring true to anyone who knows what a battlefield looks like.

Sometimes The Kneel
The salient, the gripping characteristic of men slain in battle is the utter peacefulness with which they slumber. They seem to sleep like happy, healthy children, a half smile playing on their lips. It is hard to realise that they are dead. How they lie depends upon circumstances such as the nature of the fire to which they have been subjected. Sometimes they lie face downwards, sometimes they are on their backs, sometimes they sit huddled up against a rock, fence, or hummock; and sometimes they kneel. Perhaps the most wonderful battlefield I ever saw was at Omdurman, when Lord Kitchener advanced over the ground across which the enemy

had hurled himself in unavailing fury during the earlier part of the day. The dead Dervishes did not lie upon the sand. Caught by a tornado of fire as they charged, they had quivered, staggered, then slowly sunk to their knees. And there they knelt, row after row of them, like close-packed sheaves of corn, their heads bowed until they touched the ground. They might have been at their morning or evening prayers, so serene, so devout their attitude. The finger of death had wiped all fury, all emotion from their faces. A strange and unforgettable sight. There is little outcry from the wounded. Here and there one may come on a delirious man, but, as a rule, the man who is at all badly hit is either mute or capable at most of a hoarse whisper—always, always for water. The first instinct of a severely wounded man is to crawl away and hide himself. Therefore, even an hour after the battlefield has been cleared by the inevitable advance or retreat that must follow a battle, there are few wounded to be seen, for they have nearly all crawled into some hiding place.

Litter Here, There, and Everywhere

There is singularly little blood about a battlefield – at least a modern one. Occasionally one comes across a pool of blood where a man has been blown to pieces by a shell, but the small calibre rifle bullets of the present day draw little blood. The comparative bloodlessness of a modern battlefield is one of its most pronounced features. Another, is the extraordinary litter which prevails. You see, when the final forward or backward movement comes, the fighting man's first instinct is to discard all impediments. Indeed, in the triumphant rush of victory or the sullen despair of defeat, he will jettison even things he needs. His headgear, his water bottle, his knapsack, and, in a panic, his rifle – all will be flung aside. The 'mess' that a battle leaves behind it has to be seen to be believed. All said and done, however, my abiding impression of a battlefield is of a strange and brooding peace and stillness; of calm faced men sleeping a sleep that seems too happy, to placid to have followed on sudden death; of wounded men patient and silent in their suffering, and of a colossal and grotesquely untidy litter of human belongings, trifling and precious.

TS, 09-1914

What's in an Aim?

It seems so easy to the average man to raise a rifle to one's shoulder, aim at a mark, and pull the trigger; but once the present war began the club of which I am captain has had at least a dozen novices to instruct each afternoon and evening, and it is extraordinary – I was almost saying appalling – how few there are who knew even the rudiments of shooting. Such men may be as brave as lions, but they would be absolutely useless if placed in the firing line. Indeed, it would be little short of murder to send them to the front. Many of the would-be soldiers I have had through my hands of late have at first been unable to get a bullet on the target at twenty-five yards; but there are few who have not found the cardboard after the first day or so, and still fewer who cannot get every shot inside a two-inch ring at the end of the third week. That achieved, it is simply practice that is wanted to turn them into efficient shots, for, although it is not given to every man to become a 'crack' shot, there are few who need despair of getting at least four shots out of seven on the bull. A man who is not debarred by actual physical disability should be as ashamed of not being able to shoot as he would be were he unable or read or write.

TS, 09-1914

Will Your Soldier Boy Return?

Modern warfare seems a desperately cold-blooded business. It is not now so much a question of the man. He is still, of course, a necessary unit, but efficiency of equipment and scientific war machinery are the telling forces. Swooping war-planes scatter the death-dealing lyddite into the sleeping camp. The trenches with their spitting rifles, and the whirring of concealed machine guns, or the deeper tones of the howitzers dirge, cast death at the unseen, or almost unseen, enemy. If a veteran of Waterloo could look upon our modern methods he would have difficulty in keeping the grim smile from his lips. (In his day the whole game was to get as near to your man as possible, and show what you thought of him at the point of the bayonet should your musket fail to make the desired impression.) But the old soldier would find that our modern warfare is, comparatively speaking, humane when one considers the enormous number of men engaged. So far from increasing the carnage of the battlefield; the tendency of scientific warfare is to diminish it. In the early days of hand-to-had struggles, it followed that either of the combatants must be killed or injured. In such conflicts the slaughter was terrific. The Roman legionary, in the heat of battle, got within a few paces of his enemy, hurled his deadly pilum, and the discharge of that weapon was followed by the short sword at close quarters. The almost complete annihilation of the Goths at Naissus is a ghastly tribute to the effectiveness of Roman arms. The Roman knew nothing of lyddite or dum-dum bullets, yet, it is stated, that on that day upwards of one hundred thousand Goths fell upon the field the unparalleled record of war.

To Edward I. of England is assigned the discovery of the value of the long-bow archer in warfare. At Falkirk he raked the Scottish squares with the new arm, and even the skill and valour of Wallace could not avert a defeat attended by the slaughter of nearly half his army. The English long-bow was a powerful factor in the victories of Cressy, Poitiers, Agincourt, and Flodden. At Cressy the carnage was fearful. On that day the French lost twelve hundred knights and thirty thousand footmen out of an army of one hundred and thirty thousand.

The invention of firearms gradually ousted the cloth-yard from the field of battle, and England thereby lost one of the most murderous instruments of warfare she ever possessed. The formation of troops on the modern battlefield would of course, render the effectiveness of the cloth-yard practically nil; but in the day of archery dense masses of men moved toward each other doing battle almost without thought of taking cover, and the trained archer, with a range of three hundred yards, see to it that every shaft found its billet. 'The Guards was powder, and, by God, they shall have it!' And they got their powder, or Waterloo would never have been won, yet had those British squares been composed of archers, volleying their lightening like showers of cloth-yard at such close quarters, there would have been less of the enemy in retreat.

A ton of lead to kill one man

It is computed that one ton of lead was fired away for every man killed in the Napoleonic wars, while the English yeoman could boast that for every shaft in his quiver he carried a foeman's life. It is certain that since the introduction of the breechloader the proportion of lives lost in battle has considerably decreased. In the period of the French wars the slaughter wrought by the old musket was terrific. The formation of troops in line and column, with little or no attempt to take advantage of cover, gave the musket bullet a wide chance of finding even a random mark. The fearful losses of opposing armies in the past can be better understood by a few illustrations. During the Duke of Marlborough's campaign, the allied armies at the battle of Blenheim consisted of about fifty thousand each. When the night fell the French and Bavarians left twelve thousand dead on the field, besides thirteen thousand of their men prisoners; while the English and Dutch counted their loss at twelve thousand five hundred. This means the appalling percentage of one man killed or wounded out of every four engaged. At Jena the Prussian loss was twenty one thousand out of one hundred and five thousand, and the French nineteen out of ninety thousand; a proportion of one in five. At Eylan the Prussians lost twenty-five thousand out of seventy-three thousand; the French thirty thousand out of eighty-five thousand. One in three! At Aspern, the scene of napoleon's first defeat, the carnage was still greater. Out of an army of seventy thousand one-half were left upon the field.

Ninety-five thousand casualties in one battle

But even this butchery pales before that of Borodino in the Moscow campaign, for on that field the French lost fifty thousand dead and wounded out of one hundred and thirty two thousand engaged, and the Russians forty-five thousand out of the same number. That bloody work was done on a single September day, with the old flintlock musket and smooth-bore cannon, aided by sabre and bayonet.

The only battle in the latter half of the nineteenth century that can compare with Borodino in slaughter is that of Sadowa in 1866, which ended the Austro-Prussian war. Out of four hundred thousand men engaged, forty thousand Austrians and ten thousand Prussians were killed or wounded. One in eight as compared with one in three. During the American Civil War, in the most sanguinary battle, one hundred thousand men fought. Twenty-six thousand and five hundred of their number were left on the field. That was before the era of breechloaders. Still later in the century we find that the losses at Sedan were not nearly so great. At this battle the combined forces of the French and Germans numbered four hundred thousand, and the loss in killed and wounded was only thirty-nine thousand.

Coming to the campaigns of our own times we find it difficult to arrive at figures of comparison. During the South African and Russo-Japanese wars, there were sanguinary engagements and heavy losses. But these losses never approached in number anything like the massacres of the old county's battles. Shell-fire does fearful work, and the long rifle range is effective in good hands. But the modern soldier does not walk blindly to the muzzle of the guns. He has been taught to know the value of cover, and that he can do far better work crawling on the ground than standing up before a grinning enemy to get shot for his country's sake. Comparison shows the rifle of to-day an extremely humane instrument of warfare. The old musket ball inflicted a horrible wound when it did not kill outright; while the rifle bullet kills if kill it must, but when it maims it maims lightly. In fact, too lightly, in the opinions of some experts.

But we have other instruments and machines of warfare unknown in the days of the musket. Who shall say what horrors will be experienced when the hawk-like war-plane hovers over the exposed trenches, dropping the devastating lyddite where it will? And yet the progress of the present war seems to prove that the slaughter which will take place is unlikely to furnish a parallel to former wars. Of course, the losses both on the German side and that of the Allies are being kept secret for obvious purposes. But this secrecy cannot endure very long, and when the truth comes to light it will be found that the carnage, though appalling to the peace-accustomed ears, is nothing to the carnage of the past. Though battles will be fought on in an unprecedented scale, with millions instead of thousands, the number of killed and wounded is likely to be fewer both actually and proportionally.

TS, 09-1914

Wounded on the field

I awoke at night in the midst of silence. Clouds were passing across the sky, the moon was looking down upon the deserted village, the overturned guns and the heaps of the dead as she has looked down since the beginning of the world upon the flow of water, the growth of the grass, and the fall of the leaves in autumn. Man is as nought compared with things eternal; the dying understand that better than others.

I was no longer able to stir, and I was in great pain; my right arm alone could still move. However, I managed to raise myself on my elbow, and I saw the dead piled up right along the lane; the moon shone upon them, making them white as snow. Some lay with mouth and eyes wide open, others face downwards, knapsack and cartridge bag on their back, hands clutching their rifle. I saw this with dreadful vividness and my teeth chattered with horror. I wanted to call for help. I heard a sound like the feeble cry of a sobbing child, and I sank back in despair. But the feeble cry that I had uttered in the silence awoke others in turn, and was repeated on every side.

The wounded thought that help was at hand, and those still capable of utterance groaned. These cries lasted a few seconds, then all was still, and I heard nothing but a horse breathing heavily near me behind the hedge. He wanted to rise; I saw him lift his head at the end of his long neck and then fall back.

Towards morning dew had begun to fall. The silence was full on the vast monotonous sound on the roofs in the garden, and in the lane. I thought of God. Whose doings are unchanged from the beginning of time and Whose might is infinite. Who pardons error because He is good, and I trusted that He would pardon me, for I had greatly suffered.

But what I remember best of all, what I shall never forget did I live to be a hundred, is the moment when I thought I heard the sound of voices in the distance. Oh! How wide awake I became! How I listened! How I rose on my arm to shout for help! It was still dark, but already the sky was paling with the dawn. Far away, through the rain that streaked the air, a light was moving in the fields, irregularly, stopping round about. They were only vague shadows, but others saw the light, too, for on every side sighs rose into the night plaintive cries, feeble voices like those of little children calling for their mother. Oh! God, what is life? What is it that we should prize so dearly? This wretched breath, the cause of so many tears, so many woes, why do we fear the loss of it more than aught else in the world. What is in store for us that at the least fear of death our whole being trembles? Who knows? For countless centuries men have talked if it; it occupies the thoughts of all, but none can say. Erckmann-Chatrian.

TS, 09-1914

Wounded Soldiers in Callan

Two brothers, John and Stephen Kenny, natives of Callan, are now in that town after leaving military hospitals, having been invalided home from the front. John Kenny, a private in the Munster Fusiliers, a well set up soldierly man, received a shrapnel wound in the leg during the desperate battle at Mons, in which the Munsters lost heavily, all but 120 out of 1, 100 being either killed, wounded or missing Every single one of the officers is in the casualty list. The engagement in which Private Kenny was wounded took place early in the morning. He was one of a party of 100 who were laying a bridge. 'After the Engineers had the bridge laid, the Germans attacked us with heavy guns. I got wounded in the leg and was removed by the ambulance. The next thing I heard was that the Germans had crossed the bridge. They let us build it and they made use of it.' Private Kenny spoke of the kindness shown to them by the French people in their march through France Food and wine were given to the soldiers, and as they passed through villages and towns they were cheered. The Munsters carried a green flag and their caps were decked with green ribbon. They sang Irish songs on the march, which aroused the enthusiasm of the French, who joined in the choruses.

KP, 09-1914

John and Stephen Kenny survived the war. There was a Private Patrick Kenny from Callan who died of wounds in July 1916. They may be related.

October, 1914

Mullingar Man's Experience at the Front

On Tuesday Private William Cooke, 2nd Inniskilling Fusiliers, arrived in Mullingar, wounded over the eye. Cooke, who is vey popular locally, was met by quite a regiment of friends at the train. Though he has been at the front since the earlier stages of the War he was extremely modest, and it was only by degrees he could be induced to say anything about himself though he spoke freely of the doings and bon comeraderie of his fellow soldiers. His life story is particularly interesting in the fact that he arrived at the firing lines just at the time when the advancing movement against the enemy approaching Paris was started. 'Once we got them going,' he said, 'the Germans were kept on the run all the time; it was an uninterrupted retreat, and they had little time for plunder or loot.' Cooke could not tell the names of all the places they passed through, especially smaller French villages, but says at one place the 12th Division of the 4th Brigade, to which he was attached, were in the trenches for about three weeks, the Germans being only about 200 yards from them at the time. Forty British guns bombarded one village in the campaign of dislodging the enemy at each step. The order to his (Cooke's) Division was to hold the trenches at all costs as reinforcements were coming up. The men were exposed to very heavy shell fire whilst in the trenches, and at first he had a narrow escape, a shell splinter actually chipping the stock of the rifle he held. For the whole three weeks the Germans were sniping at them in the trenches, but the British lost very few men. Eventually they were relieved by the French, and were soon on the move again. Von Kluck's forces still going on in front to retreat. After some days his division was taken to a rest camp, and later boarded a train to a place called Haganbrook, from which they marched in extended order, the enemy retreating all the time, but returning fire. At Termonde there was a very sharp engagement, and Cooke was wounded over the eye by shrapnel. 'I was somewhat dazed,' he said, 'but not rendered unconscious. My eye and nose were bleeding heavily. I saw soldiers shot down each side of me as I lay there.' Then the Red Cross people picked me up.'

The French Artillery
Cooke said the French Artillery was very effective, at times wonderful; it rendered great service. Owing to a splendid system of aerial reconnoitring, he said, the French were always able to get the proper range. The German

artillery was very fierce, and would unnerve anyone at first, but they became accustomed to it. It was for all the world like a big day's thunder storm in Ireland. 'I saw,' he added,'a shell blast and tear up a tree, and carry clean away the head of a man standing behind it. But the German infantry is not up to much. They are very poor workmen with the rifle. Their bullet always went wide of the mark. It is their artillery that is wonderful.

Newbrook Races – Discussed in Battle
'On the 14th of September,' he continued, 'we were under heavy shell fire all day. That evening Mick Dunne, another Mullingar man, reminded me in the midst of all the shot and shell, that it was the day of Mullingar Autumn Races, but I suppose, he said, we won't hear what won at Newbrook.' Cooke added that they had got great experience in trench making, and it suggested itself to him at the time that as he belonged to the Mullingar Volunteers he might be useful some time in that regard if he got safe through the War, Food was plenty, but they often got but little sleep, and of course, this was haunted by the awful sound of the big guns. It was pouring rain all the time. The French people were exceedingly kind to the soldiers everywhere. Cooke, who has no wound now, complains that his sight is bad, as the injury was just near his eye. He concluded by saying that he had found some people state that the English fought behind the Irish, but from what he has seen he had no hesitation in saying that the English soldiers fought as well as any Irishman could.   WE,10-1914

William Cooke survived the war. The conversation about the races was retold in a later article 'From the Front. Narrow Shaves' 'WE,01-1915).

From the Trenches
Exciting and Interesting Stories of Happenings

Lieutenant E N T Broadwood, of the 1st Norfolk Regiment writes:
'The Germans have been simply massacred by us and the French. A Cornwall officer, Lieutenant B (whose father is a Unionist MP), told me the other day that at the Marne one of the Cornwall companies had a hot time with lyddite and were knocked down all over the place. However, next day they reformed. They said they had 'gone to sleep' without knowing it at about 5 pm the previous afternoon, and this correspondent with the time the German attack took place. The men woke up in the middle of the night and found themselves lying among the dead. They saw Germans moving about all round them in the wood, and they feigned death. When the Germans had retired they rejoined their regiment.'

Capturing the enemy
A Corporal of the West Riding Regiment in a Glasgow hospital says: We had some leisure in our position along the Aisne, and there was a little

village near our lines where we used to go for a bit of a lark. One night coming back – there were about ten of us – we were surprised to find a light in an empty farmhouse, and were still more surprised to find sounds of revelry coming out through the window. We peeped in and there were about fifty Germans all over the shop, drinking and eating and smoking.

It was a dare-devil of an Irishman who suggested that we ought to give the Germans a little surprise and we were all in with him.

Doing our best to look fierce and create the impression that we had at least a brigade behind us, we flung open the door without any ceremony. Our first rush was for the passage, where most of the Germans stacked their rifles and from there we were able to cover the largest party in any one room. They were so taken back that they made very little resistance. We fastened them up securely, collected all the smokes and grub they had not touched, and marched them off to the camp.

Antwerp

The diary of a petty officer who was with the Naval Brigade at Antwerp is written in the breezy style of the sailor – Oct 8th:

'We seem to be in a pickle. Our baggage party have just got here. Report the town in flames and all our gear lost. Shells coming in like one o'clock. Man on my side got a bit in his leg, but says he can shoot just as well on one leg.

Belgian artilleryman reports that he and two others are all that are left of our covering fort. We seem to have nothing to do but wait for the end. These trenches would be alright against savages, but against their huge artillery like so much dust. Three shells come with a whiz like an express train, and then – crash! The spirits of our troop are top hole. No one the slightest bit excited, just smoking and yarning and dodging shells, but its rotten not coming long side them. Here she comes, rip crash! Saved again, another non-stop for Antwerp.

About thirty men of the Royal Naval Reserve who were engaged at Antwerp, returned to Kinsale. The story of one of them, a young man belonging to the town – Christy Allen – states that at 7 o'clock on Thursday evening the order was given for the retreat, which proceeded under heavy fire until they were out of range. A supposed Belgian officer was now leading them presumably to Ostend, but as afterwards discovered was leading them into a trap.

Scouts were sent out and these returned with the news that the Germans were in large numbers only a mile away. They then took a different route, which brought them safely through. In the meantime the Belgian (?) officer was put up against a wall and shot – riddled with bullets. The officer in charge of his company was Mr A M Asquith, a son of the Prime Minister.

A Dragoon officer from North East France, writes a Spanish officer, has come to serve the native land of his mother and is now attached to our patrol. We find him a very accomplished steeplechaser. He brought three Arab chargers and has been quite an acquisition with his gultas[?]. His sister, Abers of Cialrvaux, is at the head of a party of Spanish and French nuns who are nursing the wounded in the military hospitals and even tending the fallen in the firing line. These Sisters of Mercy have no fear of death.

Cavalry

Corporal P J O'Rourke, of the South Irish Horse, who is son of Sergeant O'Rourke, RIC, Johnstown, County Kilkenny, writing home, says:

'We pegged down our horses when the alarm sounded, "Germans in Town". We all ran to out horse lines, got our rifles and defended our horses with very slight losses on our side. When we got the enemy back a bit we got saddles up in a minute and dashed through the town after them. Thirteen got wounded. I must say that our chaps are very brave under fire.

Quartermaster Sergeant J Barber of the South Irish Horse, writing to his father in Fermoy says:

'A German airship passed over our lines, and when over our position showed a blue sort of light. Next morning we heard a shrieking noise, and next thing we knew was that one of the German guns had out range. Then a couple of others joined in, and we had a lively time. One shell exploded within 10 feet of us and sent splinters in all directions, wounding three infantrymen and very lightly one of ours. Another killed several of our horses and stampeded some more. Another burst some yards further on and killed one man and wounded several. Nearly the last one they fired went a bit further on and landed fair in a squadron of cavalry and killed and wounded between 30 and 40 men and horses. Some of our lot had narrow escapes. An officer, Mr Roche-Kelly, had his hat taken off his head, another of ours was knocked down by the wind of a passing shell which only burst a few yards from him; he possibly owes his life to being flat on the ground when the shell exploded.

Infantry

Private Merryweather said: 'When we were in the trenches the water supply ran out and realising the position we were in, Bugler Lovelace volunteered to obtain some water for us. He went under heavy fire a distance of fully 700 yards to a farm which was being shelled, but he succeeded in bringing water, but he had hardly returned to the trenches when he was struck in the thigh by portion of a shell and wounded'

Private T Coulon, East Lincs, of Holborn Street, Sligo, one of seven brothers at the front, writes; 'We had a great time of it at Mons. The Germans came on like a swarm of bees, and we did enjoy it. It was like firing at a m-u-talo, you could not miss it. I hope the lads (his brothers) got out safe, for it was a terrible three days. The Germans must have lost a lot of men. Our artillery fairly did it on them.'

WE,10-1914

Message from Missing Officer
Wounded and Prisoner of War

An officer of the Royal Munster Fusiliers, who was reported missing on 27 August, has written home a postcard to say he was wounded and is a prisoner of war at Paderborn, says the *Morning Post*. The message runs: 'At last we are allowed to write. I hope I have not caused you anxiety, if so, it is over now. On August 27th we were cut off in a rearguard action, nine officers were killed, and I was wounded. I got a shot through my instep, which penetrated the foot when making a charge. I would write to----, but we are only allowed to write one pc. After considerable hardships in France, and almost at time entire lack of food, I was put in a train near the frontier, and after forty hours journey reached here. We are now well treated, and have Sisters of Mercy to look after us. I, of course, must remain here till the war is over. I know nothing of the progress of the war, and don't suppose I shall until I get to England again. Don't be anxious about me. My wound is healing well, and the most pain is over. I got about on crutches, but shall not know for another month whether I am permanently lame or not. My address is;--Royal Munster Fusiliers, British Prisoners of War, 'Leo Coveets, Paderborn.'

LL, 10-1914

Our War Prisoners
Lies as to Their Treatment Refuted

Among the fantastic statements in Germany about the treatment of prisoners of war on concentration camps in England the most inaccurate is perhaps that made by Dr Karl Peters, in *Der Tag*, the illustrated supplement of the *Lokalanzeiger*. The arrangements in the camp are miserable, he writes, and it is no wonder that infectious diseases broke out there at once and that more than 300 of our people were murdered in this way. The prisoners are compelled to sleep on the ground and are not protected from dampness either from beneath or above.

The facts easily dispose of the statement. There are now between 15,000 and 16,000 Germans and Austrians in concentration camps in the British Isles. Of these, *The Daily News*, learnt at the Prisoners of War Information Bureau in Wellington Street, only three have died. There has been no epidemic of any kind. The three deaths were caused by heart diseace. The health of the camps is remarkably good, Those prisoners who are not housed in buildings are under canvas. They have three blankets each, and are protected from the ground by a waterproof sheet or other means. They are housed and fed as well as, if not better, than the new Army.

LC, 10-1914

South Irish Horse at the Front

Mr J.J. Barber, Fermoy, has received a letter from his son, Quartermaster Sergeant Barber, of the South Irish Horse. The letter is dated 28 September, 1914.

'We have seen a bit of fighting. We were in Landrecies and things were hot enough for anything and anyone. We retired, but we had the best of the affair. The British losses were very small compared with the Germans. The way our troops behaved that night was enough to make anyone proud of being a member of 'French's despicable army,' as our friend, the Kaiser called it. We have been following the retreating German Army for some days, and I am sure friend William has changed his opinion, at least he has good reason to do so. I cannot tell you where we are or what we are doing, only that we are going on well, and are very well looked after. Our system of supply is simply marvellous, and all arms are in splendid condition, very keen, and no sign of any sickness as yet. Weather here is fine, and days fairly warm, nights very cold. You might send me a pair of wool-lined gloves, also a pair of mittens. If we are there for the winter it will be rather rough.'   LC, 10-1914

Quartermaster Sergeant John Joseph Barber survived the war.

Thrilling Letter from a Limerick Lady

A young Limerick lady who is at school in the South of England, writing to her parents, says: 'There are fifteen Belgian refugees (Nuns) here and two Christian Brothers and two red Cross nurses. They came on Friday from Bruges with three sets of wounded. Oh the tales they have been telling us are something dreadful; poor things have had no rest for three months and hardly any food. When they arrived here they all cried, God help them. Some of the nuns are going back to Calais to assist more of the wounded. Are they not very good? They say the children are to be pitied over there, some of them have their eyes out, and the Germans go as far as cutting off the nurses hands so that they cannot protect the children. All that is absolutely true. Yesterday four Belgian soldiers came, and we were all taken into the parlour and each shook hands with us. They are straight from the battlefield. Such feeling as we had for them. We are all in terrible excitement at present, all the College girls got the buttons off their coats, and one of our girls got the last one they had, was she not lucky.'   LC, 10-1914

Wounded Munster Fusiliers Officer

Prisoner Amongst the Germans
Fate of the Regiment

The following letter has been received from Mrs Dawson-Thomas, Castletownroche, written by her son, Mr R W Thomas, 3rd Royal Munster

Fusiliers, attached to the 2nd Battalion, Royal Munster Fusiliers, and now a prisoner:

Etreux, France, 10 October 10, 1914

Dear Uncle Robert – I am going to write you an account of my doings as far as I can since landing in France, and I hope you will get it sometime, though it is doubtful. If you do get it you might please sent it on to mother immediately. Well, I landed at Havre on, I think, 12 August, and we stayed there in camp for two days, during most of which it rained hard and made everything most unpleasant. One night I was out on picket, and it poured rain all the night and the thunder and lightening were awful. I took shelter when I could under a motor wagon.

Well, after that we came a long way by train to Le Nouvion, and marched to a little place called Boue, where we went into billets, and stayed for five days, doing route marching, etc, every day. I had a grand time there, a lovely old farm house, and the people were awfully good to me, and fed me on the best of everything. I think I forgot to mention that all the time the French are awfully good to us. They cheer us, and give us almost anything we want, all for nothing. Well, then we marched right up to Belgium in two days, about 50 miles, to a place called La Grandreng, and the second day we did 32 miles, and it nearly---(censored). The next day we fought a small battle just on the frontier without any losses and retreated right away back to Fes, just near where we started all the marching, so you may imagine what state we were in by the time we got there. Then the fighting started. The first I knew of it was being roused at 3 a.m, one morning by an orderly from headquarters to proceed at once with my platoon (50 men) to reinforce another company on outpost who were being attacked. Then we fought for two days, and just as we thought all was over we found we were surrounded, and so a desperate battle begun. I could not describe the horrors of it on paper, but we were about three quarters of a battalion fighting six German battalions, and without any chance of relief, and I think we really did our best.

We had one section of artillery and two machine guns with us, which helped a lot, but they were very soon knocked out. Our Colonel was a wonder to see; he had absolutely no fear, and I followed him and helped him all I could in every charge, but he was blown to pieces in the end by a shell. We had, I think, 10 officers killed, 5 wounded, and the remainder prisoners. I was wounded in two places, a bullet right through my throat, and all the biceps of my left arm blown away by a piece of shell, but no bones broken. My throat of course is bad and very troublesome. They put in a tube so as to allow me to breathe, and I can eat and drink all right, but I can't speak at all, but I think it will be all right when the wound heals and they take out the tube again. The doctor says I will be quite alright and able to speak. I have no pain, and am able to be out and walk every day. The

Germans are really very good to us prisoners, and the doctors seem to be very clever, so there is really nothing to complain about. All the officers were sent off to Germany yesterday, and all the men who were able to travel, so I am alone here among the Germans, except for three of our men, who are very bad. By the way, one is a Bandon man who knows you well, his name is Harrington. He has very bad wounds in his back, and has to lie on his stomach, but they say he will get all right in time. This town where we are is about the same size as Bandon, and it is just one big hospital. Every house in it is full of wounded men, and the flies and smells are awful. I stay out in the air all day, and walk along by the canal as far as I can to be away from it all. One sees some perfectly awful sights here.

I have no clothes but a suit of reach-me-downs, and a flannel shirt taken out of a shop here, and I can't shave at all, so you can think what an awful sight I look now, I don't think you would know me if you were to meet me suddenly. My uniform was all ruined, torn, and soaked in blood and dirt, so they threw it away. I would give anything now for a decent suit of khaki uniform. Well, although we were well beaten, I believe we gave as good as we got. We killed and wounded a great many Germans, and they say themselves that we made a gallant fight of it. They also say the English fight---(deleted by censor). When O come home I will be able to tell some strange tales, but I can't write it all. Our fellows who were in the South African War say it was child's play to this, and that never was a battle so fierce as the one we were knocked out in. Now I must stop. I would be quite happy if I could get some letters, but none have reached me here. I suppose they won't either. Your affectionate nephew, Robin. LC, 10-1914

Twelve men named Harrington from Cork died in the war, none of them listed from Bandon. Robert Webb Thomas survived the war.

Delvin Man's Experience.
Right in the Battle Line
A Ride to Death

The letter, which we re-print below is an accurate copy of one written to his brother by Private Thomas Conalty, of the Fifth Lancers, which regiment formed portion of the British Expeditionary Force, and has been at the front since the commencement of the War. He is son of Mr Michael J Conalty, ex-Sergeant, R.O.C. Delvin, and brother of Mr James J Conalty, Post Office, Mullingar. It is to the latter gentleman the letter is addressed, and through whose kindness and courtesy our representative has been enable to procure an exact copy.

17-9-14 Dear Jim,

Your ever welcome letter I have received, dated 4 September. I have received three out of the six you sent all containing cigarettes, so I have not done so badly. Yes, I have been right through the thick of it, here, my job of being orderly to the Boss bringing me right in the firing line. I have had some miraculous escapes from shell and rifle fire, but came through it all unscathed. Well, about one or two of my narrow shaves. Once in a shell fire, the Boss and I were riding a few yards apart when a shrapnel burst between us, killing his horse, and wounding mine. I thought I could actually see the bullets fly out of that shell. My fourth experience was the worst of the lot. It occurred three days ago at the beginning of this great battle, which is the biggest we have had yet. We had to cross a river and canal by pontoon bridges (the iron ones being blown up by the enemy). Our duty was, to see if our infantry already in position across the bridge required any protection on their flanks. Half of our Brigade got safely over, consisting of our regiment and the Greys, when the enemy started shelling the bridges with six big guns. It was terrible. Half of the brigade that had not come over retired to safety, but not so with us. We were entrapped in the town, and had to take shelter as best we could along the streets. I tell you, Jim, it was the worst experience one could have gone through, as they started to shell the village, and to see those 60lb shells hit houses 20 and 30 yards away, and explode in the centre of our troops, it was awful. Not one of us expected to escape. One shell burst in a garden ten yards from where I was standing. Luckily, there was a heavy wall between. My horse was wounded in two places, and the chap beside me had his horse killed. I was knocked flat by the force of the explosion. Then it became too hot to hold on, as the place was in flames. Well, Jim, then the ride through death took place. Individually we had to retire at a gallop, across the pontoon, with six big guns trained on us all the time, and two or three immense explosions taking place every half minute. I was next man-after the Colonel to face it, so I set my horse to it, murmered a prayer, and was over. What a cheer we got from the chaps when we reached to safety; they had given us up for lost, but, thank God, we got across with few casualties, although it seemed impossible. But what a sight across that bridge, strewn with dead, etc. I hope never to be in the same fix again.

'So you have read about our charge. Well, all the credit is due to the Sixth Squadron and Headquarters Staff, as we were the only troops concerned in it. The Scots Guards came along when it was nearly over. We had another charge since, but then it was really more like a pursuit than a charge. We captured 240 of the lot. They can't face our spears. I hadn't the heart to stick any of them, as when they see us come, up go their hands. They all seem to get into a dead funk when they see us coming at them. "A lot of howling d----s", they call us. For instance, look at our first charge. We speared 80, while our losses were only ten. Well, Jim, I could keep on writing for hours and hours, but as I have not much time, this will give you an idea until I return. We are not taking much part as yet in this great battle, so we are having a couple of days rest, which we were badly in need of. Now, Jim, I hope you will get this account quite safely, and, remember, I have not enlarged on a singled incident. You see some ghastly sights here; one becomes hardened to it all, but it will live in my memory for ever. We have 180 casualties out of a total of 550 in our regiment. Please let father know by forwarding this to him, as I know he is anxious about me. – Your affectionate brother. Tom.'

The Irish Brigade
Reverend Father Logan Volunteers as Chaplain

A very large and enthusiastic meeting of the Volunteer Corps from Crookedwood, Ballinalack, Multyfarnham, Rathowen, etc, was held on Sunday at Bunbrosna, about six miles from Mullingar. A resolution 'condemning the action of the nobodies in Dublin who tried to get control of the Volunteer movement', was unanimously adopted.

Sir Walter Nugent, MP, who was very cordially received, dealt with the duty of the Volunteers.

Mr T M Reddy, J.P., Hon. Colonel, Mullingar Corps, said he would support the Irish Party.

Rev. Father Logan (an Irish priest from Buenos Aires) approved of Mr Redmond's suggestion that there should be an Irish Brigade formed of Irishmen who volunteered for the front. He had offered his services as chaplain in the Irish Brigade to Mr Redmond, and Mr Redmond had told him his name would be one of the first on the list.

MR, WN, 10-1914

Leinster Regiment
Surrounded and Cut up
Bravery of Private Goggins

Private Coffey, of the Leinster Regiment, says the Leinsters and the Rifle Brigade, numbering about 2,000, were practically surrounded by about 10,000 Germans, and terribly cut up. They had either to advance or be annihilated. They charged, and gained the trenches evacuated by the Germans, and held these until reinforced during the night.

Wounded soldiers in the last batch taken to Cardiff, tell stirring stories of hand to hand fighting, and acts of devotion. They state that Private Coffey and others wounded on the field were fired on mercilessly all day.

At night Private Goggins of the Leinsters crawled out and dragged Coffey under heavy fire across the field and through a drain to the trench. Goggins during the night brought in sixty wounded men and then journeyed to a neighbouring village and fetched ambulance men who conveyed the injured to hospital.

Private Brazier, of the Welsh Fusiliers, declares that the Germans threw shells into the British trenches with spring boards. (Passed for publication).

WI, 10-1914

Two soldiers named Coffey were killed in the Liensters in 1914. Private Gogins survived the war.

Soldiers Letters
A Fairly Quiet Time

His many friends will be pleased to learn that Mr Richard Brewster (son of Mr W. T. Brewster, Secretary and Manager of the Independent Newspapers Ltd, who is serving with the South Irish Horse in the Expeditionary Force in France is, to quote his won words, 'quite well and still in the land of the living'. Writing to his sister, Mr Brewster says:

'We are having a fairly quiet time just now, but are expecting more excitement shortly. We are all being inoculated to-day against typhoid fever. I believe it makes one sicker about a day, but its worth getting done, so we will often have to drink fairly unclean water perhaps.

'I heard a couple of days ago in a letter from a fellow in Dublin to a fellow here that some of us were reported dead – myself killed and another dead from pneumonia. For God's sake never believe a single report of that kind unless it is given by authority of the War Office. I can assure you that if you heard it, I am still quite a lively "corpse".

'Don't forget to send me later on a piece of plum pudding because I don't expect to be home this side of Christmas."

Writing to friends in Athlone under date 1 October, Mr Brewster, who is full of optimism, says: 'It is a great experience here and I would not miss it for worlds. We are very well fed and clothed and needless to say are in good form and spirits. No news from here of course so good-bye.'

Mr Brewster is serving with the South Irish Horse, and some few weeks ago was reported as dead or missing. His interesting letters show that he is very much alive and taking his soldiering duties very pleasantly.

Private G Casey – We are living in trenches here, all merry and gay. We are being shelled by the enemy with shrapnel, but they are not doing much damage at present. There are apple trees over our trench, and we have to wait till the Germans knock them down for us. You ought to see us scramble down our holes when we hear a shell coming. We are getting plenty of food. It is very cold at nights.

Private George Brady, Royal Irish Rifles—Yesterday we were told off to bury German dead, but we couldn't get through, there were so many and we sent into their lines under a flag of truce to ask if they would come out and help. They sent a lot of men out, and they were quite friendly. They were well supplied with cigars, which they most likely looted from some French houses, and they offered us some, which we were glad of.

Chase of 300 miles

A junior Officer in the Connaught Rangers – Well, I'm still alive and kicking, but it is a miracle that I am as the regiment has had an appalling amount of casualties un the last fortnight. It was about a fortnight ago, after having walked on our flat feet about 300 miles, chased hot-foot by the Germans, that we turned round and started chasing them instead. Our company, which was leading troop of the whole division, then came into first contact with the German and we had a scrap and drove them back. Only three men and one officer were wounded.

Three or four days after that we went unexpectedly and unprepared into our first big battle. I never thought I'd come out of it alive. We lost 200 men killed and wounded. Two officers were killed and five wounded, including Major H shot through the arm, but I think he will be all right. We captured 300 Germans in that fight. Since that day we have been shelled incessantly by their artillery, but were fortunate up till yesterday, when their infantry attacked us too.

We lost fifty or so more men and five more officers killed. It knocked us all over. I am at present in command of a company. Weather is very bad. I have not changed my clothes or boots for about three weeks, and we have been wet through and through night after night.

WI, 10-1914

Dublin man 25 year old Second Lieutenant Richard Gardiner Brewster was killed in France in March 1918. He has no known grave but is listed on Panels 38 to 40 on the Pozieres Memorial in France. The five officers killed in the last part of the above article (on 20/09/1914) are, R B Benison (Cavan), Second Lieutenant R A De Stacpoole (Galway), Lt G R Fenton (Sligo), Lt R M H Henderson (India) and W S Sarsfield (Cork). Nine soldiers named G Casey died during the war, one of these was a sailor who used Casey as an alias. His true name was G A Kaiser).

Treatment of British Prisoners

Some ill-feeling was aroused in Germany by the reports that the English prisoners were being treated better than those of other nationalities. The Berlin correspondant of the Hamburg *Friendenblatt* has inquired fully into the matter, and reports as follows

'Some 1,800 English prisoners are at Doberits (the exercising ground of the Guard regiments stationed in and near Berlin). They are in four large tents, and among them are eight officers who would not give their word of honour that they would not try to escape. The food supplied to the English prisoners is exactly the same as that given to German soldiers. They have meat once a day, namely, at mid-day, while the officers receive one mark and 40 pfennigs (about 1s 5d per day) with which they can buy their own food. The public cannot get within several hundred yards of the Englishmen, who have certain work to do. A meadow is placed at their disposal, and in it they play with footballs made of old clothes. The Englishmen are treated with strictness, but also with humanness.'

KCC, 10-1914

'Just Like Clutterbuck!'

A Sergeant of the King's Own Royal Lancashire's says his regiment, at the battle of Mons, got home with several dashing bayonet charges, one of the most brilliant being led by Captain Clutterbuck, formerly a ranker of the Yorkshire Light Infantry, who, with a handful of men, routed four times their number. He paid the price of his gallantry with his life. The Sergeant added, 'It was just like Clutterbuck.'

> *It was at Mons; the breathless fight*
> *Ran to a second day*
> *After a storm of shell by night,*
> *A fresh and furious fray;*
> *There in the hot, unpitying sun,*
> *The Germans gathered, four to one;*
> *Said our captain, "Duty must be done!"*
>
> *He summoned up his company,*
> *And keenly scanned each face;*
> *'The foe are there,' said he, 'And we*
> *must shift them from the place.*
> *Fix bay'nets. Boys! We'll let them feel*
> *Just what it's like to taste cold steel!'*
> *His smile he tried hard to conceal,*
> *Which was just like Clutterbuck.*
>
> *Fiercer the deadly fight became,*
> *But as the mouth of hell;*
> *The air around was a sheet of flame,*
> *And many a comrade fell.*
> *Up stood the Captain as shrapnel burst*
> *Over the men, who at it cursed;*
> I *n the charge he meant to be the first—*
> *That was just like Clutterbuck.*
> *Just a glance at the foe he threw,*

On the hillside looming large,
Another glance at the lads he knew-
Out rapped the one word, 'Charge!'
He didn't look, when he'd said his say,
To see if his men sprang to obey.
But he reached eight co, and led the way!
It was just like Clutterbuck.

A ringing cheer in exultant notes
And fine North Country "burrs,"
Swell from the insty, dusty throats
Of the King's Own Lancasters;
Sheer up the hill each man-jack speeds,
Nobody falters save he who bleeds,
Racing hard – but the Captain leads,
And that's just like Clutterbuck.

Never a moment now for talk,
Now is the time to do;
Into the Germans they fairly walk–
Lancashire lads all through!
Four to one! And a shirker might
Think it no shame to take to flight,
But, the Captain thought the odds about right–
Which was just like Clutterbuck.

There in the thick of all the din,
Bang in the front was he,
Like a lion loose, and wiring in--]leading to victory!
But, when the fight was just on won,
King Death beckoned his bravest son,
His time had come – but duty was done –
That was just like Clutterbuck.

Happy the land with such tales to tell!
It can be conquered never!
Happy the heroes who, like him, fell –
For they shall live forever!
When British heroes, in British ways,
Achieve great deeds in coming days
These be the forms of your proudest praise –
'It was just like Clutterbuck.'

KCC, 10-1914.

Captain A W Clutterbuck survived the war.

Burying the Dead

After the tremendous fighting near Meaux over miles of front the dread lay unburied. A force of some eight hundred firemen was despatched to the scene to perform the necessary work. One fireman in an interview said—"We were three days engaged in our disagreeable task. The experience is unforgettable for the Germans had been killed by shot, shell, and bayonet in many, many thousands. The farmers and the labourers and the women who were on the terrain had taken up the duty of burying the dead before we arrived, ad they had first placed underground the French and British soldiers. They had buried them, as far as possible, together, and had tried to make a cemetery, so that the soldiers who had fought side by side against the invaders should rest with their comrades. The heaps of German dead remained just as they had been killed, with all the debris of the battlefield, and when we arrived the country people assisted us to make great trenches for their burial. There were thousands killed in their own trenches by the shrapnel of the English and the French artillery. But at one place scores were dead fro the bayonet, and in another by the sabres of cavalry. The carcases of horses we also buried, nur in cases where we could drag them into a pile we covered them with wood and petrol ad burned them. We gathered great quantities of German guns and ammunition with unexploded shells.

KCC, 10-1914

Local Letter from the Front

Mrs Kennedy, of Annagh, has received a letter, dated 21 September, written in pencil, from her son, who is a surgeon serving in France with the 14th Ambulance, 5th Division, of the British Expeditionary Force. Having applied for permission to make extracts, Mrs Kennedy reluctantly complied from motives which can easily be appreciated:

I am about half a mile from Jurl, in a farmhouse, like Mrs Hough's, and am very comfortable; I am here eight days. The weather is cold and wet and hard on the troops. The Germans have blown up the bridge crossing the river and then entrenched on the other side. However, we expect to hunt them out any moment. The shell fire has ceased here now, but it was awful the first four days, bursting all round us; one actually hit the roof of our house. I think it will be a long war, but the Germans are bound to lose. We have killed close on half a million already, but they are very numerous and we must keep at them. I hope you will get this.

I hear the shells bursting outside as I write, but we are quite "climatized" to shell fire. The Germans ate on one side and we are on the other side of the river. I cannot name places, but we hope to drive them into Germany soon. I am with an advanced dressing station about 500 yards from the enemy's trenches. I see their fire every night and day. At times everything is very quiet, and then there is an outbreak of fire which startles us for s few moments, but it is lovely to see the shells burst round the aeroplane. The airmen are very brave, and do great work. Send me some newspapers as we don't know anything here; it is like a desert, the whole country being devastated. No cattle, no sheep, 'no-nothing', only homeless dogs and cats, and riderless horses whose jockeys have been shot. I could get any amount of German swords, helmets, etc., but cannot send them home. I ride a captured horse with German saddle.

October 1st

The weather is sunny during the day but foggy and very cold at night. We have been served out with fresh meat for the first two days. We are living under favourable conditions just now, but under the continual strain of imagining that we may be blown to atoms at any moment. I have this minute seen a large piece of shell taken from the arm of a man who was hit a mile from here. Think our Red Cross flag must have saved us. We have the Germans nearly surrounded. We, the 5th Division, are on one side of the Aisne at Ropreux, about three miles from Soissons, the Germans being on the other side. I hear a pom-pom gun firing at an aeroplane; now all kinds of guns are firing at it. We see so many fo them that they have become as familiar as bikes. Turning to another phase of the situation, this is a great place for partridge, pheasants and rabbits, but I have no suitable gun to shoot them.

Arthur P Kennedy   KCC, 10-1914

(Surgeon Kennedy is the fourth son of the late lamented Mr Richard B Kennedy, Anagh, and it will be remembered that some time ago he was for a short period Medical Officer of Silvermines Dispensary District of the Nenagh Union, and afterwards changed to a very lucrative insurance appointment in Clonmel. His enthusiasm at the first sign of war induced him to throw it up and bravely offer his service like the genuine Irishman he is. His hosts of friends wish him success and a safe return.—Ed)

An Irish Regiment Decimated

A Belfast football player, Private Michael Bennett, 2nd Batt, Royal Irish Rifles, of 114 Bryson Street, Belfast, who has returned wounded from Mons, relates how a troop of 15th Hussars came along and told them the Germans were only three miles away.

Soon the enemy were firing on them before any attempt could be made to dig trenches. "Hell broke loose," continued Bennett, "But no-one faltered, though we were in a death trap. To raise a head meant eternity." From 3 o'clock till dark the enemy swept the position with their machine guns, and it became a "furnace of fire and death." The enemy would not charge. An hour before dawn the order was given to retire, and by forced marches for four nights they reached St Quentin. He stated that out of the 1,400 composing their battalions only 300 remained after the retreat, though doubtless many were captured.

According to the official returns the loss in officers up to the last despatch sent from the field is 12. The Rifles were not the only Irish regiment which have been reduced. The Connaught Rangers, Royal Irish Regiment and the roya Irish Fusiliers have paid their toll. The and Battalion of the Leinsters appear to have been so far the most fortunate of the Irish regiments, as only two casualties have been reported, that of Captain Boyd, son-in-law of Captain Burdett, Coolfin, Banagher, and the return received last Thursday gives the name of Lieutenant W.F.Morrogh, also wounded. He is son of Mr Walter Morrogh, Cork. (KCC, 10-1914.Private Michael Bennett, and Lieutenant Walter Morrogh survived the war. Captain Boyd, unfindable).

What our Allies Eat and Wear

In summer the Russian soldier wears a loose, cool white linen blouse. In spring and autumn he is hardly ever seen without his long khaki great-coat. With the coming of wintry weather he changes this for a sheep-skin, which is the warmest, most comforting overcoat imaginable. The fleece is worn inside. Outside the appearance of the roughly tanned skin is yellow. With trousers tucked into the top-boots of pliable water-proof leather with which all Russian soldiers are supplied, and with a camel's hair "bashlik" (scarf) tied round the head, the ends being wound round the neck, you lave no chink in your armour of wool and hide for the cold to creep in at. Officers wear fur-lined leather waistcoats and tall caps of grey astrakhan, with a flap running three parts of the way round which can be unbuttoned and brought down over the ears and the back of the neck. Few of them trouble about thick shirts or underclothes.

They were off to the front, this sturdy, stocky regiment on that snowy, slushy country road. Russian rifles have their bayonets always on them, with a hunge which allows them to be 'fixed' or 'unfixed' in an instant of time. They carried their packs on else had them strewn on the transport carts which rumbled behind. Every man had his kettle. Many carried them in their hands. These are for making tea in and to hold 'stchee,' too, the famous cabbage soup which is their usual fare. With meat boiled in it and potatoes floating about it makes a good meal by itself. Rye bread of dark colour and nourishing substance is eaten with it, or else a biscuit made especially for the army, succulent and sustaining. If they can get it they like 'kasha' for a change. This is sometimes what we call porridge, sometimes a dish of buckwheat eaten almost dry. Of meat the Russian soldier eats little even in peace time, and he seems to be all the better for it. He is generally a peasant, and it is seldom that peasants taste meat except that which has been boiled in the 'stchee.' This is tender but not large enough to go round a bog family. Peasant fathers and mothers need the help of plenty of children. As with all nations which are on the up-grade, the birth rate in Russia is high. She adds to her population at the rate of some three millions a year.

KCC, 10-1914

Bravery of Catholic Priests
Ministering to Dying
Heedless of Shrapnel

A remarkable tribute to the offices of a kindly priest is contained in a statement made by Gunner C Ayres, of the 29th Battery, Royal Field Artillery. He was wounded at the battle of Mons.

'Not long before the ambulance chaps took me away I was surprised to hear close to my ear a gentle voice half whispering to me. As the figure came round my feet into the line of vision I soon made out the cloak and hat of a kindly-faced priest.

'He knelt down by me, and, heedless of the shrapnel all flying round, said what I could easily guess was a few short prayers. Then in very poor English asked if I was ready to die and quite honestly, I was.

'He then opened my shirt and took out the metal disc which gives my number and name on it and he attached to the cord a little cross with the Virgin Mary stamped in relief upon it and said, "Blessed for you by the Pope."

'Soon after that the ambulance came. Nothing will ever lead me to believe other than that the priest saved my life. I can only think that after leaving me he saw the Red Cross men and directed them my way. I like to believe that anyhow.

'Although I am Church of England myself, still the Christian son of these brothers of the Cross prove them all to be made of the right stuff.'

WE,10-1914

Wounded Five Times
A Grim and Sad Discovery

Corporal Patrick Hyland, of the Signalling Staff, attached to the Second Battalion of the Connaught Rangers, arrived in Granard last week on furlough after some weeks in hospital in France. He says the Connaughts were in the thick of the fight at Mons, and inflicted great loss on the enemy. For fifty hours they held the trenches. He was wounded by bullets in four places in the left side. He had his wounds dressed and then took part in the battle of Cambrai. His brother, Thomas Hyland, fell in this enagement.

'We were both,' he said, 'were in the same regiment and had fought side by side. He was unscratched. We had been speaking of home and our mother. He was cheerful, and was encouraging me with the remark that my wounds were not more serious. During a stiff engagement we became separated. Soon afterwards, I went to look for him with members of the Red Cross, and we came across his body. It was cut in two by shrapnel.

Three hours afterwards, Corporal Hyland was knocked out of action by a shrapnel wound in the right leg. He was removed from the battlefield by the ambulance of the Red Cross, and afterwards taken to hospital in St Nazareth, where he was also laid up with pneumonia. He says he can never forget the attention received from the doctors and nursing nuns. The one draw-back during his fighting time was the want of a bit of tobacco. He received gratefully in the trenches two cigarettes from a comrade. He says that when it comes to a hand-to-hand engagement with the Irish troops the Germans are afraid. His regiment suffered severely. The losses were about 700 men and 25 officers out of 1,200. Corporal Hyland was two years and nine months in the South African War, and was afterwards some years in India. He was married in Granard some months before the war.

WE,10-1914

Patrick Hyland also served in the Lincolnshire Regiment under the alias George Taylor. His brother Thomas Hyland was reported KIA on 21-10-1914 and subsequently found to be a prisoner of war. He was repatriated in December 1918.

The Irish Soldier's Patriotism

Remarkable Letter From Carrick-on-Suir Man at the Front

Corporal Michael O'Mara, of the Irish Guards, a native of Ballinagrana, Carrick-on-Suir, who has been at the front with the regiment since the outbreak of the war and who has been through some hard fighting, sent an interesting communication to his relatives a few days ago. It is headed 'The Irish Soldiers Patriotism,' and was written on ordinary notepaper, in a neat hand, and filled four pages of the sheet of paper. Corporal O'Mara, and his comrades clearly do not forget their native land in the midst of war's alarm.

The following is a full text of the communication from Corporal O'Mara:

It is only a square piece of cloth, but its colour is green, and on it is the harp of Ireland inscribed in a wreath of shamrock, underneath are the words 'Eirinn go Breagh', once bright and clear, but now faded and obliterated beyond recognition. Such is the description of the flag which the Irish Guards procured when a few months ago they received information that they were for the front and from the moment they set foot on foreign soil that treasured emblem of Irish Nationality is displayed at the head of the battalion, the pride and admiration of the regiment. Shall it be said to-day, as it has been persistently insinuated in the past, that the patriotic sentiments of the Irish soldier undergo a complete change when he enlists in the ranks of the British Army. Those who are disposed to believe so may find enlightenment in the following facts which an Irish Guardsman and a British soldier I have not only witnessed, but taken an actual part in. While testifying our loyalty by discharging our duty faithfully and consciously, we never can, nor never will, forget, in this supreme struggle, when the mighty nations of Europe are engaged in deadly combat, we are Irishmen, and as Irishmen we must live up to tradition. We are British soldiers, proud of the name, and throughout all our battles foremost consideration is to add more lustre to the fair name of Erin, always remembering that the glory and honour of the Empire depends largely on the men in the field. We strive to contribute our portion. Recent years have closed the chasm which separated the sister Isles, and to-day all Irishmen feel proud to belong to the greatest nation in the world, the British Nation. But to return to our flag, which is now faded, though treasured far more than ever. I will endeavour to describe how on occasion at C---, when the fate of the day seemed to waver in the balance, and the ruthless enemy, by sheer weight of numbers, were pressing onward at every point of vantage, this faded flag turned threatened defeat into a decisive victory. On our left were the Munsters, and on our right were the Leinsters and Connaught Rangers. They were all hard pressed and about to retire, when suddenly from the firing line rose the stalwart figure of an Irish Guardsman flourishing the old green flag and shouting excitedly "Eirinn go Breagh". With the blood coursing fast through my veins, I watched with pride and admiration the marvellous effect produced by those simple words. With a mighty cheer that rent the heavens, a cheer that rose and swelled above the din of battle and the rattle of artillery, those sons of Eirinn charged down on the advancing enemy with bayonet fixed and every nerve tense with excitement. The enemy hesitated, staggered by such a turn of events when victory was almost within their grasp. But they were given little time for hesitation, for, to use the lines of an old Irish ballad.

Like lions leaping at a fold

When mad with hunger's pangs
Right up against the German lines
The Irish heroes sprang

The enemy turned and fled in all directions, completely routed and wholly disorganised. Such is only one of many incidents which occurred in the present campaign, but it is sufficient to show that though loving and fighting for the Empire to which he is proud to belong, the Irish soldier still cherishes his true nationality.   ME, 10-1914

Michael O'Mara survived the war. 'Eirinn go Breagh' means Ireland forever. The ballad lines above come from 'Fontenoy' by Thomas Osborne Davis).

At the Front

The following postcard has been received in Limerick from an officer connected with this city who is in the fighting line:

'Thank you very much for the No 5 Adares. Every fellow was short of cigarettes when they arrived, so I was one to sit next to at meals. The situation is favourable. Every day we sling bricks at the Germans and they sling more back. But everyday I think our tails wag harder and their's less, everyone of our three arms is individually superior to them. Their guns and machine guns are excellent and they use them most efficiently. The Uhlan and infantryman don't count for much beyond numbers, and they have a surprising lot. I have received at least two letters from ---and the last one had a nice little cake of soap in it. Yesterday I had a good wash for the first time for ages. I got a pair of socks from – yesterday, and will write to thank her soon.'   LC, 10-1914

Communications from Prisoners of War

We have received (says the *Cork Examiner*), the following, which we believe is the first communication received from British soldiers who are prisoners of war in Germany. It is dated 14th inst, and comes from Sergeant W Murphy, Royal Munster Fusiliers, English Lager, Sinnelager, via Paderborn, Germany. The communication says that "the regiment on August 27th suffered heavily, in fighting a rearguard action which lasted almost eleven hours. There were about 140 killed and 90 wounded. We had no assistance against superior numbers. The artillery fire of the enemy was most deadly. Communication is now established between home and the prisoners of war here, and the names of those here have been forwarded to the British Red Cross Office. I cannot account for about 120 men who escaped with the transport in the early hours of the 27th. We are being well treated here by the Germans. This will be of interest to your large circle of readers. Friends writing here will find tobacco and cigarettes most acceptable. We have also received the following, which we believe has come from a prisoner of war, giving the regimental numbers of C Company, 2nd Battalion Royal Munster Fusiliers, survivors, and now prisoners of war, and quite safe and well. It will enable readers to identify their friends, who are, though prisoners of war, safe and sound:

> 5911, 8133, 7392, 8874, 6955, 7033, 8023,
> 9276, 9258, 9061, 9834, 9963, 6872, 9240,
> 6875, 9885, 9252, 9870, 10079, 7104, 9263,
> 8871, 6346, 8031, 7085, 6303, 6355, 7568,
> 7640, 7774, 10072, 10046, 5580, 9830, 10050,
> 7563, 6151, 10070, 9954, 7542, 6516, 9793,
> 6389, 7346, 6445, 10011, 9595, 7771, 9102,
> 9154, 7709, 9289, 7097 10043, 7255, 8075,
> 7130, 4497, 7922, 6052, 10064, 7822, 5955,
> 9973, 7904, 8675, 7761, 6016, 6564, 4432,
> 7917, 10059, 7960, 5999, 7146, 9971, 10076,
> 7991, 6560, 6889, 7289, 8483, 4541, 7532,
> 9118, 6570, 7539.

LC, 10-1914

Killed in Action

29 AUGUST, 1914

My Dear Mrs Chute,

I am most deeply grieved to have to write and give you a few little details of the death of your most gallant husband, as I am, unfortunately, the senior officer who survived the action. The regiment was left in a somewhat exposed position, and the orders for a withdrawal seem to have gone astray. Chute, with his guns, which he handled during the day with really wonderful skill, covered the withdrawal of my Company at mid-day. It was pouring with rain, and with entire disregard to personal comfort, characteristic of him, he lay down in six inches of water to manipulate his guns the better. The Germans were crossing the front, and he never neglected an opportunity of delaying their advance. He withdrew them from one position to another, all day forming an invaluable escort to the two field guns we had attached to us. The withdrawal continued through a village at about 5.30 pm and at the other side of it he came into action again, firing right down the road, on both edges of which Captain–'s

Company was withdrawing. Owing to the help of your husband's guns, the Company got safely through, and rejoined the Battalion. The enemy was now on three sides of us, and their artillery opened fire.

Chute brought his machine guns back at the gallop along the road under a positive hail of lead. It was a splendid feat and was successfully accomplished and once again the guns were placed in position. We were now completely surrounded and your husband crossed the road to try and find a target to aim at. As he crossed he was shot in the right side and thigh, and fell dead. Up to the last he was cheery and full of spirits as ever; in fact he was the life and soul of the Mess. It is impossible to realise that we'll never hear his voice again. He will leave a large gap not only with the regiment, but in each and all his brother officers hearts. Yesterday, the 26th, the Germans allowed us to send out a burial party of our own men, and they found Chute and buried him with the eight other officers of the regiment who were killed.

May I on behalf of the surviving officers and men of the regiment, now prisoners in the German hands, tender our most sincere sympathy for a loss which we know only too well is one which can never be replaced. Personally, though I have known him so short a time, I feel as though I had lost my best friend. I can say no more.

Believe me, yours very sincerely.

H.S. Jervis

Mr Challoner Chute was son of the late Mr Francis Blennerhassett Chute, of Chute Hall, County Kerry. He was stationed in Limerick a few years ago with his regiment, and was very popular with all ranks, and a wide circle of friends in City and County.

LC, 10-1914

Lieutenant Chaloner Francis Trevor Chute, Royal Munster Fusiliers, was killed in action on 27/08/1914. Husband of Maud Emily St. Clair Carew (formerly Chute. nee Hobson), of 3, Howes Place, Cambridge. He is buried in Etreux British Cemetery, Etreux, Aisne, France

Interesting Interviews

A Press representative has had an interview with some of the wounded soldiers in St John's Hospital.

Samuel Cowery, 2nd HLI, a North of Ireland man, said he was injured on the 20th inst between Ypres and Langemarck.

'The Germans made a desperate attack early in the morning, but we made just as desperate resistance. The Germans kept up reinforcements all day, and we had a strenuous time of it. I was wounded and subsequently removed to Boulogne, and then conveyed to Ireland. I received an injury to the knee cap. I fought with an Irish regiment – The Connaught Rangers –

and they can fight.

'Nothing,' he added, 'Could stop them – they fight like hell. Since the battle of Mons a great many of them have been wiped out. The Irish Guards, too, made a name for themselves.'

Henry Doherty, of the same regiment, stated he was engaged in the attack on Lille. The attack lasted a day and a half, when the Germans had to leave the trenches. 'We were within fifty yards of them at one time. The fighting was simply slaughter.'

Private W. Mall, Lancashire Regiment said he believed the Germans have all classes – old men and boys – in the ranks. There was one German boy captured under 16 yearsof age. The Germans are cruel and cowardly fighters.   LC, 10-1914

Interesting Letter

From a Limerick Officer.

Lieutenant Commander Robert Cooper, RN, (Cooper Hill, Limerick), Embarkation Officer at Marseilles, writing to a friend here says:

'The coming of the 30,000 Indian troops which has already appeared with photos in the papers caused great excitement. Crowds came as near as they could to the docks. I disembarked myself about 1,710, British Soldiers, and about 500 horses and mules and lots of guns and stores. When one thinks that this transport will be about 7,000 miles by the time the men get to the front, and often 8,000, it really makes one proud of being a Britisher. I do not think we took much over 40 hours, say 42 hours, to put all that crowd with horses, guns, stores, victuals and followers on shore.'

Dealing with the staff the writer says:

'Six of us are English and fifteen of us are Irish, and more or less interested in farming or sport. The head of our department is a County Wexford man, and is really a very good head. People here are very nice to us, and we are made members of the Phoceens and other clubs.

'The farmers Association,' the writer continues, 'will be interested to hear that supplies here are plenty and cheap, but the eggs produced in Algeria seem very bad. Butter A1, and cheap meat of all sorts-a-plenty, but I am sure it is horse meat sometimes. Soap, matches, and tobacco are the scarcest.' The letter goes on 'it is wonderful how out here, as at home, the British and French Fleets have such a complete command of the sea.'
                                                                    LC, 10-1914

Lieutenant Commander Robert Cooper survived the war. His brother, Fleet Paymaster, John Cooper, of HMS *Monmouth* was lost in action when the ship was sunk in Battle off Coronel, three weeks after this article was published. He has no known grave.

Rear-guard Fighting

There have already been numerous advance-guard actions in this war, and several fine examples of rear-guard fighting. Any force marching against an enemy is preceded by an advance guard, the strength of which, although varying with circumstances, is usually about one-sixth of the total force. Thus a column of 6,000 men would throw put an advance guard about 1,000 strong. The duties of the advance guard are to prepare the way for the force in rear; for example, by repairing bridges that have been destroying 'obstacles', to guard the main body from surprise, to drive off the enemy's scouts or patrols, to gain information about the enemy, while preventing him from obtaining any, and, finally, if necessary, to take up a defensive position, and hang on to it like grim death until the main body has time to come into action. For these purposes any advance guard is divided into van guard and main guard. The van guard is usually composed of cavalry or mounted infantry, and its chief duty is to give the earliest possible intimation of the presence and whereabouts of the enemy. To this end the van guard covers itself with a widely-extended screen of mounted scouts and patrols. The main guard, on the other hand, is meant to attack or strongly to defend itself, and therefore is generally composed of infantry supported by light artillery. Above all things, the commander of an advance guard must avoid being drawn into action from which he cannot extricate himself with assistance. If he makes this blunder he may force the commander of the main guard body either to sacrifice the advance guard or to fight when he does not wish to do so. During an advance the functions of a rear-guard are humdrum enough and usually confined to shepherding stragglers and keeping an eye open for any possible attack from behind.

In the Post of Honour

But when a defeated force is retreating the post of honour is with the rear-guard, and it should be composed of officers and men of the highest courage, resource, and experience. A rear-guard may have to sacrifice itself in order to give the main body time to make good its retreat. The rear-guard's object is to delay the enemy by blowing up bridges, constructing obstacles, and by successively occupying defensive positions of sufficient strength to compel the enemy to deploy—that is, extend his troops for attack. As soon as the enemy has developed his attack, the rear guard swiftly retires to another position, thus forcing the foe to reform and begin all over again, all of which, of course, takes time.

TS, 10-1914

A Tale from the Trenches

Private Paddy chewed the hard biscuit that served him for breakfast, and growled because the only liquid available was water from a river from which a dead horse lifted its hoofs to heaven. 'An' it's my birthday, too! Twenty-one I am to-day, and if I'd been home being Sunday there'd ha' bin a cake as big as a haystack, an' a drop o' rum to slip in the tay. '

'Oh, chuck yo'r brousin', Paddy, an' give us a bit o' peace, afore the enemy begin. If they was to hear yo'...'

A bugle broke on his utterance, and as the men looked up, the command ran down the line to 'Man Trenches!' Private Paddy looked at the trench distastefully. He had slept there the night before, and had dreamed evil dreams, dreams which he remembered in daylight, and which even as he stepped into the trench sowed seeds of fear in his heart. That fear grew amazingly as he couched behind the earthen epaulement(sic), waiting for what was to follow – for in his dreams he had seen himself a corpse, lying exactly where he crouched at that moment, and had heard the man on his right hand to say, 'Poor Paddy a gonner!' For a moment the thought came to him that he would change places with one of the men on either side of him, then he remembered the foolish saying that every bullet has its billet, and decided that the change was not worthwhile.

'If it's got to come, it will,' he muttered to himself and then looked across the river with eyes that had in them a gleam of despair. There was a thunder of distant guns in the air, telling that somewhere on the wide front the battle was already joined, but on the immediate front of the Fusiliers there was nothing doing, and the men, whilst they waited, talked and smoked, and watched the other side of the river, wondering where the enemy would show himself. Many of them were young, the most had never been in action, and all found the waiting trying to the nerves – Private Paddy not least of all.

He chewed the end of an unlighted cigarette to pulp, tore it off, and then began the process over again, and finally threw the fag away – a sodden wreck. At first his mouth showed a tendency to water, so that he could not swallow fast enough, then it went suddenly dry, for overhead there came the sudden unexpected screech of a shell, a quick explosion, and then a hum of shrapnel bullets. Private Paddy was so startled that the too-ready flow of saliva dried up instantly, and in fear he started to his feet.

'Lie down, Paddy, you fool!' said a voice behind him angrily, and as another shrapnel shell burst behind him, he tumbled back into his place, shaking with fear.

He was not the only man who had jumped to his feet, and was far from being the only one over whom the spasm of fear passed. It ran in a broken wave down the whole line, leaving untouched here and there a man who had been in action before, and the nonchalance of these helped to steady those to whom the experience was new. As Paddy fell back into his place the man on his left, an old hand, grinned.

'Bit of a startler, eh, Paddy!'

A Quick shame came in Paddy's heart, and he felt it borne upon him to explain that sudden access of funk.

'Well, yo' see, Bill. I wasn't expecting it!'

The man Bill accepted the explanation without question. And perking his head upward, offered comment on the shells, which now shrieked in a steady stream. 'If it wans't for the bang, it 'nd be like listenin' to th' six o'clock factory whistles whilst you're lyin' in bed. ' The resemblance was certainly striking, and the mere association of the terrible sound with something altogether familiar helped to steady Paddy, without altogether driving the fear from his heart.

That fear grew gigantic when immediately following a shell which burst clean over the trench, a man four paces removed staggered to his feet, shook his fist at the unseen guns, and then dropped backward. Private Paddy's face went white as chalk. He felt as if he were going to be sick, and probably would have been so but for a chum's intervention. This calm acceptance of a terrible thing steadied Paddy once more, and the voice of the Lieutenant behind him, a lad newly-joined, and but a little older than himself, helped amazingly.

'You're not smoking, Paddy! Have a cigarette?'

Dumfounded at the honour, Paddy helped himself from the silver case, and striking a match on the rifle-stock began to smoke. He smoked nervously, glancing now and again to right and left as shells burst, and the old hand, recognising his trouble, gave him sound advice.

'Don't look about yo' so much lad. What th' eye doesn't see, the heart doesn't grieve about. Keep your eye on that patch o' the wood across th' river there, that's where the Germans'l show up. I'll lay a bob.'

He fixed his eye upon the wood indicated. It was something to know that if one waited long enough a vulnerable enemy would appear; it was the enemy overhead, appearing from nowhere, and which could not be fought that shook the nerve. He watched the wood as if fascinated, puffing at the cigarette unconsciously, and, as it was consumed to the wax tip, it burned his mouth. He spat it out with an oath, and as he did so Bill spoke excitedly.

'J'hoshaphat! They're comin'!'

A shout of exultation ran the whole length of the trench as a line of grey emerged from the wood, and men, in excitement, stood to their feet, some of them to be struck by the humming shrapnel. The officer shouted to them to lie close, and whilst Private Paddy did his best to obey, he could not resist the temptation to peep over the edge of the trench. What he saw was merely thick lines of men swarming forward, a mile away at this distance looking like so many sheep. The sight reassured him. But for the bursting shell's overhead he would have been quite unafraid. He fingered his rifle eagerly, burning to kill his man; then a shell burst almost directly overhead, and as he ducked instinctively, something ripped the pocket if his tunic and there followed a miniature explosion, and immediately after a strong smell of brimstone. For a moment he too astonished to speak, then he tore at the pocket, and dragged out a much damaged box of French matches of the stinking brimstone variety. The brimstone was still spluttering, and the reek of it filled the trench. There was wrath on his face.

'Th' only box in the company – almost, an' those bloomin' beggars...'

'Chuck it away, Paddy!' laughed Bill. 'It stinks worse than Lyddite. You'll poison th' whole blessed trench if...'

'A thousand yards!'

As the order ran along the line, Paddy threw the box towards the advancing Germans, and automatically adjusted the sights on his rifle.

'Ready' Present! Fire!'

The volley from the trench broke the advancing German line, and as volley followed volley in quick succession the enemy wavered. But already other men had poured from the wood, and, sweeping onward, carried what was left of their first line forward.

'Lor'!' cried Bill, 'there's millions of them!'

The artillery fire increased. Shells burst steadily over the trenches, doing a great deal of harm but in the excitement of firing, Private Paddy forgot all about them. Steadily he joined in the volleys, which, however, failed to stop the advancing hosts; and as he fired, in the background of his mind there was a wonder how men could advance in the face of such a withering fire.

'Independent firing!'

Steadily he picked his man and fired. A shell burst overhead, and his cap was carried from his head as by a sudden gust of wind. He never felt it go. The man Bill rolling over and fell against him. He glanced towards him and caught a twisted smile on his face.

'They've got me, Paddy, this time. If ever yo' come up wi' them d--d gunners, just give 'em...'

Bill's eyes closed. Paddy knew instinctively that he was dead, but the knowledge in no way appalled him. Very gently he pushed his dead comrade away so that his own actions should not be impeded, and with a white-hot rage in his heart gave himself to the work of destruction. Still more Germans. They were across the river and coming up the hill now. Their first line was very near, and the shell fire suddenly ceased.

'Fix bayonets!' Magazine fire!'

The orders were obeyed successively, and after the second, as each man pulled out the 'cut-off' of his rifle the fire became terrific. A couple of machine guns were playing havoc with the advancing enemy. Before the terrible stream of lead the forward ranks wavered and broke, then turned to flee. For a full three minutes, as they met their advancing comrades behind, there was a scene of indescribable confusion. The opportunity was too good to be missed.

'Charge!'

With a roar of delight the men poured out of the trenches and down the hill into the tangled mass. The Germans saw them coming, and at the sight of that line of steel fear entered their hearts. More of them tried to run, and the confusion grew worse. A minute later, yelling like madmen, the Fusiliers were on them, and the gleaming bayonets were at their deadly work.   TS, 10-1914

About a Rifle

We need rifles – good ones. We need to be able to handle them and to shoot straight. When taking position to fire keep the body rigid but not stiff. The firer should be at right angles to the target, legs slightly apart, with his elbows and lower part of chest forming a triangle. Rest the stock of the rifle in the hollow of left hand, the thumb slightly resting on the side of or just under the barrel, holding the gun firmly but not tightly. It is the right hand does all the work, and keeps the sights straight and true on the 'bull. ' The ball of the thumb should be pressed against the thick part of the stock, the fingers should grasp, or partly grasp, the 'hand, ' and the first joint of the first finger should rest lightly on the trigger, whilst the heel; of the stock is held, by steady pressure of the right hand right into the shoulder. You thus avoid the kick. Having thrust your cartridge into the. rifle and closed the breech with a smart snap, the rifleman must first get the stock comfortably fixed against his shoulder, then – though the mode of procedure here varies – bring your foresight down from the top of the target to about an inch below the 'bull, ' then, fixing your attention on the little black disc, get your foresight; seen through the V in the backsight, just touching the 'bull, ' pull – not jerk – the trigger, and your first bullet has been sent, at some 2,000 feet per second, towards its mark. A bullet does not travel in a straight line, but, under the influence of gravity and friction, begins to drop almost as soon as it leaves the muzzle. The bullet of a service rifle drops six inches in the first 100 yards, but when it had gone 200 yards it will have dropped not twelve inches but two feet. The drop increases with the distance. Were there no sights, on the rifle and you wanted to hit a mark at 200 yards you would have to aim two feet above it. The sights of a rifle enable you to keep your eye on the mark although the muzzle of the rifle is actually pointing above it. The movable slide of the backsight enables you automatically to point the muzzle just so many feet above the mark aimed at as is necessary to counteract the known drop of the bullet at various ranges.

Judging Distances
Soldiers, volunteers, everybody, need to be able to judge distances. In war a man's life may hang on his ability to estimate the range of a foeman. It's an interesting business to be able to judge distances. To learn measure out a distance of, say, one hundred yards, and carefully study it. Then pick out objects in other directions which in your estimation are one hundred yards away, and test your judgment by actual pacing. In this way you will come automatically to recognise a distance of one hundred yards or thereabouts, and you can then estimate a longer distance by reckoning it as being so many times one hundred yards. Another exercise is to get a friend to show himself standing, kneeling, and lying down at various known distances. You should then carefully note and memorise the different appearance he presents according to the distance. You will find that at one hundred yards you can clearly see details of his clothing, which are only partially visible at 150 yards, and quite invisible at 200 yards. Distances are over estimated when the observer is kneeling, sitting, or lying; when both the back-ground and the object are of a similar colour; when heat is rising from the ground; when the ground is undulating or broken, or when looking over a valley; when the object lies in the shade, is only partially seen, or is viewed in mist or a bad light. In long streets, avenues, and ravines, things look farther away than they really are. Distances are underestimated when the sun is behind the observer; when both the background and the object are of different colours, and again when the object is large or is seen in a bright light or clear atmosphere. Should the intervening ground be level, or covered with snow, the object will appear nearer than it is. The observer should also add five to ten per cent, on to his original estimate when he is looking over water or a deep chasm, or, again, when looking upwards or downwards.

TS, 10-1914

This article is obviously written about pre war black powder rifles and not the SMLE).

An Old Campaigner Gives Useful Hints

When I left for my first campaign, I asked an old sergeant for a useful tip 'Travel light – and carry light, ' was all he said. I took the hint as regards the former – that is, I took with me as little as possible; and as regards the latter I took a tiny silver electrical lighting arrangement, and was the most envied man in the regiment throughout the campaign. Next to this in importance I place a really good knife, with strong blade for cutting wood, a pair of scissors to make your inevitable tailoring neat, and a trusty tin-opener for tins too profound to explain. The last corner of your haversack should be consecrated to meat tabloids and spare buttons – the former to support the inner man, and the latter the outer man, both in an emergency.

For your Army 'emergency ration' must only be opened on the direct order of an officer in the last resort, and, despite all the varied opinions as to the best concentrated foods to take, you will find it hard to beat good meat tabloids. For you can get sustenance by sucking them for hours on the march, and at night you can turn them into hot soup. For preventing sore feet a hundred things can be recommended, and those are best which can be easiest procured, such as soap, starch, or ordinary Vaseline in salt and water. Perhaps simplest of all is fullers earth, dusted over the inside of the socks, and I mention this because the same dusted over any part of the body where the clothes or equipment are tight will save painful chafing on the march. Feet can be hardened by immersing them in salt and water, or spirits. It is surprising, however, how little you will need to remember these tips if you have good-fitting boots and socks, and bathe the feet daily.

The various methods for making doubtful water drinkable and enteric-proof number millions. Here is one worth all the others put together for simplicity, quickness, and cheapness. Get from a chemist tabloids of bisulphate of soda, sweetened, each thirty grains, and flavoured with oil of lemon. One to a soldier's water bottle, or $1\frac{1}{2}$ pints of water, and in twenty minutes you have a perfectly safe drink, not unlike lemonade, and quite as healthy. If you cannot get the tabloids, remember in a crisis that even putrid water can be made drinkable by boiling it along with charcoal or charred sticks. Or get a piece of canvas, or coarse sacking, dust the wood ashes from your camp fire over it, and pass the water through that. To keep your water cool in the hottest weather, hang it up in the shade in a canvas bag and wet the outside of the bag all over. But beware of the false thirst, especially, on dusty marches. Sucking a pebble, or, better still, a plum-stone, is a sure preventive of this false thirst. But if it is a real thirst and yet only filthy or sea water is at hand, remember that you may get relief by immersing your arms in the latter.

When Minus a Doctor.
When marching through dust, damp your handkerchief and apply it to your nostrils to breathe through. Never drink after a dusty march until you have rinsed you mouth out, unless you want a minature morass with assorted germs in your inside. Carry one or two simple medical hints in your head, as you may be days without sight of a doctor. For a burn, apply cold water first, and then mild oil or potato parings, and keep the air out. For a sprain, lay clothes dipped in cold water on the place to reduce the swelling, and rest the part. For a bruise, apply brown paper dipped in vinegar, or soap. For stomach disturbance, try the soft ash of burnt wood in water, or hot water, slowly sipped, and any sweets containing peppermint, or ginger, or bismuth, try warm water or a little gunpowder, if you can get any – not cordite, or explosives – in water. If an attack or sunstroke is feared, inhale tobacco smoke. But prevent it by wearing a

piece of red paper under the crown of your hat. For a wound, to stop bleeding, hold the limb up, and apply cold water to injured part; make a pad of a handkerchief, or cotton wool, apply it to part, and bind tightly. When halting on a long march, if equipment, belt, or clothes are too tight, it is best not to loosen them, or they will be much harger to do up when you start off again. If you want to be sure of a cap fire and a hot meal at the end of your march in wet weather, let every man of your section carry a couple of dry twigs in his pocket. These will start a blaze, even if everything else is wet.

When in camp, bank up the earth round the bottom of your tent outside to keep the wind out if the weather is cold, and, if the weather is very wet, bear in mind three points. First, dig a shallow trench all round the tent bottom to catch the rain water off the tent sides, and make an outlet in the trench to bear the water away. Secondly, slacken the tent-ropes to ease the great pressure put upon them by the saturated canvas. Thirdly, do not run your finger down the wet tent wall inside unless you want the water to come in. Never select either a rain-collecting hollow or a wind-swept hill crest for your camping site. A slight rise is the best.

Between the Blankets.

A thick sheet of brown paper spread between your two blankets will make them nearly as warm as three. To roast meat in an ordinary camp kettle, place some fat at the bottom of the kettle, cover it with clean pebbles, place your joint on the pebbles, close the lid down and set on the fire. Roasting in this manner will take a little longer than the usual way. To find the north with a watch, align the XII, on the sun, and then the line bisecting the angle between the XII and the short hand points north and south.

(TS, 10-1914)

Carrickman's Experience

Mr James O'Donnell, Main Street, Carrick-on-Suir, a sapper in the Royal Engineers, returned home from the front a few days ago suffering from the effect of a wound in the arm and from rheumatism contracted in the course of his work with the Engineers making trenches, pontoon bridges, etc. Mr O'Donnell, who is a very intelligent and modest and retiring young man, in the course of an interview with our correspondent, gave some interesting details of the work of the Engineers in the war and the dangers they encounter although they are not actual combatants. He had not been quite a year in the Engineers when the war broke out. His company left England on August 15th and arrived at Rouen in France on the 20th. From Rouen they marched to Wasseigne, and arrived before Mons on the 23rd. They were sent at midnight to make trenches for the Highland Light Infantry, one of the regiments of the Brigade attached to their company of

Engineers. The other regiments in the Brigade were the Connaught Rangers, Berkshires, and the Irish Guards. During the next few days they were constantly engaged digging trenches, blowing up bridges, and constructing pontoon bridges over rivers and canals. In the course of their work they were repeatedly shelled by the Germans, and so fierce was the shelling at times that the work had to be temporarily abandoned. Mr O'Donnell witnessed some fierce fighting by the Infantry of the Brigade to which he was attached. In spite of their bravery and disregard of danger, the German heavy artillery proved too much for them and wrought terrible havoc among them. The Connaught Rangers and Highland Light Infantry suffered very heavily, and the losses of the Irish Guards and Berkshires were also very heavy. He was with these regiments in the retreat from Mons to within a few miles of Paris, having every moment miraculous escapes from death by the German shells which fell around them like hailstones, now bursting and doing little damage, and anon laying many a poor fellow low. On 14 September, at Ventuleuil, a few miles from Paris, his company and the Brigade with which they were associated had a terrible time from the German shells, few of them escaping minor or major injuries, and many a one getting his last glimpse of La Belle France, and their bones now mingle with her blood-sodden earth.

It was at Ventuleuil that Mr O'Donnell received the bullet wound in the arm that put him out of action. The bullet entered the soft part of his arm about three inches above the elbow, and passed out about a inch below the shoulder. Just before receiving the bullet in the arm, he had a miraculous escape from death. German shrapnel shells had been whizzing and bursting all around them without a moment's intermission. He was lying flat on the ground expecting every moment that the fate that had overtaken many of those who lay around him would soon be his. The familiar sound of whizzing of a shrapnel shell was heard right over is head, and in a moment it fell within a couple of feet of where he lay, and exploded. The shrapnel bullets flew in all directions.

A man who lay beside Mr O'Donnell had his leg badly broken and his rifle smashed. One of the bullets grazed Mr O'Donnell's cheek, passed through the collar of his coat, and through a pocket-book in his breast pocket. That was his narrowest escape from death or serious injury. Immediately afterwards he felt the sting of a rifle bullet in his arm. He was removed to the temporary hospital, which, he was informed, was before the war, the country residence of Madame Cailleux, who figured so prominently in the recent sensational trial in Paris. Whilst in hospital he and the others there were visited by Sir John French, who chatted with the soldiers on their adventures, and expressed the hope that they would soon be quite fit and well.

When making trenches for the Irish Guards near Mons, Mr O'Donnell had the pleasure of meeting a fellow Carrickman and school-fellow, Mr

Michael O'Meara, of Ballinagrana, Carrick-on-Suir, who is in the Irish Guards and has been at the front since the beginning of the war. Mr O'Donnell says the German heavy artillery is the most effective thing on their side. They send their shells with deadly precision and without a minute's interval. The shelling usually follows the visit of a few German aeroplanes.

Mr O'Donnell was most enthusiastic in his praise of the heroism of the French and Belgian priests who work with the 'Red Cross' and also in their spiritual capacity on the battlefield. Their splendid bravery and utter disregard for danger and death in the discharge of their duties are wonderful. They are to be found everywhere that men fall, succouring the wounded, preparing the dying to face their God, and hurriedly uttering a short prayer for the repose of the souls of the poor fellows who have passed into the valley of the shadow of death never again to be troubled by shrapnel or steel. Many of the priests wear their surplices and stoles in the battlefields.

The soldiers watch with much interest the discharge of the German shells at a distance by night time. They present a very beautiful sight as they pierce the darkness in a long red line. Mr O'Donnell gave some interesting details of the life in the trenches for several days and nights, sleeping and eating there, and encountering whatever kind of weather the heavens send them. Officers and rank and file alike share the same comforts or discomforts in the trenches. The food was excellent, and was well and regularly served, considering all the difficulties that had to be faced.   ME, 10-1914

James O'Donnell, and Michael O'Meara survived the war.

Clonmel Man's Narrow Shave
Cap knocked off by German Bullet

Private W. Roberts, of the 2nd Battalion, Royal Irish Regiment, writes to his mother, residing at College Street, Clonmel, stating that he had a narrow shave of it at the famous battle of Mons. 'I wasn't shot last night – the cap was taken right off my head by a German bullet!' He adds that he is now in a rest camp at St Nazarene, in France, where 105 British soldiers are in charge of 1,695 German prisoners.

                                                                TS, 10-1914

Private William Roberts was killed in action the same month this article was published.

Diabolical War Plans
Devices Which May Make War Impossible

There is a story that one of our newspaper correspondents, following in the wake of the retreating German armies after the battle of the Marne, came upon trenches filled with German soldiers kneeling apparently in position to fire. Some had their rifles at their shoulders. There they remained, lifelike in attitude, yet one and all dead as the clay in which they knelt. Whether this be true or not, this much we know – that the French actually possess a weapon capable of producing such an appalling result. Turpenite is the name of the explosive used. It is a chemical composition which, when the shell containing it explodes, liberates arsenious(sic) gas. A single bubble of this poison will slay the person who inhaled it as swiftly and surely as a lightening stroke, and one shell will spread its death-dealing contents over a space of forty acres. Sentimental folk declare that such a weapon is too terrible for warfare. But why? Death by turpenite is painless. The object of warfare is to subdue the foe by killing. If warfare becomes too deadly, the peoples of the earth will, and must, combine to see its end.

Too Inhuman to Disclose

Most folk have probably heard of the 'Secret War Plan' devised by that wonderful soldier and leader, the first Earl of Dundonald. For this he claimed, at the time of the Crimean War, that it would, within four hours annihilate Cronstadt or Sebastopol. Twice it was submitted to Committee, whose verdict was that it was irristible, infallible, but too, 'inhuman. ' To this day the details lie in the War Office archives. Devices of a similar kind are plentiful. It has been the dream of many inventors to perfect apparatus which would destroy armies at a stroke.

Twelve years ago the Italian scientist M. Emile Guarini, chanced to receive a shock from a wireless telegraphic apparatus through an umbrella that he was carrying. This led him to make experiments, and he soon found that, with quite moderate currents, shocks could be conveyed through the air. He has invented an apparatus by which the energy of 1,000 horse-power at 100,000 volts can be concentrated by antennae, so as to destroy all life over and area of several square miles. He declares that, given a free hand, he can construct an apparatus, throwing forward deadly waves which will kill every living thing over a fan-shaped area twelve miles in length. A few years ago there was submitted to the American War Office a shell which, its inventor claims, will not merely destroy a ship, but a whole fleet.

Almost as bad as an Earthquake

It is a ten-inch shell charged not with the usual lyddite or cordite, but with two gasses, one of which is hydrogen. The charging is done in much the same way as a sparklet soda siphon cartridge is charged, but the pressure is enormously greater, being 3,000 lb. To the square inch. No fuse or percussion cap is used. The method of explosion is the inventors secret. According to the inventor, the 5,000lb. Pre4ssure is increased two hundredfold when the shell strikes, giving the almost incredible explosive force of a million pounds. The gases liberated mix with the air, causing the instant generation of combustible gas in huge volumes. Such a shell would have results somewhat similar to the eruption of Mont Pelee, which instantly destroyed St. Pierre and its thirty thousand inhabitants.

Mr Hudson Maxim, the inventor of the silent rifle, has a plan for finishing off a hostile army in very short order. He suggests a huge shell or aerial torpedo loaded with sulphuric anhydride. This would be packed in metabolic capsules, which by a small bursting charge, would be scattered – like shrapnel – over a large area. Each capsule is provided with a number of tiny holes, and the result would be that the anhydride would at once begin to send up a dense fog of sulphuric acid gas. This would burn, blind, and suffocate everyone within its zone and force them from positions. Then, under cover of the vapour, the force using this amazing weapon would be able to charge and finish the deadly work.   TS, 10-1914

Dodging the Shells

The following striking description of life in a 'dug out' by an officer at the front has been sent for publication:

'We have been very busy lately waiting and continuously moving from those beastly shells. The last week we have been in support, which is far worse than being in the trenches. One sits in dug-outs at the back of a hill or in a wood, and shrapnel, varied by lyddite, comes and stirs one up. I have not had my boots or any clothes off for over two weeks now, and to-day is the first chance of a wash for hands and face, as the water is precious and difficult to get up here. Of course you know our position for the last three weeks by the papers. We have been fighting with the Guards the whole time practically; a great honour.

Watching and Sniping.

' I have been sent to the trenches with my platoon and have got a fine place. The enemy's trenches are 250 yards in front and one can see any movement. We watch them as cats watch a mouse, and I have an observation post where I have been watching and sniping. I have had several shots, but no bullseye yet; the devils are too cute. They have four big guns in front which go banging off at all times. They have a huge big gun which we call Black Maria. She has a shell of 230 lb, and a range of over ten miles. I was greeted by her on my first day. I had a lucky escape there from a splinter.

'I got my first wound about ten days ago; we were in support on the side of a hill and an aeroplane went over and gave the show away. We got tons of high explosive shells and shrapnel. Three big explosives kicked within ten yards of me and a chunk hit me on the side of the arm and the rest buried me in my dugout. I had to be pulled out and only just in time, as I had two cartloads of stuff over me. So you can imagine I have a holy horror of some of those things. I have not had any sleep for the past six nights, as I stroll around my position at night to see if they are awake and if anything is happening. You bet I shall be jolly glad when this show is over. There is not much truth when a chap writes home and says he is having a topping time; it is only swank. To be moved on all day by shells is no fun. My teeth are a bit sore from the biscuits. This regiment has had the devil's own luck so far. They have been in every engagement from Mons and the retreat and have only lost four officers wounded, but we must not boast, as we say every shell has its names written on it.

'Very funny coincidence; we had to go through a big wood, beating it for any spies, and this was on 1 October, pheasant day. This caused great amusement.

'I find huge relief in a pipe in the trenches, waiting for the unknown. We get a Government issue of navy cut once a week of 2oz, which lasts me easily. Don't forget a letter, paper, or anything is most acceptable out here to pass the time and divert thoughts. Also food in any shape is very acceptable, as our food is rather curtailed, although excellent. A piece of milk chocolate is what I should like more than anything. All small parcels get through, no big ones. Please do not send equipment, as there is nowhere to put it and no chance to change. I wear all I can. Chocolate or a few chocolate biscuits next time you write, if you please. It is a great thing to know that one is taking part in the biggest battle in the world. Will you send us some envelopes and paper, as there is none to be got here?. You will get this in your old envelope.'   KCC, 10-1914

German Prisoners At Templemore

The number of German prisoners of war here at the time of writing (Wednesday) comes to between seven and eight hundred men. An additional body of 300 or 400 is expected before the end of this week. The number of soldiers belonging to the Arish (sic) Army, who are guarding them is about 150. About half a dozen officers are amongst the captured.

A considerable number of the prisoners of war interned here belonging to the German navy and their uniform is practically the same as that worn in the English navy. The other prisoners are dressed in grey. About half of them are Roman Catholics and attend Mass regularly. Every possible precaution is taken to prevent any of the prisoners making their escape and over a ton of barbed wire entanglements has been put up within a few yards of the windows where they sleep. A few sentry boxes have been got up in the barrack yard in places which command a full view of where the prisoners sleep and work.

The officers are allowed a ramble through the country districts nearly every day, but they are always accompanied by a couple of English soldiers armed with rifles. The work of the other prisoners consists so far mainly in cleaning the grass off the barrack yard which had been allowed to grow since the barracks were vacated about three years ago. Judging from a view which I had at the barrack grounds on Wednesday that work is now almost completed, and it is difficult to see how the prisoners are to be provided with work inside the barrack walls much longer.

The prisoners are quite gay and happy looking and sing and whistle at their work. Only a few of them speak English. It is said they did not like the change from the good Tipperary beef with which they were supplied up to a few days ago to that of the foreign frozen stuff. They are paid the full value in English money to which they were entitled whilst bearing army for the Kaiser according to their ranks, and they spend a considerable portion of it in purchasing goods from a store which has been set up in the barrack yard by a local trader.

The people of Templemore are delighted at having so many German prisoners in their midst. In fact the Germans have made the name of Templemore more famous than ever it had been before and the fine weather is bringing tourists from all parts to see the town and its cosmopolitan inhabitants.

TS, 10-1914

How Airmen Fight Duels

When a few weeks ago, news came through that duels had been fought in the air between aeroplanes, everybody was vastly surprised. The average person never expected that aeroplanes would ever do anything more than scouting and occasional bomb-dropping, and, as a matter of fact, they are not really constructed to fight. True, some are fitted with machine guns, but those weapons are intended more for the destruction of airships than for duels between opposing heavier than air machines. So unprepared are they for warfare that the actual fighting has to be done by the passenger who, in scouting, acts as an observer, and he uses either a revolver or rifle. The outcome of the fight, however, depends to a far greater extent upon the skill of a man who is piloting the machine than upon the man with the gun.

The best machines for fighting are monoplanes, in which the fighter sits behind the pilot. In such a machine he has a clear range through which he can fire, spreading from one side, right round the back, and so over to the other side, with only the tail to stop him firing backwards. Biplanes in which the fighter sits in front of the pilot are bad fighting machines for the fighter is unable to fire anywhere at all without running a great risk of hitting the pilot or some part of the machine. The only man who can use a firearm at all on these machines is the pilot himself and he only has a very limited range.

In an aerial engagement, a pilot has one main thing to do, and that is to get his opponent in such a position that he cannot strike, and yet at the same time to try to give his own man a clear range. The pilot of a monoplane, for instance, will endeavour to get just above an opposing biplane. In this position he is perfectly safe from the other machine, because the top plane prevents the man in the biplane from firing upwards. The fighting man of the monoplane, however, can easily fire downwards, and has an excellent chance of wrecking the other. The best position for the biplane would be right behind the monoplane, on the same level, for then the marksmen in the monoplane cannot fire, for fear of hitting the tail of his own machine. Here the machine gun of the biplane would be of inestimable value, but, in any case, everything has to be done quickly, because, owing to the enormous speed at which they are travelling, the machines cannot keep in range for long. Two rival 'planes approaching each other from opposite directions, are quite unable to fight, because they are not level for more than a second or so. They pass in a flash and neither is able to get in a shot, let alone an accurate one. It, therefore, follows that fighting must take place while the machines are both going the same way. As they are only travelling in one direction, then one pilot has continually to be on the look-out to see that he is not going away from the country his own side is occupying, and getting over unfriendly territory. So he has to manoeuvre, and change his direction frequently, for it would not do to have to land in hostile ground. This is yet another instance of how much depends upon the pilot. The very best fighting men of all are the trick-flyers. A man who can loop the loop, or turn his machine at an almost vertical angle has immense advantages over the ordinary airman. If a biplane were behind a monoplane, for instance, he could, by turning sharply and 'banking, ' get out of the way of the fire from the biplane, whereas an ordinary pilot would be absolutely at the mercy of the man in the other machine. Although his machine would be lopsided for a moment, the trick-flyer would not mind – he is used to it, but an ordinary man would have no chance.

As a last resource in a fight, an airman rams his enemy. This means absolutely certain death to himself, but if it is necessary, he does it. To 'ram' a machine, the airman climbs up above it until, when he thinks he is sufficient distance above, he does one terrific volplane(sic) on to his enemy's machine and rams it – at the sacrifice of his own life.

TS, 10-1914

In the Trenches (2)
Thrilling Stories

Raining Bullets

Some of the most thrilling stories from the front are related by Irish soldiers. Private D. Geoghegan, of the 2nd Battalion King's Royal Rifle Corps, describes how his company ran into a Maxim gun of the enemy on 14 September, 'I got two bullets,' he said, 'through the left arm; and one made a slight wound on my chest, and one across the top of my finger, knocking the rifle out of my hand. The arm and fingers are healing up wonderfully, but I have one in the chest to come out yet, but it does not seem to affect me much.

I think the French and English airmen are the most plucky and daring in the world. We saw one the day after the French beat the Germans at Lucy. He encircled the German position three times at a height of about 4,000 feet, and while he was up we counted 3,111 shells burst all round him. They were above, below, and each side of him, and he sailed through the lot. The Germans have a gun simply for firing at aeroplanes. It fires a kind of shrapnel, which bursts in the air, but I have not seen them hit anything yet, and I have seen hundreds of shells fired. We have more than held our own against the Germans. They have done the 'white flag trick' on us several times, but they paid dearly for it. They seem 'fed up' and glad to surrender when they have a chance. We heard of a case the other day where some surrendered on a river bank, and six of them swam from the other side to surrender with them.

Private George Brady, Royal Irish Rifles, In a letter in the *Evening News* says:

'We were told off to bury the German dead, but we couldn't get through there were so many, and we sent in to their lines under a flag of truce to ask if they would come out and help. They sent a lot of men out, and they were quite friendly. They were well supplied with cigars, which they most likely looted from some French houses and they offered us some, which we were glad of.'

Awful Sights

Writing to his brother, Private Morgan, RFA says: 'There are many awful sights to be seen here after our last fight, when we beat the Germans badly. Their dead lay so thick at one point in front of our trenches that we couldn't get our guns across, because we were too squeamish about riding over their dead in case there should be wounded men mixed up with them. Everywhere for miles around us is choked up with dead. Some were in the river, some of them were thrown in by their mates, but in other cases they were wounded men who crawled to the river to drink and fell in. I think there's no doubt that some of their wounded deliberately drown themselves rather than bear the agony of their wounds. The Germans are terribly callous about their wounded. We came on a chap of theirs who had been pinned down under a gun carriage that had to be abandoned. He could not extricate himself, and he simply had to lie there with two loathsome vultures waiting to nibble at him when the last spark of life had gone. Whenever we see vultures we always kill them, but they are always hovering about battlefields.'

Irish Officer's Story
A Second Lieutenant of the 2nd Battalion, of the Connaught Rangers, writing to his mother at the end of September, says that he went quite unexpectedly and unprepared into 'our first big battle, and I never thought I'd come out of it alive. We lost 200 men killed and wounded. Two officers were killed, one very great pal of mine; five wounded, including Major---- shot in the arm; but I think he will be all right, We captured 300 Germans in that fight. Since that day we have been shelled incessantly by their artillery; but were fortunate up till yesterday, when their infantry attacked us too. We lost fifty or so men; five more officers killed. It absolutely knocked us all over. We have only six officers left in the whole Battalion now. I am at present in command of a company. It has been a miracle that I myself have so far escaped. While there's life there's hope. I have not changed my clothes or boots now for about three weeks, and we have been wet through and through night after night.

Crawled for Aid
Private G. Sims, of the 1st Battalion, South Wales Borderers, relates he was wounded at the battle of the Aisne. 'It was almost impossible for a wounded man to get back from the firing line without being riddled, 'he says. 'I stayed in the trench until five in the evening. The noise was deafening, shrapnel bursting all over the place and raining bullets. I determined to try and get back to have my wound dressed and I crawled back somehow, rolled down on to the road, crawled along again for a few hundred yards, and presently got in touch with some stretcher-bearers, who carried me to a doctor.'   TS, 10-1914

Pte Daniel Geoghegan, Pre George Brady, and Private George Sims survived the war. Sixty-four soldiers named Morgan died in the RFA during WW I).

Irish Rifleman's Adventures
The following are extracts from a letter written by a non commissioned officer in the Royal Irish Rifles:

'We fought a rearguard action until within ten kilometres of Paris, and then turned about and fought the Germans to the river Aisne. The Rifles were not at the battle of the Marne, but had a rough time getting across the Aisne, which we crossed after four attempts. About three miles beyond the Germans had entrenched themselves on heights. We captured the trenches at the point of the bayonet, and occupied them ourselves. For five days we held the trenches under continued shell fire, and were at length relieved by the Argyle and Southern Highlanders. Then we went down to the village expecting to have a beanfeast of bacon and jam – a nice change after five days on emergency rations. We lit fires and made our tea; everything seemed comfortable, when suddenly a shower of 'Jack Johnsons' came over the hill. The first lot buried our transport, and they kept it up until not a house was left. The hospital was shelled and blown up, but all the wounded had been removed to the cellars. A bunch of five 'Jack Johnsons' landed within five yards. The last one killed nine men and wounded twenty-six and a piece of shell struck my knee.

'The Germans plunder and destroy everything they can. Some of them are simply beasts. One night I was in charge of a scouting party, and on entering a village we saw a light in a house. On looking though the window we saw thirteen Germans, all half drunk, and empty wine bottles were scattered over the place. An officer was sitting on the mantelshelf, and in the middle of the soldiers was an old woman and two girls. We rushed in. Every man in the room was killed. I bayoneted one, and he toppled through the window, and I then shot the officer. We then captured their horses and rode them back to our own lines.'

KCC, 10-1914

Leinster Officer's Letter

An officer in the Leinster Regiment writes:

'I spent my morning potting at Germans in a turnip field across the way. Awfully cute chaps. They had the tops of the turnips stuck in their helmets and through my glasses I could see a turnip growing very rapidly. and then have a crack at it, and it would disappear like a shot.

'I hung my shirt out all night to dry on a tree (writes Corporal Laird, Medical Corps), 'at daylight I found a piece of shell had taken the elbow off it. Good job I wasn't in it. '

KCC, 10-1914

Methods of Advance That are Irresistible
Graphic Description by Wounded Soldier

Paris, Thursday

A graphic account of the French's method of fighting is given by a soldier who has arrived from the front:

'We advanced,' he relates, 'by successive bounds. It was very funny. We are rather scattered about in little parties of five or six. We consult one another. 'Are you there?' 'Yes, ' 'Come along, then.' So we rush along for a hundred yards without looking at anything, our knapsacks in our hands in front of our faces like a shield. 'When we get out of breath we fling ourselves down flat in the mud. We hold a muster of our force, and on the right and left we see a few parties of the company. Everybody has climbed at the same time. Everything has gone on well. We hide behind trees to watch for a favourable moment for a fresh advance. Bullets are whistling, but they pass well above our heads. The Germans are too near us on the side of the hills, and they cannot touch us. Besides, they fire too badly. They do not raise their guns to their shoulders, but fire from the hip without aiming.'

Intoxicating Rush

'One, two, three! We are now right at the top. We keep on looking to the right and left, and find we have not got ahead of our comrades. A few moments rest and it is time for us to dash forward. One of us, a private, lifts his rifle in the air. Everybody understands. At the same time we all show the point of our bayonets over the ridge. They gleam, though there is no sun. We rush forward shouting. This time there they are in front of us. It is intoxicating. We don't know where we are. We do not see our comrades who are falling at our side. We only see those grey tunics, those spiked helmets which are falling back. However they do not turn their backs on us, but how badly they fire! All at once shells began to arrive. They have got our range. We cannot hold out any longer.

So, without turning our backs either, and continuing to fire, we withdraw, all help the wounded to come with us. We form again on the other side of the ridge, but above on the top our places are taken by another force of our men, a kilometre nearer the enemy than we were.'

Force Always Intact

The journal which prints this narrative, explaining the last section, says that, as a matter of fact, the units engaged go into the firing line in relays, in a sequence of movements minutely regulated by the central intelligence section, which regulates the whole machine. It is a marvel, 'the story goes on, 'to see the suppleness of these masses which succeed each other without cessation, without disorder. Accordingly the heaviest fighting leaves us masters of an intact force. The flesh of our army grows again under the very blow that tears it, and the enemy may strike all he can. He cannot weaken our grasp, which is already beginning to crush it.

TS, 10-1914

Royal Irish at the front
Castlecomer Private's Mishap
Tribute to Captain Smithwick
Interesting Story

Our Castlecomer correspondent writer, Private Thomas Tynan of the 4th Battalion, Royal Irish Regiment, who left Shanvally Camp, County Cork, about three weeks ago for the front is back in his home in Castlecomer on a 15 days sick furlough, he having been invalided close at Lille on marching to the fighting line.

Private Tynan spent about two days in hospital in Manchester, and though has had a strenuous time of it, his regiment being kept marching in quickest time from time of landing in order to reach the fighting quarters. He was just at touch with the enemy when crossing an irrigation field over a ladder in the night time close to Lille, he slipped from the ladder and seriously injured his thigh. He had the experience of seeing his comrades make a dash with the bayonets at the enemy, and previous to his accident came at close quarters with the enemy and in the shades of the night saw a big German sat in a trench and, not giving him a chance to make a corpse of himself, shot the German through the heart and when he got up saw that the German had already been shot but was in the position as if he were about taking aim at the foe.

Private Tynan, when he got close to the battle line was shocked to see thousands of cattle and horses in dying conditions, but this sensitiveness wore off him when on another day he saw hundreds of corpses of Germans lying on the fields in all stages of death struggles. He pays a great tribute to the bravery of Captain Smithwick, of Kilkenny, who is his officer, and who shows the greatest pluck and courage in the field. At the time of his accident he is happy to say there was no fatality amongst his company. Private Tynan expects to be going back to the front in a few days.

KP, 10-1914

Thomas Tynan survived the war. Captain James Arnold died of consumption brought on by injuries received 20 October, 1914, at Le Pelly.

Sky Pointing Cannon and Aircraft

The recent official announcement that the defence of great Britain against aircraft had been undertaken by the Royal Navy raises the interesting question as to what will prove the most effective method of fighting foes in the air. The tremendous speed at which aeroplanes travel must necessarily make them a very difficult target to hit, whether the gunner be on land on in the air. For this reason it is naturally desirable to have a weapon with a charge that spreads as far as possible after leaving the muzzle. The reason for this will be obvious to you, if you apply the idea to an ordinary sporting shot.

Suppose you were armed with a rifle and a snipe got up, your chance of hitting so small a bird was a single rifle bullet would be practically nil. But aim a sporting gun at the same bird, and you have a much better chance of bringing it down, because the shot spreads. This is the idea which will most probably govern the construction of the ultimate sky-gun. In the same way, a duel between aviators in mid-air would most likely be brought to a definite conclusion in favour of the man armed with a weapon that spread its charge as already indicated. But perhaps even more important is the question of bringing down aircraft by means of guns planted on the ground, or on the roofs of buildings.

Following along the lines already indicated, such guns must create as large a danger zone in the air as possible, most likely by means of shells which explode when well up. But the problem is how best to employ these sky guns.

Even supposing that a number of sky guns, charged with shell, are employed against one or more 'planes or airships; the result of their shooting might easily be far from satisfactory. This possibility has already been recognised, and in order to make air batteries more certain, a suggestion for combining sky guns has been put forward.

Roughly, the proposal is to place a number of guns together, each one of which must point upward at a slightly steeped angle than the one in front. They would be discharged in a bunch simultaneously.

TS, 10-1914

Testing the Guns
Explaining how weapons of warfare are
tried and proved before acceptance

There is no weapon in use by our forces to-day which has to stand so terrible a strain as the quick-firing gun (not the maxim). This fires a projectile weighing about eighteen and a half pounds. It has a range of over four miles, and the shell, on leaving the muzzle, travels more than three hundred yards in the first second. In all great gun factories there is a special department where this testing is carried out. First of all the barrel, from bore to muzzle, is accurately gauged with most delicate instruments.

Inside the Barrel
Next, a gutta-percha impression is taken of the inside of the barrel. This is kept – filed, you might say – together with full particulars and description of the fun to which it belongs. If all appears correct the gun is sent to the proving ground. Here the testing is most severe, the charges used being considerably heavier than those employed in actual warfare. It speaks well for modern workmanship, that very few cannon show any signs of damage from this treatment. Guns that have withstood the tests ate then returned to the works, where the gauging process is gone through all over again.

Inside and out, the whole barrel is carefully measured to see if there is any enlargement due to the heavy charges. If the expert pronounces that the gun is satisfactory, off it goes, to the grinding shop, where the bore is lapped out with lead blocks in order to give a perfect polish and finish. The final process is the 'browning, ' which consists in treating the whole of the outside of the weapon four or five times with a certain acid. This enables the metal to resist weather in a remarkable fashion.

From Solid Steel

As in a cannon, so in a rifle, the bore is the all-important part. While cannon are built up, the barrel of a rifle is made by boring out a solid rod of steel. These rods are fixed in a lathe, and bored out by drills which enter at opposite ends and almost meet in the centre. The first testing of the bored-out barrel is most ingenious. The breach end is sealed and made airtight. The at the muzzle end is inserted a gauge which exactly corresponds to the correct bore. If the diameter be absolutely true the air compressed in the barrel will support the weight of the gauge. If there is anything wrong the gauge drops. After passing this test satisfactorily, the barrel goes to a man termed a 'viewer, ' who places it on a stand so arranged that light from a mirror is reflected down the barrel. The viewer notes whether any of the rings of light reflected on the polished inner surface are irregular.

Passing the Viewer

If they are, he marks the barrel accordingly, and sends it along to another man who makes the required alteration. His tools are so delicate that he can work to within the thousandth of an inch. Back goes the barrel to another viewer, who, by means of magnifying glasses, is able to judge as to its perfect straightness to within the ten thousandth part of an inch. Watch one of these men at work, and what strikes you most forcibly is not so much that he is able to gauge the barrel; with such marvellous accuracy, but that he seems to discover by magic the exact spot where there is any departure from the straight. He wastes no time about it, and, with a couple of sharp blows with a hammer will instantly rectify a small error. Every rifle goes through the hands of half a dozen experts before leaving the factory, and afterwards is put through severe firing tests, not only to make certain of the soundness of the barrel, but also to ensure that the sighting is as perfect as workmanship can make it. TS, 10-1914

The Awful Invention

What will happen when everybody will be using the pocket wireless telephone.

People are talking of inventing a pocket wireless telephone. According to the optimistic inventor who has been talking about it till he must have got a bad pain in the neck, the new freak will be so cheap and handy that everybody will be using it. I have no gift for scientific descriptions myself, but speaking in general terms I understand that the apparatus will be nothing more than a couple of wires and an indiarubber band, and you wear it round your neck. In fact, the idea is that you put it on in the morning with your collar and tie, and from that moment you become a sort of animated telephone-receiver. You will be able to hear all the conversation that is taking place along your particular air-current, although of course you will be too much of a gentleman to listen on purpose to any remarks not intended for yourself. If you want to talk to anyone, all you will have to do will be to take from your waistcoat pocket the transmitter, which will simply be a rounded piece of metal having all the guilty look of a bad half crown. You will hold this piece of metal in both hands, and address to it and remarks you may have to make. Your words will then travel along the ether waves in all directions for any distance up to about fifty miles, and anybody with a receiver tuned up to your particular pitch will hear what you have to say. It is all going to be just as simple as that. A long experience of telephoning on the present wired system, however, gives me a hint of what is likely to happen when the new invention has finally awakened and stretched itself, so to speak. When you have put your wireless receiver on in the morning, and find that you have drifted into half-a-dozen cross-currents of very animated conversation not intended for your private ear, you will realise that the world is indeed a cold, hard spot. For instance, you rise in the morning and, in accordance with the instructions given away with every packet, you hang your wireless receiver lightly round your neck. And there it is in case anyone wants to talk to you. And just as you are sitting down to breakfast the air-currents will get mixed up for the usual unknown reason, and you will finish your ham and eggs to a tune something like this:

'Of course, I told him, dear, that we shouldn't be able to marry yet, because three hundred a year isn't –. I'm Mrs Jones, of 'The Laurels…. Why haven't the pork sausages come yet? You promised. Are your Dr Squills? Yes I said Squills! Come on; hurry up, my good man. The nurse assures me positively that---. Ah, yes, old man; but you never said anything to me about the little girl with the yellow hair who was walking with you at—. My dear sir, you have got the wrong air-current. You have indeed. I'm Professor Guff, the geologist. I don't know anything about staring-prices or,. Well who 'did' take my umbrella then? I left it on the –. No, I'm not the garage. I'm Mr Black, the undertaker in the High Street. Can I oblige? What? WHAT? Oh, well, if it comes to that, rats to you, too you ill-bred… ' And so on.

Apart from the babel of mixed air-currents there will be a grave liability to trouble in an opposite direction. That is to say you will get on to a single current and will not be able to get away from it anyhow. When you left home in the morning your wife probably asked you to bring back from town a few housekeeping details. And just as you are sitting down to discuss an important project with a likely customer who has more money than he likely needs, the still small voice that is hanging round your neck will remind you that the turkey must not weigh more than ten pounds at the very most, and that you must be sure and taste the cheese before you buy it, as the last lot you had sent home had to be disinfected before it could be used even for the mousetraps.

I do not wish to discourage inventions where they make for the general well being of my fellow men; but, speaking in calm and calculating terms with a vote and an bad cold, I say that the pocket wireless telephone is not good enough. Not half. Why, you may be sitting quietly in a restaurant munching your mid-day chop (or nuts and bananas, as the case may be), when the pugnacious-looking man opposite you, who is twice your fighting-weight, will lean over to you and exclaim; 'Don't you dare say that again!' You will explain weekly that you have said nothing yet, and he will demand to be told, with a sceptical smile, who was it that has just called him a welsher. While you are suggesting that the dispute had better be referred to the waiter, the pugnacious –looking man will remember that he is wearing a wireless receiver round his neck, and that everyone of his clients is talking to him in very plain English.

And he will scowl at you and hurry away, but not before he has probably spoilt your appetite for the rest of the meal. And then suppose you should happen to borrow a fiver from Jones till Saturday, and (by some unaccountable oversight) have omitted to settle up at the promised date. Every time Jones could get a message through on your particular air-current he would be cooing gently into your ear. As you sat in your office, as you walked along the street, or as you hung by your strap in the train, the automatic receiver round your neck would be singing the old sweet song; 'What about it, old chap? Saturday was the day. ' I do not think there will be such an enormous public demand for the pocket wire-less telephone as the optimistic inventor seems to think. I may be mistaken, but that is my impression.   TS, 10-1914

The Enemy's Sugar
How we are doing without it

By L.G. Chiozza Money, MP

The dear food scare has largely passed away, although it is to be feared that there is still a very large number of people who entertain a vague idea that the war is likely to drive the price of food to an extraordinary height. As far as our bulk of food is concerned it may be well to repeat the assurance that there is nothing whatever to worry about. Beef is going to be dear for a short period, but that is an incidental matter, and the price will drop again. Wheat may be very dear after the war for a temporary period, owing to an extraordinary call by European peoples who will have been unable to carry on their normal agricultural work. Broadly speaking, however, during the war, with exceptions here and there, our food supply is secure, and even last month, in the first shock and dislocation of the conflict, our food imports were excellent. With this very brief reference to the general case, which I may expand on another occasion, I want here to direct particular attention to sugar, because what we are doing in the matter of that delectable commodity points a tremendous moral. Between them last year Germany and Austria supplied the United Kingdom with 25,900,000 cwts, of sugar out of a total of 39,300,000 cwts. From the point of view of the sugar consumer, therefore, it would appear that a bitter fate has compelled us to go to war with two exceedingly sweet countries. In these peculiar circumstances, what was to prevent the price of sugar from rising by leaps and bounds? And, indeed, how were we to get sugar at all? Nothing is more certain than that, if the matter had been left by the nation to the play of ordinary 'economic forces, ' sugar would have been at least one shilling per lb, before many months had passed. What a chance for the 'corner' men! Fortunately for sugar consumers we did not resign ourselves to the play of those factors which, at a time not long removed, we should have been quite content to see play havoc in the matter. What the Government has done has been to appoint a Sugar Commission to see to it that the nation is provided with sugar. Just as in peace we sacrifice far more lives than in war, so in peace we permit commercial depredations to proceed which we do not now permit in time of war. In war it is impossible for sugar to be better managed than in peace. We could, if we cared, manage sugar a good deal better than it is managed now. We are dimly realising that in at last using the powers of the development Commissioners to further sugar production in the United Kingdom. We are doing it very timidly, but we are actually moving. What is true of sugar is true of tea, of wool, or timber, and of every other natural product. It is merely stupid for a great nation of forty-six millions of people to depend for these necessaries upon private and irresponsible speculators, whose object it is not to supply the nation but to make profits for themselves. TS, 10-1914

The Munster Fusiliers
Letter from an officer

The following is an extract from an officer which the 'Morning Post' prints from a young officer of the Royal Munster Fusiliers, who is now a prisoner:

'The Germans are really very good to us prisoners, and the doctors seem to be very clever, so there is really nothing to complain about. The other officers were sent off to Germany yesterday, and all the men who were able to travel; so I am alone here among the Germans, except for three of our men who are very bad. By the way, one is a Bandon man; his name is Harrington. He was very bad wounds in his back, and has to lie on his stomach, but they say he will get all right in time. This time where we are is about the same size as Bandon, and it is just one big hospital. Every house in it is full or wounded men, and the flies and the smells are awful.... Well, although we were well beaten, I believe we gave as good as we got. We killed and wounded a great many Germans, and they say themselves that we made a gallant fight of it.

ME, 10-1914

Private Denis Harrington, Munster Fusiliers, from Cork, was killed in action in Gallipoli in August – 1915.

The Post in War

The Army Post Office Corps, as its name implies, consists entirely of Post Office employees, organised so that in times of emergency a sufficient number of expert postal officials would be at the disposal of and come automatically under the control of the military authorities. The men start in drafts of fifty with the mails at definite intervals, and go right up to the firing line. The sorting is done en route, which necessitates working from twelve to sixteen hours or even more out of each twenty-four, whether on sea, land, or is the train. The return journey involves the same hard work with the mails which have been picked up from the men at the front for delivery at home. The number of parcels now going to the men is reaching gigantic proportions, and it is only necessary to realise the amount of labour which this entails to appreciate the trouble of handling them under the conditions. The military operations are being conducted over a wide field which varies from day to day, so that when the scene of hostilities is reached the corps is even then faced with the serious trouble. Moreover, in case of necessity the men are called upon for military duty. For instance, at Mons, where every available man was needed, they were employed digging trenches and in the firing line. In this engagement some were killed and others wounded. In the case of the navy and Post Office have little or no responsibility. All letters and parcels for the ships of the Fleet are handled in the same way as for ordinary provincial delivery. The Admiralty ask for the mail bags to be despatched to various east coast ports, where they take them over for delivery to the different ships.

TS, 10-1914

The Torpedo

Describing some of the wonders of the
modern submarine weapon

A torpedo is about the most terrible and wonderful thing that has ever been devised for spreading death and destruction during war-time. In outward appearance it is a metal tube sixteen feet or more long, and eighteen inches in diameter. One end is pointed, and the other has a fin at the top, and one at the bottom. Set horizontally to these perpendicular fins are two rudders. And behind these are set two propellers which work in opposite directions. By altering the angle of the rudders the torpedo can be made to travel at any depth required, and the upright fins and the two propellers revolving one to the right and the other to the left help to keep the torpedo from turning over or revolving in the water. It is the interior of a torpedo which is so wonderful. It is almost like a little submarine boat. About a quarter of the length of the missile, consisting of its pointed end, is the warhead filled with wet, compressed gun-cotton, and in the very nose of the torpedo is the striker, a little rod which, as soon as the torpedo hits a ship, plunges down like a piston into the centre of the gun-cotton, which at once explodes and blows the ship sky-high. In the ordinary way this striker is held in place by a pin which prevents it from being driven inwards, but, on firing, this pin is automatically withdrawn so that the torpedo may deal its deadly blow. The centre of the torpedo, for about a third of its length, is filled with compressed air, which works all the intricate machinery filling the after-compartment. The popular opinion is that a torpedo is fired at a ship in a manner similar to that in which a shell is fired, and it gets its motive power in the same way; but this is not so.

It was true that a torpedo is stared on its journey by being fired from a tube, but if it had to depend on this firing to carry it to its destination it would not travel more than a hundred yards or so. Directly it is discharged from the tube, and as soon as it gets in the water, the machinery is the interior of the torpedo is automatically set in motion, the two propellers start to whirl at a dizzy rate and drive the torpedo onward to its mark. If it is deflected slightly from its course a gyroscope, spinning round in the interior, works a series of levers which bring it back to the right direction. The compressed air drives a four-cylinder engine which in turn drives the propellers. Then on the nose of the torpedo are knives which will cut a way for the torpedo through the torpedo-net with which a battleship tries to protect itself from being torpedoed. The machinery of the torpedo will drive it for about 2,000 yards, and it traverses this distance in about two minutes; so a torpedo-boat or submarine has to get to within a mile of its victim before it can launch the torpedo, and this brings the torpedo-boat within point-blank range of the big and little guns of a battleship. Thus it will be seen that torpedo attacks are best made at night, when the torpedo-boats have a chance of stealing upon their victims unawares. The torpedo has buoyancy chambers so that the missile floats when the machinery runs down. Another clever device shows a light as soon a it comes to a stand-still, thus indicating its whereabouts to the boat's crew told off during practice to pick it up. A torpedo costs a big sum – £500 to be exact.

TS, 10-1914

The War and Wild Game

One curious effect of the war has been noticed in Switzerland. Wild animals and birds of all kinds are fleeing from Western Germany and parts of Austria, frightened by the incessant cannon and rifle shots, and seeking sanctuary in the Swiss forests and Alps. They include wild boars, deer of various kinds, goats, as well as wild fowl, while in the lower Engadine even bears have been seen. The Swiss lakes and rivers are crowded with terrified birds pf all sorts, but the authorities have very properly prohibited shooting on these waters so that the poor birds may get a rest before continuing their flight to safer regions. It is said that large numbers of wild boars from the Black Forest have entered the Jura Alps, passing through the ranks of the contending armies in Alsace without being noticed. On the Russian frontier a more ominous sign of war is reported. There it is said huge packs of wolves are to be seen prowling around the battlefields and adding to the terrors of the helpless wounded. Vultures are plentiful along all battle fronts waiting to eat the unburied dead.

TS, 10-1914

This Ship for Sale

Have you ever, during you annual visit to the seaside, noticed a ship lying at anchor in the harbour, or roads, with a broom fastened to her mast head. Most probably you have, and wondered whatever it meant. There is quite a simple meaning to it, however, for it is a sailor's sign which tell seafaring men that that particular ship is for sale. Although the average person would be absolutely at a loss as to what the sign conveyed to a sailor the meaning would be quite clear.

TS, 10-1914

Those Silent Orders
Why military instructions are nowadays so often passed by signal

Were the Napoleon Bonaparte to come to life again and visit a modern battlefield, among the many things he would see calculated to startle him would be the extent to which the word of command has been replaced by signals of one kind or another. This is an inevitable development of war. The widely-extended formations – the enormous fronts on which battles are fought, the incessant and frightful din of modern artillery all tend to make it impracticable for leaders to give their orders by word of mouth, or by flag-signalling or heliograph, and so whistle or manual signals are resorted to. The bugle, by the way, has largely gone out as a means of giving orders, if only because its call is easily heard and interpreted by the foe. Anyway, the only war bugle-calls now authorised ate the 'charge' and the 'alarm. ' The Germans give most of their orders by whistle, and, British officers and non-coms, are also provided with whistles. The following are the official whistle-calls:

(a) To draw attention to a signal about to be made – a short blast.

(b) To denote 'cease fire' – a long drawn-out blast.

(c) To denote 'rally' in wood, bush, fog, or darkness, when the signal 'close' cannot be seen – a succession of short blasts.

(d) To denote alarm – a succession of alternate long and short blasts.

Signals by hand or arm are largely used in skirmishing, warning that a signal is about to be made being given, as already explained, by a short blast on the whistle, on hearing which the skirmishers will look towards their commander. Thus, if he extends his arm at full length above his head, and waves it slowly a few times from side to side, this means 'extend. ' But an extension may be made from the centre or from one flank or the other.

Mute Directions

If the commander gives the signal in the manner already described, and then drops his arm to his side, this means 'extend from the centre, ' that is, the centre man of the line or squad stands fast or moves straight forward, while the remainder incline outwards from him. If the commander finishes the signal with his arm pointing to the right, this means 'extend from the right, ' and, similarly, 'extend from the left' is indicated when his outstretched arm remains pointing to the left. The 'close' is signalled by placing the hand on the top of the head, with the elbow square to the right or left, according to which arm is used. This means 'close on the centre, ' 'close on the right or left' being signalled by finishing the signal with hand pointing to right or left. 'Advance' and 'retire' are respectively signalled by 'arm swung from rear to front below the shoulder, ' and 'arm circled above the head. ' A sort of jumping movement with the clenched fist rapidly moved up and down between the thigh and shoulder tells the men to double. To stop an advance or retreat, the commander raises his arm at full extent above his head; while, if he wishes his men to lie down after halting, he makes two or three movements of the open hand towards the ground.

Scouts and Skirmishers

It is the duty of skirmishers and scouts to give the earliest possible intimation of the presence of the enemy, and whether he is in force or in small numbers only. 'Enemy in sight in small numbers' is signalled by holding the weapon up above the head and as if in the act of guarding a blow. If the weapon is similarly held above the head, but us frequently raised and lowered, then the message reads 'Enemy in sight in large numbers. ' Perhaps reinforcements are wanted in which case the arm is swung from right front above the shoulder. To let your own side know that there is no enemy in sight, the rifle, or other weapon, is held up at the full extent of the arm, muzzle or point uppermost. German airmen, one reads have been signalling the position of French and British batteries, etc, by dropping(. . unreadable word...)discs, giving the required information.

TS, 10-1914

Up-to-date War Dodges
How the war game is being played on either side

The present campaign is helping to prove the value, or otherwise, of many military theories; but for the man in the street perhaps one of the most interesting studies in this connection consists in the methods adopted by the various combatants for deceiving one another and dodging destruction while fighting in the progress. During the operation in Belgian towns, for example, soldiers and townspeople alike quickly grew accustomed to the continual arrival of shells in their midst; and so the art of dodging shellfire was very soon mastered by all those concerned. A shell explodes upwards in the shape of a rough V; therefore, in order to avoid the results of the explosion, it is necessary to lie down flat on the ground. To remain standing means that you will be killed. A successful ruse adopted by the Germans in battle lately was that of hiding. They placed their guns just inside a wood, but in this position the artillery would have been visible, so the following plan was adopted. The guns were hidden from view by means of great piles of fodder, with the result that they presented the appearance of miniature hayricks. The result was terrible, for the British troops marched within range, never suspecting the true position of affairs, so that when the guns opened fire Britishers – and Irish suffered severely, and were obliged to withdraw as quickly as possible. One of the most trying ordeals with which troops have had to put up with is shown in the use of the German aerial range finder. The German air scout flies over the British trenches, dropping, dropping, as he goes, an explosive which gives out a big white smoke cloud. This cloud provides the German batteries with the exact range required, and they then proceed to pour a destructive fire into the enemy lines. This move of the Germans has naturally given rise to certain counter-moves on the part of the Allies.

When the Allies perceive a German air scout coming towards them from the horizon they hastily take up a false position and the scout conveys the information to his own artillery. As soon, however, as the scout flies back to his own lines, the British and French troops evacuate the false position. The result of this manoeuvre is that the German artillery wastes its fire upon the empty trenches. In a country where there are trees advantage is taken of such natural cover, and trenches are dug under shelter. Troops entrenched thus are invisible to the hovering air scout, who is therefore unable to give his own side the exact range required. Thus, by stroke and counter-stroke, the men on either side seek to outwit each other in the great game of war.

TS, 10-1914

Watching a Battle from the Air
From the journal of an aeroplane observer at the front

We ascended from the aerodrome half an hour before the great artillery preparation was scheduled to start. As we swept around in a broad climbing spiral I cast an anxious eye towards the sector of the front where the attack was to be made. It was quiet. There was a stray 'universal shell' to keep up the tradition of 'daybreak hate. ' The first rays of dawn had seen the disappearance of the last of our motor transport. All was in readiness. As we climbed beyond the first fringe of low cloud I could see the enemy's lines and the area of his field artillery. Shell-bursts and gun-flashes were infrequent. There was no sign of preparation. No hostile aeroplane was in sight. After twenty-five minutes of climbing we got ready for the artillery. In a few minutes the area which was now so quiet would be literally like the mouth of hell. Hardly had I indicated 'all clear' when a dozen guns discharged below and behind. I counted the seconds up to twelve – the bursts fell with regularity and precision on the area. These were the 'rangers. ' They were duly checked. In less than a minute our errors were corrected and the bombardment commenced. From the hedges, wood fringes, and villages for miles around batteries of all kinds began to speak. It was still just dark enough to see the different coloured flashes. The effect as seen from the air was just as though the whole countryside was illuminated in some weird way by great swinging Chinese lanterns. The concentrated horrors of bombardment are best seen form the air. Houses, trees, trenches, and natural features seem thrown and shattered into piles of common ruin. Human life would appear impossible. But there was little time for contemplation. Behind the enemy's lines there was movement. He had been caught napping, and was now rushing up heavy artillery to hold the sector. I a moment we had spotted the region pf his 'movements, ' which became 'registered targets' to be harassed by our batteries. The bombardment had now become general. Great salvos of enemy high-explosive began to heave and tear at our front line trenches; series of shrapnel searched our reserve trenches, where the enemy knew only too well that the infantry concentration was being completed. But meanwhile the tremendous advantage of artillery preparation could not be denied. The enemy was suffering terribly, and, although he searched our field artillery area repeatedly, the gun positions were so carefully selected and so readily changed that our fire did not slacken. A hostile aeroplane was sent up to find those positions, to direct fire on the flashes, and to retrieve the situation. We saw his 'crosses' distinctly as he swung sunwards into his spiral. He was an 'extension-Aviatik,' a lumbering bi-plane with great powers of endurance, but with little speed and less ability to manoeuvre. The Aviatik had seen us, and started his regulation of targets as safe distance behind his own lines. Before he had had time to engage the targets he had registered we bore down wind and got round him – a manoeuvre which by some strange chance he had failed to observe and to encounter. He did not, indeed realise our proximity until we had actually dived at him and opened fire with our machine gun. Then he had to fight. Both machines drifted side-wind over the lines, blazing at one another with all weapons available. A vast crackle of rifles and machine-guns greeted us from the area of the trenches. We were not more than 4,000ft up and were losing height rapidly. By persistently closing with him on his turns we gradually forced the Avaitik oder to our side of the lines and then bore down on him. After resisting for about three minutes the Aviatik thought better of it and decided to get back at all costs. Although we slid almost on top of him he managed to clear beneath us by a dangerous nose dive. He just crept back over his trenches and landed so close up that our 12-pounders hammered him to bits before he had some to a standstill. The meeting in the air had occupied nine minutes. During that time so intense was the interest of the many thousands of 'spectator-combatants' on both sides that there was a distinct lull in the battle. The moral effect of the result was considerable. The moment of infantry attack was now at hand. The gunners had done their work. Trenches and obstacles were alike in ruins. I gave the signal. Receding shrapnel took the place of high-explosive and dropped with deadly precision a few yards in front of our first line of attackers. The ground seemed to vomit men. From the air they looked animated dots as they scrambled ant-like across the few yards which separated the trenches. There was little there to meet them, and less hostile infantry.

Here and there a man fell, but the line of attackers as virtually whole when it reached the German trenches. Reserves were rushed up in perfect order. The attack was pressed home into the reserve trenches and beyond. It as here that the grim fighting began. Hidden machine-guns began to enfilade, snipers began to spit. In a few minutes our original front line of attack was badly shattered, but there was the grim flash of the sun on hundreds of British bayonets. There was no flash when the bayonets had found their first mark. Here and there, as the battle began to wane and the enemy resistance had broken down, I could see machine-gun crews running for dear life in the direction of their artillery dug-outs, with the bayonets on their heels. Then the enemy began to rain high-explosive and shrapnel on the whole area, killing both friend and foe; but our '...'s' had the last word to say, and the enemy was again stifled. The new position was soon consolidated. The bombardment died down on both sides. Smoking shell-holes, heaps of dead, and increased desolation were the only changes in the general scene as I had surveyed it two hours before. But our line had been straightened out and the enemy salient removed.

We circled once over the battle zone. A score of angry 'Archies' spat at us. We went home to the aerodrome for breakfast. TS, 09-1915

Archies is a RFC slang word for anti-aircraft guns.

Watching and Sniping

'I have been sent to the trenches with my platoon and have got a fine place. The enemy's trenches are 250 yards in front and one can see any movement. We watch them as cats watch a mouse, and I have an observation post where I have been watching and sniping. I have had several shots, but no bullseye yet; the devils are too cute. They have four big guns in front which go banging off at all times. They have a huge big gun which we call Black Maria. She has a shell of 230lb, and a range of over 10 miles. I was greeted by her on my first day. I had a lucky escape there from a splinter. I got my first wound about ten days ago; we were in support on the side of a hill and an aeroplane went over and gave the show away. We got tons of high explosive shells and shrapnel. Three big explosives kicked within ten yards of me and a chunk hit me on the side of the arm and the rest buried me in my dugout. I had to be pulled out and only just in time, as I had two cartloads of stuff over me. So you can imagine I have a holy horror of some of those things. I have not had any sleep for the past six nights, as I stroll around my position at night to see if they are awake and if anything is happening. You bet I shall be jolly glad when this show is over. There is not much truth when a chap writes home and says he is having a topping time; it is only swank. To be moved on all day by shells is no fun.

My teeth are a bit sore from the biscuits. This regiment has had the devil's own luck so far. They have been in every engagement from Mons and the retreat and have only lost four officers wounded, but we must not boast, as we say every shell has its names written on it'.

'Very funny coincidence; we had to go through a big wood, beating it for any spies, and this was 1 October, pheasant day. This caused great amusement.'

'I find huge relief in a pipe in the trenches, waiting for the unknown. We get a Government issue of navy cut once a week of 2 oz, which lasts me easily. Don't forget a letter, paper, or anything is most acceptable out here to pass the time and divert thoughts. Also food in any shape is very acceptable, as our food is rather curtailed, although excellent. A piece of milk chocolate is what I should like more than anything. All small parcels get through, no big ones. Please do not send equipment, as there is nowhere to put it and no chance to change. I wear all I can. Chocolate or a few chocolate biscuits next time you write, if you please. It is a great thing to know that one is taking part in the biggest battle in the world. Will you send us some envelopes and paper, as there is none to be got here?. You will get this in your old envelope.'   KCC, 10-1914

Waterford Soldier's Story

Private Michael Whelan, of Ballybricken, who is in the Victoria Hospital. Cork, graphically related how last week his regiment, the Royal Irish, as well as some of the Northumberlands, West Surreys, Lancashires, and a Scotch regiment were at the front of the fighting line in Belgium. They had been continually engaged attacking all the time. On Wednesday last they were engaged pressing back the enemy successfully when towards evening the shrapnel, which struck his and injured is hand so badly that he was unable to use his rifle. As quickly and possible he sought the shelter of the trench and lay there till night, and about 9 o'c he crawled back as well as he could to where the main body of the British force was stationed. Here he got first aid, and after being roughly bandaged, was conveyed back to the base hospital at Bethune next day. As an indication of the severe nature of the fighting he said that on the following morning, when the roll was called, out of a party of 350 who went out the previous night day only 75 returned. After being attended to at Bethune he was sent down in a train to the coast and brought in the 'Oxfordshire' to Queenstown, the journey from France taking two days in a smooth passage. On Tuesday, as he lay in bed at the hospital, was the first tile he experienced anything like comfort since he met with his injuries, and, in company with others in the hospital, he highly appreciated the skill and attention which the matron and staff bestowed on them.   WN, 10-1914

Michael Whelan survived the war.

With a Routed Army
Showing what occurs to a military force that has suffered defeat

Running away sounds, a very simple operation, and so it is, but it results in a state of being for the individual soldier that is very complicated, and one which, if he were in the frame of mind for reflection, should make him wish that he and his fellows had gone with less hurry and a little more kick. The first thing that happens to a routed army is that its feeding arrangements break down. Even where all is going well, it is sometimes not easy to get food to the various units, especially if the lines of communication be lengthy. Every wagon sent full to the front has to return empty to the base, and this, of course, congests the lines with vehicles doing no effective work. There is a system by which each regiment draws its food and ammunition from the supply force, whose business is to keep in touch with the fighting men, and frequently, even when all is going well, there is delay in this. But when the fighting men are panic-stricken doing all they know to put a large distance between themselves and the enemy, and are hurrying towards home in broken detachments along every road that is open to them, then how is the supply force, even if it be itself unfrightened, to get food to the nerve-wrecked warriors? If it knew in the morning where they were, it could only be quite certain that by midday they would be somewhere else. Therefore, to run away is but to cut oneself off from one's bread-and-butter – probably the worse calamity of all.

Every soldier is supposed to have on his person emergency rations to keep him fit for a few hours, but after they have been eaten – and beaten soldiers always gobble up what food they have – the only hope of getting more is to rob the houses one passes. A soldier, especially a European conscript, relies for his efficiency upon the discipline that binds himself and his fellows into a coherent, effective army. Once that goes, he is Hans the cobbler, or Schmidt the commercial traveller again, and he finds the world a distressing and dangerous place to live in. Great guns have shot away the foundations of his universe, and, as his pricked-up ears tell him, are booming away behind him with the unkind determination to blow him, too, into chaos and the night. It is when that comes home to him that his scampering feet positively twinkle a he speeds off to safety, or to where he desperately hopes safety is. Until the ranks broke down and scattered before the punishment of the enemy game Hans Schmidt had not to think – he only had to do what he was told. There were no officers and non-commissioned officers with lethal weapons to see that he did it. To flinch meant certain death; to go on against the foe was the safer thing. He had, therefore, as much mind of his own as a bee in a swarm. But when terror disrupted discipline, and he and his fellows ran from the silver-grey steel, he was amazed to find that his officers were speeding quite ad fast in the same direction, with no thought of giving any order to anyone on the whole wide universe. In that crowded moment Hans found himself a free agent in a world full of despair.

Thundering behind him were the guns, and loosed at him, on the terribly trampling feet of swift, incredibly swift, horses, were the cavalry sent to stop any effort towards reforming into disciplined bodies once more. Hans, with one eye over his shoulder, ran in the direction he thought the enemy's horsemen were not going, was sent still another way by shell-fire, got headed off yet again by fear of a bayonet charge, and then, bowed down by the complexity of things, simply ran with a pounding heart and sobbing breath.

With utter longing de desires the friendly night to come down on him. Anybody can have the pomp and panoply of martial pride. He has no use for them. What he passionately desires is a whole skin, and no more shells, bullets, or any other form of sudden death. Now, the commissariat, having been told that the enemy has become a rabble, has only one thought- to get where the enemy cannot capture it. The ammunition wagons march off at a gallop with the same passionate impulse.

TS, 10-1914

Wounded Irish Guardsman Returns to Birr
His experiences at Mons and Landrecies

Private Benjamin Walsh of the first Battalion Irish Guards, arrived in Birr on Friday evening, having been wounded at the front. He tells an interesting story of the severe fighting in Belgium and France, between Mons and Laundrecies, having taken part in the now famous retreat of the latter position. He graphic descriptions of the bursting shrapnel and the heavy rifle fire to which the Guards were subjected. 'The German maxims and shrapnel fire he describes as deadly. The rifle fire of the Germans was not so accurate, and to him they seemed to fire mostly from the knee or hip, not sighting their rifles as the British soldiers do. The Guards of the first Battalion, left Wellington Barracks one morning early, and were despatched for France.

From the Havre base they were sent by train, and arrived at a town, tha name of which our informant does not now remember. Here they rested for about half an hour. They arrived there at 3, 30. From this they marched to Longville, which is about 4 miles from Mons. When about two miles from their destination they saw the artillery fire. They continued on, were formed into platoons and were ordered to load their rifles. He belonged to the twelfth platoon of the third company, and his officer was Lord Guernsey. It was explained that there were four platoons to the company. When going into action the village, with the farmhouse around were on fire. They got an object to march on, and on arriving there they were ordered to lie down in extended order. Here the German artillery shots and shrapnel were passing over their heads and bursting behind them. At this point the firing was over their heads, so at that time no one was injured.

They then passed up along the German left flank, all the time the shrapnel shrieking over them. They arrived at what he thought were castle grounds, and passed up a long avenue. Captain Bernard was in charge of his Company, No 3. They were now for two and a half hours under fire, and got the order to fix bayonets, and to reinforce other regiments which he believed were the Scottish Borderers, Irish Rifles and Coldstream Guards. Several men were now falling around him, and the German rifle men were but 400 yards away, that being the sighting ordered for the rifles. They concentrated their fire on the German Infantry. The Maxims of the British did deadly execution in their opponent's ranks. The German attack drew off, and his company had about three hours rest. It was now Monday, and the men were in an exhausted condition. They then fell back for about 30 miles to Landrecies where he formed one of the Fourth Brigade of Guards. They marched this 30 miles, and were not under fire at the time.

At Landrecies the Irish Guards were on the right flank, the Coldstreams being on outpost duty. The Germans came on to the attack, and passed outposts by speaking French to the officers. When it was discovered that they were Germans a very heavy fire was opened on them. He believes that there were a thousand Germans killed at Landrecies, and at about 4 o/c on Tuesday morning the Irish Guards were ordered to relieve the Coldstreams.

It was at landrecies, that he was hurt. He got a severe sprain, and a bullet also grazed his knee. He was taken by members of the Fourth Brigade Field Ambulance Transport to Leon, where he was entrained for Rouen where the Base Hospital was situated. After about a day and a half the Base Hospital at Rouen was broken up, the Germans coming within about 30 miles of it. At Roeun he was taken down the Seine on the St Patrick, a steamer belonging to the Great Western Railway. They left Roeun at about 11 o/c on Monday, and landed at Southampton at about 8, 45 on Tuesday morning. From thence he was taken to Brighton where he remained until he joined the second Battalion of Guards at Brentwood, and was recommended for sick furlough.

The Commanding Officer of the Guards was wounded.

Private Walsh speaks very highly of the treatment given to the British soldier by the people of France and Belgium. On the march they supplied them with food, milk, and other necessaries.

Part of the time the Guards were not in touch with the convoys. Their army rations were biscuits and bully beef. He shows a piece of French biscuit which appears not to be quite as hard as the English stuff. On the way down from the front the French were also very kind to the wandering Britishers, meeting them at the station, and supplying them with hot coffee, cheese, bread, cigarettes, etc. In the party who returned home with him were sixty-four wounded Coldstream Guards.

Before the war broke out he was on the railway with his brother Daniel who also belonged to the Irish Guard Reserve, and who was also called up to the Regiment. The last he saw of his brother was at Landrecies. When he was wounded, his brother was still uninjured in the fighting line. Nothing has been heard of Daniel since.

Some very pathetic incidents were told to our representative. Two brothers of an English regiment were in the firing line. One was killed and the other brother went over to see him, and received a bullet, and fell dead across the corpse.

The time was a very rough one. 'I could not describe all my experiences; the din was terrible. Private Walsh showed our representative his jacket, and pointed out where the buttons had been cut off it as souvenirs. He also showed a medal which he had received in Belgium from some people there, as well as a tobacco pouch belonging to a Belgian farmer.

On his uniform cap he wears the Belgium colours which had also been presented to him. After being wounded he lost his puttees and other articles, and said that the great coat he had at present was not his own which had also been lost. The wounded man is at present at home in Seffin.

He is brother of Mr William Walsh the popular Guard between Birr and Roscrea.

MT- TS-KCV, 10-1914

Benjamin Walsh and Captain Bernard survived the war. Daniel Walsh, his brother, was killed in action a few weeks after this article was written

November, 1914

From Roscommon Soldiers to Friends at Home

We have been forwarded by Mr Heverin, Secretary of the Roscommon County Council, copies of letters received by Mrs Lynch, Roscommon, from her son lately serving with the Enniskillen Fusiliers, now in hospital in Paris, who was wounded at the battle of Mons; and, a copy of a letter from the clergyman who attended him. The further letter given has been received by Mr Smith, Roscommon, whose brother is serving with the Royal Engineers:

Hit in a Bad Place

My Dear Mother, – I have just received your very kind and welcomed letter all right and was very glad to see you are all well as this leaves me at present, thank God. You have no cause to fret over me now. I had the bullet taken out just over a week ago, and I am getting on grand, thank God. I was surprised to see my father was called up; I thought he was too old for service, but he will be alright.

When you are writing again send me her address. I am sure she would like to hear from me. We do have a lot of people coming in to see us. They do not know what to make of us, they are very kind and the Sisters are very good to us. Dear Mother, I was very bad after the operation. I hope I will never have to have one again. I got hit in a very bad place, it was not like the arm or the leg. I got it very hard to breathe until I got the bullet out, but thank God I am all right for another while. I must now close with love to all. Hoping to hear from you as often as you can. I am, your fond son. Paddy.

P.S.—Put my name on your next letter

Clergyman's Letter

St Joseph's Church.
50, Avenue Hoche
Parism VIII.
27-10-1914.
Dear Mrs Lynch,

I am sure you are glad your son is making such good progress. I was with him to-day, and I have seen him almost every day since his operation. He is looking better than I have seen him before. I gave him the last Sacraments a week ago yesterday, as he felt as though he wound never get over his operation. I told him Extreme Unction was for the health of the body as well as the soul and I told him he would get over it all right and to-day, only eight days after his operation he is looking quite well and is feeling well. I hope you will have him home with you before Christmas. The Cardinal Archbishop of Paris gave him his blessing about three weeks ago, and to-day I brought His Lordship, the Bishop of Sale, Australia, to see him. He is well taken care of. May God bless you and yours.—I am, yours sincerely in J.O. Father Clifford.

PS: I am posting a letter from Patsy to you – WC.

These two men survived the war.

A Gurkha Charge
Germans Flee in Terror

It is a tradition of the Indian army that Highlanders and Gurkhas work together. It is because they are both men of the mountain, or that they recognise with mutual admiration in each other the same grim, dour fighting qualities? No matter. The fact stands. Where there is fierce, desperate work to be done, there are the Highlanders, and the Gurkhas are quick on their heels. Here is a description given by a correspondent of 'The Journal' of a charge of the Highlanders, which, in spite of unflinching heroism might have failed but for the timely interventions of the terrible 'kukris' of the terrible little men. The writer had seen a Highland regiment sent forward to carry a line of hostile trenches, had seen their heroic charge checked – but not repulsed – by a murderous fire, still more by the intricate barbed wire entanglements on which they had stumbled unawares. 'It is certain, ' he writes, 'that the Scotsmen would have maintained their charge till not a man was left standing, had they not received sudden and conclusive aid. Between the gaps in their ranks slipped the Gurkhas, and insinuating themselves like cats between and under the barbed wire, their kukris in their left hand, disappeared in the enemy's trenches. Then arose a terrible medley of cries – the harsh battle cry of the attackers, the groans or scrams of the attacked, as the terrible knife went home and heads rolled around. In the tumult of carnage, the commands of the German officers, who sought to rally their men, were lost. In the mud and slime of the trenches a terrible struggle, hand-to-hand, body-to-body, was proceeding. The end came quickly. In a mad frenzy of fear, the Germans broke, and ran, throwing their rifles from them, blundering into their own wire entanglements, caught in their own traps. ' Such prisoners as were taken bore in their eyes a nameless terror. For hours after they had been brought into the British lines, they trembled constantly. There was hardly need to guard them. The terror of the charge had deprived them of volition, almost power of motion.

Are big guns tested before being used in battle – and if so, how?

Every big gun, even every rifle, before it is used in actual warfare, is thoroughly tested for any weakness. There may be a flaw, an air-hole right in the middle of the metal, ad this flaw, if not discovered, would result in the bursting of the gun when fully charged, and the killing of its crew. The guns are tested in a specially constructed shelter made of heavy iron rails. There is a special screen at the back of the shelter, also made of rails, to prevent fragments flying out in that direction. The gun is fired by means of an electric wire from the firing butt. Every gun is tested with a charge which is 25 per-cent stronger than the gun will ever have to stand in wartime. If it comes through this test successfully there is very little danger of it bursting in actual warfare.

TS, 11-1914

A Waterford Merry with the French Army

Mr Robert G Merry, a son of Mr Joseph Xavier Merry (the oldest living representative of the Waterford family of Merry) and a brother-in-law of the eldest son of the Editor of the 'News,' has since the outbreak of the war been engaged in piloting a motor for General Gourrand. Writing to 'The Autocar' Mr Merry says: 'I am pleased to think that I am doing my share for my own country and for France. I have long been waiting for the opportunity, and now it has come. My fifteen years as manager for Dunlops on the Continent is now very useful to me, as I know Europe well and speak quite a few languages. Also my trips to India, Siam, the Straits Settlements, Surinam and Ceylon for Napiers, and South Africa for Mors, have been good training for this war, as they taught me much about motoring under all sorts of difficulties. But, all the same, this war is quite another matter, and I am even beginning to feel the strain. My first day of service totalled 600 klometres(372) miles in about ten hours, then 1, 100 kilometres (683) miles without a stop. My total mileage up to the present (21 October) is 12,000 kilometres (6,452) miles. The motor service plays a most important part in this war. Armies and towns are moved by motor car. The French have no fewer than 45,000 motor vehicles, so many with each Army Corps, each with their supplies and travelling repair shops and staffs almost to build a new car if necessary. It is a new arm of the Service, but it will be quite believed that in this respect the French are right up-to-date. The repair trains are always full of work, for the service is much too severe for many cars. Take my own car, for instance. Without consideration of the distance covered, I have run my engine for days and nights practically without a stop of any importance, and frequently over roads so frightfully cut up that I have had to cover miles and miles upon first and second speeds, and six times in two days I had o be hauled out of morasses by horses. We have now received sets of hauling rope and sets of Parsons chains with a supply of glycerine for the radiators. This looks as if we were in it for the winter. I am more than lucky to be driving General Gourand, as I have to take him in the very thick of it. Sometimes it is a little too thick. One night I shall not forget in a hurry, for I spent most of it driving through a huge forest without any light, as the Germans were thick about. In addition to much road obstruction, we are frequently held up by the prone bodies of the dead and wounded lying all over the road, to say nothing of artillery trains, troops, and transport. Dead horses, too, are not nice at night. The poor animals are having a very bad time of it, but, thanks to motor cars, they are spared a lot. Motor cars supply us with light, post, telegraph, food, etc., and, indeed, the progress of the war would be still slower without them, but sometimes they are too fast. One night the Germans brought a few thousand troops forty-two miles by means of motor cars. We have captured many German cars, but they now find it very hard to get any of ours, as we are advancing all the time now. But even when we were retreating we carried the broken-down cars with us. I am more pleased than I can tell you to be in the French Army and to wear French Uniform, as I get a big reception everywhere. My French comrades always offer to share anything that they have to drink, or half their straw when they are resting, but, in addition, I have thoroughly acquired the art of getting a refreshing sleep in a car. I am beginning to feel that I have almost seen enough of the horrors of this war, and, like many others, I shall be more than glad when we arrive at the finish, which must be at Berlin. Destruction reigns wherever the Germans have passed, and we have shot many of their spies that they left behind. The German shells are terrible enough, but from what I have seen our French shells are even more effective. . I will not give any details, as they are too horrible to mention. It is a fearful thing to see our officers and friends struck down all around you, but notwithstanding all these trials, everybody is as bright and happy as possible, borne up by the cheering thought of attaining in due course the great end we have in view.'

WN, 11-1914

Are Sheds for Zeppelins Easily Constructed?

When the German had occupied both Brussels and Antwerp and it was reported that they were busy building sheds to house Zeppelins, many people scoffed at the idea. 'They can't do any such thing in a hurry, ' was the general opinion. But general opinion was wrong; a temporary shed or hangar for military dirigibles or other aircraft can be put up in a very short time – in two days, as a matter of fact. But it is comforting to know such quick mounting is only possible where all the various parts necessary in erecting a 'house' for airships or aeroplanes can be got to hand ready-made. It is not possible, for instance, to cut down a few trees, saw them into planks, and proceed to build a structure of new timber. A great quantity of folding metal work, as well as a expanse of metallised cloth, is required, and where this has to be transported by rail a train of twenty trucks is needed. An Italian firm is responsible for the introduction of one of the most recent portable hangars. The component parts are iron angles made in sections, and the necessary cloth for the covering. The sections are joined together on the ground, and when the two halves of an arch are completed they are raised up by means of a 'tower, ' ropes and pulleys, clamped to the ground at their base, and 'locked' at the top by means of a 'pin. ' When the arches are in position they are securely bound together by cross-brace pieces. The metallised cloth, very strong and weatherproof – if not actually bomb and shot-proof – is then fixed over the arches, and the temporary shed or hangar is ready for use.

TS, 11-1914

Back From Douai
Kilkenny Lady's Thrilling Experience

Miss Mary F. Doheny arrived in Kilkenny on Saturday morning last from Douai, where she had been residing from the outbreak of the war till the early part of last week. She has had a very trying experience, and is, needless to say, glad to be home with her mother, Mrs M. G. O'Keeffe, Nore Villa, St John's Quay. We have published many extracts from letters written by Miss Doheny while in Douai, where she was a daily witness of the sad havoc wrought by the disastrous war. The last few days of her stay in the old French city were full of excitement, and indeed of danger, and a large number of the inhabitants fled the city at the same time as Miss Doheny. The family with whom she was residing have gone to Paris – that is the women and children, for the men folk have, of course, been called to the colours.

The German army occupied Douai on what they regarded as their triumphal march to Paris. Foiled in their design, they are once more – and this time a beaten and retreating army – in the district of Douai, Lille and Arras, and severe fighting is taking place all along the line. Some days before miss Doheny left she was in the garden after dejeuner when she heard the booming of the German guns in dangerously close proximity. She beat a hasty retreat to the house, and, with the members of the family, sought refuge in the cellar. The firing lasted from about two o'clock to six, when it ceased. Next day the family decided to leave the city (a large number of the inhabitants taking a similar course) for Paris. It was thought wiser that Miss Doheny should try to get home to Ireland. She travelled with the family as far as Lille, where she remained one night. Thence she got to Calais, but being late for the boat there she proceeded to Boulogne. Here she had some difficulty in getting her passport, but she fortunately met Colonel of a Scotch regiment who was of great assistance to her, and a French Boy Scout conducted her to the office of the Prefect, where the necessary papers were obtained, a most minute description of the young lady – her age, height, colour of her hair, eyes, and eyebrows, shape of her nose (which is 'droit'), and of her mouth(which was 'petite'), not to speak of her complexion (which is 'frais') being entered thereon. She got safely to London, whence, having rested with friends for some days, she returned home.   KP, 11-1914

Miss Mary Francis Doheny is in the 1901 census living with her family in Walkins Street, Kilkenny. She was born in Kilkenny and is not in the 1911 census. Also see 'Carrick-on-Suir Lady's Thrilling Experience at Liege'.

Ballyhale Soldier's Experience

Private P. Brophy, 18th Royal Irish, of Ballyhale, County Kilkenny, writing to a friend, states:

'My leg is improving greatly. I expect to be up shortly. The wound is not healed. I will be six weeks in bed on Monday. I would like to get a chance of getting up. '

'P----D---- must have been wounded in the second battle at a place called Cordai on 26 August last. I have not seen him since. It was a big battle. There were a lot killed and wounded. I did see some terrible sights after that battle which I would not like to see again. It was all artillery fire. There were shells bursting everywhere. There was a party to reinforce us. A shell burst in the middle of them. We passed by them. It would make you sick to look at them. We got a bit of our own back in the third battle. Both positions were the same, The Germans were on one hill and we on another, and the valley between. The battle lasted only five hours, when the Germans retired. We captured 350 prisoners, a machine gun and ten lances. We were kept on the move until 10 o'clock that night.

'We had not gone far when a shell burst in front of the first section of fours. We were then opened up in ten sections thirty yards apart and ordered to be down under their artillery fire, The regiment was in luck that day, no-one got hit, but they came near enough to us. We then had to advance under artillery fire. We were sent along the road one after another, ten paces apart, as quick as we could run. We got safe into a deep cutting, when we had to cross a bridge, but when we came to it it was blown up in the middle. We got across however, on the side rails. I think I will be home for Christmas.'   KP, 11-1914

Private Brophy survived the war.

Boy Labour

Owing to the huge numbers of lads who are working in Woolwich Arsenal, there is a famine of boy labour in South East London. There are 6,000 now employed there in making bullets and so on.

TS, 11-1914

Carrick-on-Suir Lady's
Thrilling Experience at Liege

A young lady, a native of Carrick-on-Suir, who returned last week from Leige, Belgium, where she had been for the past two years, gave to an interviewer some interesting details of her experiences in Liege during the famous siege of that town by the Germans. The first intimation she and her fellow-pupils got of the advancing Germans on the town was when at midnight during the first week of August they were aroused at midnight and told that the Germans would be in the town in a couple of hours. The pupils and nuns proceeded to the Convent Chapel, where they remained praying for some hours.

The Germans did not arrive as soon as expected owing to defence of the forts made by the Belgians. All the girls in the Convent were sent from there to the house of the house of the Convent Director, Fr Simone, about two miles away, where they remained four days sleeping at night on straw. At the end of that period they were taken back to the Convent. On the night following their arrival they were awakened by the whizzing of a shell over the Convent grounds, and before they were out of bed the shell exploded with a loud noise. The only damage caused by it was the demolition of a chimney and the carrying away of a small portion of the roof of one of the Convent buildings. Next morning they heard the noise made by blowing up of Leige bridge and by the explosion of shells around the city. The nuns and children took refuge in a large cellar under the Convent and remained there for several days and nights.

The Sisters going up to the main building every day to prepare food and to attend upon some exhausted Belgian soldiers who were taken into the Convent. At the end of the bombardment some German officers came to the Convent and took away for use of their troops a number of beds and a quantity of bedding which they gave a cheque to the Superioress. The Superioress was however unable to procure cash in any house in Liege for the cheque. The German officers, the young lady in question added, were most polite and courteous to the nuns, and the latter were heard on several occasions commenting favourably upon their treatment at the hands of the officers, who called at the Convent.

After the visit of the German officers life at the Convent resumed its normal course. Asked what she thought of the German soldiers, the young lady answered that when passing through Liege on her way to the

Convent from Father Simeone's residence she saw great numbers of them. 'They were all very fine looking men, splendidly built, with rather rough looking, but good natured faces. ' In reply to a question as to how Liege looked when she was passing through it, she stated that what most attracted her attention was a large number of cattle in the boulevards in charge of German soldiers. The cattle were eating the flowers in the boulevards and parks. They had been driven in from the adjoining country districts, and were killed in Liege for the use of the German soldiers. Some difficulty was experienced by the Superioress in procuring passports to leave Belgium for the lady interviewed and for eight English girls and a French girl who were with her at the Convent. The Superioress of the Convent was a German, and after a couple of interviews with the German Commander the passports were procured by her. The girls were driven in a brake to Maestricht in Holland, just beyond the Belgian frontier. On their way to Maestricht they passed through the little town of Visey, which had been burned down. They were frequently stopped by German soldiers and their passports and luggage examined. 'How did these German soldiers treat you?' asked our correspondent, 'Most politely and gentlemanly, ' answered the young lady. From Maestricht they went by rail to Flushing, where they took the boat to Folkestone. On landing at Folkestone they were given refreshments by some boy scouts, who meet refugees away from Belgium daily. They then went to London and spent two days at the Notre Dame Covent, Leicester Square. The young lady in question is, needless to say, very pleased to be home again in peaceful Ireland. When she was leaving Liege, the nuns were all at the Convent, and everything there was quite normal. The Convent is one of the most important educational centres in Liege, and its educational work cannot of course be resumed for a long time to come.   KP, 11-1914

Also see Back From Douai.

Clara Rangers Story

Frank Hill and Paddy McKeon, privates in the 2nd Connaught Rangers, have just returned to Clara suffering from wounds which they received at the battle of the Aisne. The former was wounded by a portion of the casing of a shell in the leg and also in the neck, while the latter received a bullet wound in the back. According to Private Hill, the battle of the Aisne was a veritable hell on earth. It began on the morning of 14 September. When a small party of sharp-shooters were selected from each company to pick out the German commanders. The main body of the Connaughts began the advance half and hour afterwards.

'We had to fight our way to a small canal branching off the – River Aisne and when we got to the canal the Uhlans commenced sniping us. We succeeded in crossing the canal and when we got to a big bridge across the

Aisne we had to sling our rifles and get down one side and got through the water to the other side. After crossing the river we advanced for about 8 miles when we came in contact with the Germans who were about 2, 000 strong. We opened fire at about 550 yards and continued to advance up to within about 200 yards of them when they commenced a deadly fire on us. Every now and again five or six of our fellows would be knocked down. The Germans showed a white flag and even turned the butts of the rifles towards us and we continued to approach them. They seemed as if they were about to surrender but when within fifty yards of them they again opened fire and knocked us clean out in fact. We then got the order to retire, but some of our chaps refused to retire and continued banging away with their rifles. All of a sudden I felt myself hit in the back, under the right shoulder bone.

A Narrow Escape
Private Hill then related that he was afterwards brought to a building adjacent where there were several other wounded soldiers. It was a kind of old stable he said and he was left there until 2 o'clock the following morning. 'When I got shot, ' he continued 'I was put on a stretcher and just as the stretcher-bearers were about to bear me away, one of them was hit with shrapnel and flattened out. The other dropped the handles of the stretcher and fled. When a lull cam in the firing I was carried away to the stable referred to. We had not left it three quarters of an hour next morning, when the Germans started shelling the whole place. They had the range from the day before and they did not leave as much as a stone upon a stone in the building. We were then shifted to a big farm house and put to lie in about three feet of corn and where we were treated for our injuries by Lady Dudley's hospital corps. We remained about three weeks there when we were sent home.'

Private Hill mentioned that in the advance at the battle of the Aisne the Connaught Rangers had to advance through a mangold field on their hands and knees. The magazine of his own rifle got clogged with clay and he had to throw it away and get a dead comrade's. It also got clogged and became useless, when he had to get another with which he continued to fire away. It was while he was on his knees that he was wounded.

KCC, 11-1914

Frank Hill survived the war. Patrick McKeon was killed in action in May 1916 in Mesopotamia.

Clareman's Letter from the Front

Mr T Kelly, Clare Castle, has received the following letter from his son, Corporal T Kelly, who was one of the 500 or 600 Munster Fusiliers taken prisoners on Aug-27. It is dated 'France, 31-August-1914' and from the tone one can understand why it was let through so soon. A German censor was not far away when it was written.

'Of course I told you I was going to the war in France. Well I left on 13th August along with my regiment. I was 14 days in France, and on 27th August the Munster Fusiliers had a great battle with the Germans, where we lost a few men, but there was a lot of us captured by the Germans, about 500 men, and I was lucky to be amongst them. Of course I cannot give you any information. Tell the Hynes in Ennis that their son is all right. A brother of Paddy Moroney's that works at Howard's in Ennis, is all right also. We are kept as prisoners of war by the Germans until the war is over. The German soldiers are very nice people. They are giving us all the privileges they can, and plenty to eat. I will be sorry to leave them, I think, when we are leaving… But won't I be delighted when I am on the boat for England again. Pray for my safe return, soon, and sound. You can imagine what it is to be a prisoner of war. I shall laugh when I'll be telling ye by word of mouth… I have a terrible story to tell ye when I get home, …I can't give ye any address, being a prisoner. Cheer up as I am as happy and cheerful as can be.'   CJ, 11-1914

Thomas Kelly was killed in action in September-1916.

Elephants as Work-Horses

Elephants are the only animals left alive in the Zoo at Antwerp. They are being used for hauling guns and so on.

TS, 11-1914

From Catapult to Cordite
The Evolution of the Modern Explosive

When the first man, in the old Stone Age thousands of years ago, threw his first javelin against a hairy mammoth, he put his foot over the threshold of the problem of explosives. For it seemed to him – and our feelings today are with him – that it would be more pleasurable if one could hurt and kill one's enemy without the gratuitous thrill of having to sit on the massive tusk on the verge of a cavernous mouth, or of having to approach within a few paces of the huge legs which might the next moment descend upon him. It would be more convenient to stand at the cave entrance, on a dizzy ledge of rock, and hurl a weapon at the distant enemy.

The Chemical Catapult
So man was driven to invent the catapult; and a gun is merely a chemical catapult. The trigger is pulled back like the leather of the catapult, and the sudden and extraordinary expansion of the explosive corresponds to the elasticity of the rubber or spring, the essential feature of both instruments being the employment of some source of more than human power which

Waterford Court House when John Redmond was nominated as Member of Parliament in 1910. He used his influence to persuade the Liberal government to introduce a bill granting Ireland Home Rule.

In April 1912, the Prime Minister, Herbert H. Asquith, introduced the Third Home Rule Bill which foresaw granting Ireland self-government. That government would have been centered on Dublin. Below are the Dublin streets in 1911.

Irish Volunteers was a military organisation established in 1913 by Irish nationalists.
John Redmond, leader of the Irish Parliamentary Party (Home Rule) inspecting the Irish Volunters in 1914.

Inset: Poster advocating Home Rule.

August 1914 and German armies sweep through Belgium. The issue of Home Rule is
put to one side for the duration of hostilities.
Belgian civilians flee from before the invaders. *Inset poster:* Redmond supports Britain.

Belgian civilians
scramble to leave on
the last boat as the
Germans press closer
to Antwerp.

Dublin joins the call to arms and these young boys show the way with the camera capturing their impromptu parade.

Full page newspaper advertisement ran in many papers.

A Dublin tram bedecked with recruiting slogans to join the British Army.

Irishmen!

YOU cannot permit your Regiments to be kept up to strength by other than Ireland's sons! It would be a deep disgrace to Ireland, if all her regiments were not Irish, to a man

A Call to 50,000 Irishmen

Excluding Munition Workers

TO JOIN THEIR BRAVE COMRADES IN IRISH REGIMENTS

Lord Kitchener has told you—his fellow-countrymen—that Ireland has done magnificently; and all the world knows of the splendid valour of the Irish Regiments, horse and foot. So glorious is the record that it must be maintained by the men of our race—by Irishmen alone.

It is your proud duty to support your gallant Countrymen who have fought so well. Ireland must stand by them!

You are asked to SERVE FOR THE PERIOD OF THE WAR ONLY.

Your relatives, whom you have looked after, will be looked after while you are away—your wife, your parents, your children.

You will be fed, clothed and boarded, and your pay will be 1/- per day. Married men will receive the same, subject to a deduction of 6d. per day, which goes to their wives entitling them to receive 12/6 per week and 5/- for one child; 3/6 for the second child, and 2/- each for others. The dependents of unmarried soldiers will receive substantial allowances.

You will be equipped and receive your preliminary training in Ireland, completing your training in different parts of the World, and serving with Irishmen wherever you go.

Pensions may be given to disabled Soldiers discharged in consequence of disablement by wounds or disease due to War Services. If wholly disabled, weekly rates, according to rank, 25/- for Privates, 40/- for Warrant Officers. If partially disabled, Pensions may be granted to bring the wages of Soldiers capable of earning to the rate referred to above. Extra Allowances for Children.

Every famous Irishman urges this duty very earnestly on you. Every Irishman should answer the Call—farmers' sons, merchants, men in shops and offices, all must act a man's—an Irishman's part.

JOIN AT ONCE : TO-DAY

To the Dept. of Recruiting, c/o G.P.O., Dublin; or Belfast Recruiting Office.
FILL IN AND POST THIS FORM; NO STAMP NEEDED

Mark with a X the Irish Regiment you wish to join:

CONNAUGHT RANGERS
ROYAL DUBLIN FUSILIERS
    1st to 9th Battalions
10th or SCHOLARS BATTALION
Professional, Men & Clerical Workers
ROYAL INNISKILLING
ROYAL IRISH FUSILIERS
ROYAL IRISH REGIMENT
ROYAL IRISH RIFLES
LEINSTER REGIMENT
    1st to 5th Battalion
5th or Farmers' Battalion for Farmers' Sons
ROYAL MUNSTER FUSILIERS

I undertake to enlist when called upon for the PERIOD OF THE WAR ONLY in the Irish Regiment mentioned.

Age _____ Height _____

Occupation _____

NAME _____

ADDRESS _____

German infantry launching a mass attack in the opening stages of the Great War.

British soldiers take on the assaulting German formations at Mons.

Wounded men of the British Expeditionary Force being transferred from a French hospital train to a hospital ship for the Channel crossing.

WEXFORD SOLDIER MISSIN

BANDSMAN MICHAEL FARRE

A walking wounded Tommy waits his turn to board the hospital ship to take him home to Britain.

Gunner Albert Edward Baker, RGA and his daughter.
Courtesy of Christy Archer (Albert's only Grandson), Galway.

Right: Michael Fahy from New Inn. Left: Thomas O'Grady from Clashamhadra, Tipperary. Thomas survived the war but was wounded in the foot.
Courtesy of Frank Fahey, New Inn. Tipperary.

Sgt John Doyle Twelveacre, Tagoat, killed in action.

Pte Robert Farrell Wexford killed in action.

Lt John O'Dwyer Thurles killed in action.

Pte Michael Fitzhenry killed in action.

Cpl Patrick Roche killed in action.

Cpl Patrick Dempsey killed in action.

Lt T. K. Walker killed in action.

Pte Maurice Cullen killed in action.

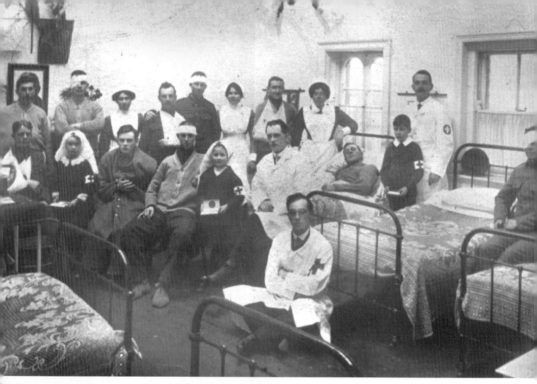

Patients in City of Dublin Skin and Cancer Hospital.
Courtesy Eoin O'Brien, Irish Skin Foundation.

Cashel-born *Médaille Militaire* winner, James Francis O'Brien, RFA, died of wounds at home. Buried in the Rack of Cashel.

Seaman Patrick Murphy, RNR, drowned on the East coast of Africa while serving aboard HMS *Orbita*.

can be made yield up its energy at a given moment in the required way. Explosives are, therefore, tabloid energy or power, and this is just a reminder of the fact that some substances are explosive generally, whereas quite a number of common things may be made explosive by some particular kind of treatment. When water boils on the fire there is no explosion as it is changed into steam; but if the spout were sealed and the whole of the water could be changed into steam in a second there would be an explosion. And the instance is good because it is really a kitchen model of a volcano. Moreover, steam guns were used in America in the 'sixties. The essential idea of an explosive is then the violent release of some pent-up thing; just the opposite, from this standpoint, of the catapult, which works by allowing a distended thing – the elastic – to contract and distract suddenly, whereas all explosives release a compressed thing. The release gives rise to a wave, and this, of course is experienced as a sound. It is the sound which is popularly called an explosive.

What is 'Tabloid Force'?
Now, it has been said that an explosive is tabloid force, power, energy. Howe is it available? It is easy to follow the mechanism of an explosive further. Explosives, as commonly used, are solid substances which, by burning produce almost instantaneously an extraordinarily large volume of gases. The heat and pressure of a blow cause the burning to start, and the burning also produces heat which, acting upon the gases, increases the volume still further. It may be suggested that there is no obvious reasons why even a sudden and enormous expansion should cause the damage of an explosion. And the suggestion is quite just. It is only when they are confined that explosives are really dangerous. Gunpowder burned in the open merely causes a noise like 'pouf, ' and burns quickly. Guncotton may be burned on the hand – it is not to be recommended as a fashionable hobby – without any serious inconvenience. Indeed, gunpowder was first used as an incendiary composition. But a fire-work or a gun charged with gunpowder will explode with a loud report and may cause fatal wounds.

'High' and 'Low' Explosives
Gunpowder is the best-known explosive mixture. It is made from the commonest ingredients; carbon, sulphur and saltpetre. There are several modifications of gunpowder, other nitrates being substituted for the saltpetre – potassium nitrate. The nitrates give the oxygen to the mixture without which it would not burn at all, other explosive mixtures containing chlorates which have the same nitrates. The different powders are used in different circumstances where a more violent or a slower or a safer explosive is required. For it is not always the same effect which come from an explosive. Velocity may at time be sacrificed, say, in favour of a higher weight of common shell. Gunpowder is a 'low' explosive; its explosion is slow and its effect is less violently disruptive. Dynamite is

probably the best-known 'high' explosive; and the name does not stand for one particular substance but for a large class which are, in effect, diluted, nitroglycerin, and which are generally used for blasting.

Germany's New Explosive

Guncotton may be described as a nitrate of cotton-wool (which the chemist would call cellulose). Both nitroglycerin and guncotton are less useful as explosives themselves that their derivatives, although Russia and the United States use compressed wet guncotton in their high-explosive shells. One of the most famous derivatives is the smokeless propellant used by the British Ar, y and Navy, cordite. Germany is reported to be using in the present war a 'new' explosive. Its chemical name is Trinitro-toluene (picric acid is called trinitro-carbolic); but it is commonly called T. N. T., or in Germany, Tyrotyl. It is not at all new. It is, in fact, a well-known member of a series of aromatic explosives, and toluene is a derivative of coal tar. It has long been known that it much improved the ordinary detonators and that detonators made with T. N. T were being used in Germany.

TS, 11-1914

German Dead, Furnaces Kept burning

Gruesome details are given by the *Echo Belge* as to how the Germans dispose of their dead. It states that many trains have been seen coming from the direction of Charleroi having as their sole loading the bodies of German soldiers, stripped of their clothing. At the Usine Sambre et Morselle(sic), at Montagn-sur-Sambre, two huge furnaces have been constantly burning, 'and they never cease consuming the bodies of Germans brought from the Yser. '

In a café the proprietor refused to seve soldiers who had become noisy. They appealed to an officer, who while he admitted that soldiers should not in accordance with the rules, have any more drink, added;--'Give liquor to these – they have need of forgetfulness.' These were the men charged with the duty of putting the bodies in the furnaces.

TS, 11-1914

Getting Food to the Trenches.
All about the risky work of the Transport-Wagon Driver

An inky black night in a rather wild, open country. Lines of wagons stand in readiness to start. To each wagon there are attached a couple of horses – Dublin cab-horses some of 'em. There is a bugle call; a number of men in the raggiest khaki you could imagine come up from out of the darkness at the double. They line up before the wagons, an order is shouted hoarsely, and away they go, jolting and rattling across the trampled wasted corn lying thick ad dank on the sodden ground that three months ago was a yellowing cornfield. The wagons contain bully beef, biscuits, apples, and cold tea in bottles, and the drivers have got to deliver eleven miles away. The men fight, sleep, eat, live, and die in the trenches, until the moment comes for an advance or retreat. For, once entrenched in such a war as the present, there is no coming out day or night. And getting these food wagons to the trenches is perilous work, for the Germans do all they can to prevent the food wagon reaching our soldiers. The danger of what is called food-transport work is, of course, far greater in some places than others. In some places there may be shelter to be obtained right up to the trenches, and the wagons are never seen by the enemy, but in others the wagons may have to reach the trenches by way of open and difficult ground, over which headway can be made but slowly. Many a driver has perished, many a baggage wagon been destroyed, in such places. When the wagons are within about four miles of the trenches, the Germans try to locate them with searchlights or fireballs, and then begin shelling them. They use fireballs now altogether for this purpose. The fireball as a sort of immense firework. When it bursts it turns into a glaring ball of blue fire which hangs in the air throwing a brilliant light about the ground beneath it, and enabling the German gunners to get the exact range of the food-wagons. A comrade of mine saw a shell burst within a foot of a wagon. It simply wiped the wagon and driver and horses out of existence. They were all blown to smithereens. The wagons, of course, spread out as far as possible from each other, and if one or two meet with disaster, some always reach the trenches in safety. Often the food has to be distributed under shell-fire, but in the trenches one is fairly safe; at any rate, the danger never effects the Tommies appetites, and more than do his ragged garments, the mud with which he is caked, or the other hundred and one discomforts of living in the trenches. All sorts and conditions of young men may be found among the food-wagon drivers – from 'Varsity undergraduates to men who, not long since, were clerks in City offices, or driving wagons about London, or checking tickets at railway stations – all glad to do their bit, ready to die if necessary doing their duty to their comrades and their country.

TS, 11-1914

Giant Gun's That Shatter Steel like Tin Cans

The surprise of the great war is certainly the new German and Austrian howitzers. One of the m has a mouth 17 inches in width, that hurls a ton of the most terrible explosive over miles of country. All the principal successes of the huns have been won by their terrific siege artillery. Liege, Namur, Maubege, and other French fortresses, and then beautiful old

Antwerp, have fallen quickly under the tremendous shells from guns made in secret in Germany and Austria, and hidden till war broke out. Most of us thought that the long siege guns of Port Arthur had proved that a great modern fortress could keep back an invading army for months. The French and the Belgians built on this fact, but they built on something worse than sand. For the more strongly constructed a modern fortress is, the more terrible is its fate. It is usually built with a roof of very thick armour plate, and walls of armoured concrete thicker than a house. The roof lifts and falls by powerful machinery, and when the guns of the fort fire. It is like a turreted battleship, fixed on land and cemented thickly, with trenches and slopes and barbed wire entanglements and machine guns to beat off a storming party. What chance has an unprotected gun, firing in an open field, against a great armoured fort? Yet the unprotected gun always wins. The thing is so unexpected, so contrary, it seems, to reason. Now we know, however, that even with smaller siege artillery than their huge 17 inch howitzers the Germans could have blown their way into any fortress.

Valueless Forts
The invention of smokeless powder has destroyed the value of every fort. When an ordinary gun is now fired no cloud around the muzzle betrays its position, but the direction from which the shell comes is some indication. With the piece of artillery known as a howitzer, the shell is a rather stumpy thing that stands almost upright. It sends its shell high into the heavens, and the shell falls like a thunderbolt from the sky on to the place at which it has bee indirectly aimed. No one can trace where it comes from. So with smokeless powder and a light shelter of boughs or straw to hide it from aerial scouts, the modern howitzer can fire without being discovered. It is away from the object it is shelling. The noise it makes cannot be distinguished from the roar of other distant artillery. But the fort it is attacking is a plain fixed mark. With modern range-finding instruments, and with a man in a flying machine or balloon to watch the shots and report if they fail to hit, a battery of modern howitzers can rain shells on a fort all day long.

The guns in the fort are no good. Nothing can be seen for them to fire at. Moreover, the great new howitzers have a longer range than the older guns in many forts. They can fire openly throughout the night, with their flaming mouth proclaiming their position. For the opposing guns cannot send a shell far enough to reach them. This was the case at Antwerp. Shells rained down from the sky – night as well as day – tons and half-tons of picric acid and exploding steel. Nothing made by man could withstand the shattering, horrible force of the constant explosions. The thick steel dome bent and crumpled under it like a top of a tin can, The concrete was rent into rocky masses as big as a fallen cliff at Moher. Sometimes the steel dome was so battered in that the hydraulic machinery could not lift it. If a shell got inside, the havoc made was ghastly. The gunners died before they were struck, by splinters, falling walls, or broken overturning guns. Merely the enormous force of the explosive gases, killed by the shock of their explosion. It was like being blown out of a gun. The gases got between the body and the clothes of some gunners and stripped them naked, while killing them. If a man was not immediately killed by the shell the poisonous fumes of the explosion finished him off. Men in neighbouring chambers fled from the forts at times screaming like madmen. Designed as places of strong defence, they had become terrible death traps. The all-conquering big howitzer, firing in the daylight without been seen, and capable of being moved in pieces on motors from place to place, from country to country, was the lord of the battle

Flying Man Helps

All the great French fortresses on their eastern frontier, from Verdun to Toul and Belfort have suddenly become almost useless. In most cases the best guns have been taken out of them and placed in new earthworks that stretch for miles round the old forts. The French garrisons have come and dug trenches in the forests and fields, and it is with hidden rifle-pits, hidden machine guns, and hidden howitzers that they are now beating off the Germans. The latest and best kind of fortress – such as the French have rapidly made from Verdun to Belfort – is formed of lines of open-air trenches, behind which the movable artillery fires without being visible. The great new gun hides itself and compels everything and everybody to hide. That is why a modern battle lasts for a month or more. It is a terrible game of hide and seek with death.

If a flying man discovers the position of one of the enemy's guns, his own gunners suddenly mass the fire of half-a-dozen howitzers on the position. When the big gun has been killed, the smaller guns are attacked; then the troops in the trenches are swept with shrapnel till they run for their lives. Then an army advances. It takes about a month to move forward two miles in this way.

TS, 11-1914

How are Big Guns Conveyed Across Rivers?

As a general rule strong bridges have to be constructed in order to convey big guns across rivers, guns which, with their carriages, may weigh anything up to ten tons. These heavy guns are often taken across one at a time on specially constructed rafts. Many of the guns that have had to be taken over canals during the fighting in the north-west of France, for instance, were conveyed by being lashed to empty barrels. Three barrels lashed together will float several tons. A fourth barrel helps to keep the gun on 'an even keel' as it were, as well as taking off part of the weight.

TS, 11-1914

Dead in Vistula

All day long in Warsaw people are thronging the bridges which cross the river Vistula, watching the dead bodies of Germans floating by. Thousands of them were drowned in the Vistula during the German defeat of Poland.

TS, 11-1914

How are the Huge Shells for the German 17-inch Guns Moved?

Many of the shells used by the big German siege guns – 'Jack Johnsons' as they are called by the British on account of the dense black smoke they throw out when bursting, weigh close on a thousand pounds. It is, of course, impossible for one man to lift such a weight, so each shell is placed in a special wicker-work basket. The lid for the basket is generally made of metal, and fastened on with leather straps. Each basket has four handles, for it takes four men to carry the shell to its gun, each man practically lifting between two and three hundredweight. These shells cost '1, 250 each, so that is another reason why they are so carefully protected in transport.

TS, 11-1914

Men of Straw

A man living near Metz, who at the outbreak of the war was taken to Hanover, states that he saw the Germans fill railway carriages with dummies made of straw and dressed in French uniforms, to make believe they had captured numerous prisoners.

TS, 11-1914

Impressive German Funeral at Templemore
Soldier Buried with Military Honours

It was announced in Templemore on Friday morning that one of the German prisoners or wad had died of wounds. The deceased was one of the last batch that arrived in Templemore. He was a Roman Catholic. On Sunday at 3 o'clock the barrack gates were thronged with people anxiously waiting to see the funeral. A couple of minutes after 3 o'clock the barrack gates yawned and the firing party of the Leinster Regiment marched in front of the hearse. The coffin was wrapped in the German colours; next came the Kaiser's Prussian Guards who acted as the bodyguard, marching each side of the hearse, and after the hearse came the German officers and some of the men, guarded on each side by the Leinster Regiment. There was a very large number of the townspeople present. As the funeral proceeded to the new cemetery it was met by Rev. Father Kiely, P. P., Templemore, who read the last prayers at the graveside. When the coffin was laid in the grave the German soldiers sang two hymns; then the firing party fired three volleys over the grave and the 'Last Post' was sounded. When the men were ordered to line up each of the German soldiers and officers dropped 3 handfuls of clay on the coffin, a custom peculiar to the German people. There were four wreaths of flowers with streamers of the German colours placed on the grave. – RIP.

TS, 11-1914

Is There Any Danger of a Torpedo Exploding Accidentally?

Before a torpedo can be discharged, a little pin or safety catch has to be removed. This makes it impossible for the striking-pin of a torpedo to be driven in by something or other while the torpedo is being handled. If it were not fot eh little idea this might mean that the torpedo would explode and cause enormous damage. To prevent such an accident the pin is locked by a small 'safety pin. ' This pin slips through a hole in the fore part of the torpedo, and also through the striking pin, and thus keeps it secure. Before the torpedo is fired this pin is, of course, withdrawn.

TS, 11-1914

Is There Any Special Apparatus Used For Destroying Barbed Wire Entanglements?

A special motor-car, which has fitted to it an arrangement for cutting through the barbed wire, is being largely used during this war. A huge 'knife' extends from the bonnet of the car, over th e top, and down the back. The car drives right into the entanglements, and the knife cuts away the wire.

TS, 11-1914

Letter from Corporal Downing

A further interesting letter received from Lance Corporal Downing, 2nd Field Squadron, 2nd Cavalry Brigade, is as follows;--' I had your letter on returning from my work at the quarters of the Scots Greys;. It was a terrible afternoon – a regular snowstorm that covered the whole country with a white mantle in a very short time, and the farm houses, trees, and landscape, generally reminded me at once of Xmas time at home. It brought back my mind the stories I read long ago of the Crimea and the picture regarding the retreat of the Grand Army from Moscow (Lady Butler's, I Think), though there were no wounded or dead in this one. The farmers here worked away through it all and I thought what a silly people they must be, not to seek the warmth of their homes, when they were not compelled to be out. I especially noticed one man ploughing – in a blinding storm – a farm but a couple of hundred yards from home. However, when we reached our billet a warm stew and some hot tea, and a letter from home, soon banished all care. The R. E. are in the firing line, all our work is done except that attending to our horses and baggage, and getting ready our stores, and I may tell you that so far we have had some warm corners, although the lot that left England with me have been only 6 weeks in the country. Still the R. E. have been very lucky so far, but have had their share of casualties in proportion to their numbers, and they have been very useful in this war. I have just changed a 5 franc note, that is 4s 2d, and bought some coffee at the farm house on which we are billeted. It is good to be in a barn butt of straw those nights, the weather became so cold. We have however been partly broken into it.   TS, 11-1914.

Lance Corporal A. S. Downing survived the war. Also see, Letter from Corporal Downing. Letter from the front. (1) and Letter from the front. (2)

Letter from the Front (1)

In a letter received on Monday from Lance-Corporal A. S. Downing, of the Cavalry section, Royal Engineers, dated 11tgh inst., and headed from 'somewhere in France, ' the following interesting passages occur:

'We are at the front and of course in the firing line where we work generally at night and I am quite used to having 'coal scuttles' bursting round me. We have had to lie down when constructing barbed wire entanglements while the German fire and the fire from our own trenches passes over us. The spirit of all troops is surprising under the circumstances and we argue and chat as if nothing unusual was happening. We get a 'tot' of rum each night and work together each doing his share. Although unused to the work at first we can do it now. The older soldiers can, and do work, but the young lads want a little persuasion, which is only natural. Were it not for our splendid reserves, all men of substance at home or in the colonies, we should not have such a fine though small fighting machine and when you see that 'French's contemptible little army' are able to put the 'comether'(sic) on the splendidly organised German millions who are by no means to be despised as soldiers you can sing truly that a little bit of khaki goes a long long way and gets where it wants to. My word can't I eat and smoke and there is no wind up. Send me some Irish twist for the boys who are keeping our dear little homesteads free from the crunch of the heel of the invader and in future remember that the word England stands for justice in spite of the fact that her laws may be badly administered in our own green spot. One thing has been again reproved and that is that Ireland can breed soldiers.'

TS, 11-1914, A. S. LANCE CORPORAL A. S. DOWNING SURVIVED THE WAR. ALSO SEE, LETTER FROM CORPORAL DOWNING, AND LETTER FROM THE FRONT. (2)

Letter from the front (2)

A letter received this week from Lance Corporal A. S. Downing, 2nd Field Squardon Royal Engineers, Cavalry Division, British Expeditionary Force, who acted as correspondent here contains the following passages about the war:

'It is the same routing every day, marching and working and fighting when it comes our way, and of course it gets monotonous. It is wonderful to think that there is such a big war raging so near home. Fighting is going on every day and night and the artillery fighting is terrible, nothing but the sound of guns and rattle of rifles all the times. Massy wrote and sent me a cutting about a Roscrea man (Jackson) who has been awarded the Cross of the Legion of Honour. All our letters are censored so that we can only write generally, and I, therefore, could find nothing to say that would touch on our whereabouts. The country is very like Ireland and the farmers work away in the fields when the Allies are in their districts, but they scoot as soon as the Germans put in an appearance, and it is pitiable to see the women, and children fleeing towards us as we advance. You would want to be an eye-witness of it to believe it. Several attempts by the Germans to break through our lines have failed and we have hammered them well during that time. We get plenty of tobacco. I got a Rosary beads from a Belgian and carry it in my pocket.'

TS, 11-1914

Lance Corporal A. S. Downing survived the war.

Also see, Letter from Corporal Downing, and Letter from the front (2). For Jackson see A Roscrea Soldier's Experience at the Front).

The Glorious Flash of the Cavalry Charge

Cavalry charges have been described in glowing prose and thrilling verse, beside providing the subject for many a richly coloured canvas. It is noticeable, however, that more often than not the painter portrays a galloping mob of horsemen riding in wild disorder brandishing their uplifted sabres – for usually it is light cavalry that figures in these pictures, possibly because the flashing sword is capable of more artistic treatment than a row of levelled lances. It may be that these paintings are fairly faithful representations of the particular scenes which the artist has sought to reproduce, but they certainly do not give an accurate impression of a cavalry charge today. In the first place, the prime consideration of cavalrymen in a charge is to preserve their alignment, and this they will not fail to do if mounted on their own well-trained horses, unless the ground is so broken as to be unsuitable for cavalry operations, or unless large and frequent gaps are made in their ranks by artillery fire. In the second place, cavalry (whatever they may do in pursuing a broken enemy) do not, in charging, wave the sword above the head, but hold it extended at arm's length straight out in front, so as to give the enemy the point.

Uncertainty that Proves Fatal

A great deal of the training of cavalry is directed to obtaining absolute steadiness in these two matters, for it is an axiom that the result of a charge between opposing bodies of cavalry is decided some instants before the actual collision takes place and that, given equal numbers, the advantage will lie with the side which best preserves its formation and is the steadiest in the handling of its weapons. In other words, the issue is decided by moral effect. The effect of the training of horse and man tells throughout the charge, but it is within a second or so of the impact that the steadiness of the men in the use of their weapons is out to the supreme test. A trooper may find himself confronted by an enemy standing in his stirrups with uplifted sword. He is probably tempted to thin he can more quickly disable his opponent by striking at him with his own sword, and it is only as the result of perfect training that he continues to rely upon his point. Any uncertainty during the last few instants as to the manner in which the weapon is to be fatal. In this connection it is interesting to note that most of the swords with which British cavalry is armed are longer than any used by the other contending armies on the Continent, and they are the heaviest in Europe. They are made in two sizes, the longest measuring 35 ? in., and the other 34 7/8in. ; they weigh 2lb 13 ? oz, and 2lb. / 15 ? oz. Respectively. The French cavalry sword ost nearly approximates to these, being 35in, long, but weighing only 32in, 2lb, 6oz., while the German sword is only 32 in., in length, it weight being 2lb, 8 ? oz.

So far the British Hussar regiments have been more particularly referred to, as light cavalry alone uses the sword exclusively in shock tactics. In their engagements with the enemy's cavalry they have, on most occasions, had lancers opposed to them, for the whole of the German cavalry has been armed with this weapon for a quarter of a century. The lance, of course, is the more formidable weapon on account of its length, and the Hussar must parry it before he can disable his opponent. Unless the squadrons are charging at top speed this is comparatively easy, but when the horses are fresh and fast the utmost skill and coolness is required to avoid its point. Now, although British cavalry has the advantage so far as the length pf the sword is concerned, it is in exactly the reverse position in regard to the length of the lance, for the British lance is shorter than any used by the great European Powers. The German lance is 11ft. 9in, in length; the French lance, 11ft; the Cossack, 9ft, 10in; while the British is only 8ft. 8in.

The Modern Cavalry Charge

A cavalry charge nowadays is a much more strenuous business than it was a hundred years ago. In the Napoleonic wars, when the range of musketry was little over half-a-mile, the advance usually commenced from a distance of about a thousand yards, and the cavalry would trot for the first 80 yards before breaking into a gallop for the last 200 yards. Since then the effective range of rifle fire has bee quadrupled, and cavalry may have to advance from a distance ten times as great. They are therefore trained to trot for 8, 000 yards, and to gallop for 2, 000 yards. One of the cavalryman's chief concerns throughout the campaign is to keep his horse fit for severe tasks such as this. He never rides when he can walk and, when on the march, if circumstances will permit it, he even relieves his mount of the weight of the saddle, which he stows away in a transport wagon. The double line in which cavalry charges is separated by just a horse's length has been found by experience to be the best formation, although it has the disadvantage that if a front rank horse falls it probably brings down the one immediately behind. A second line has, however, been found to be necessary because, in the event of the enemy not being ridden down or through at the first onset, and a melee ensuing, a reserve is essential. This is particularly so in the case of Lancers, for in a press, where the rider has no room to turn, the lance is practically useless. The rear rank riding in gives the front rank men a better opportunity to discard their lances and draw their swords.

Distinction of Weight
In the German Army the distinctions between the weights of the various classes of cavalry are strictly observed, but in the British Army the differences are not so marked. The British Hussars, it is true, are regarded as the light cavalry, but between the Dragoons (medium cavalry) and the Lancers (heavy cavalry) there is little to choose.

TS, 11-1914

The 'Silent Death'

The latest, and one of the most terrible inventions for warfare ever conceived, is the 'silent death. ' It is a weapon which is intended to be used from aeroplanes or airships, and is made of steel about three-eights of an inch thick. The length is about five inches, and one end of the rod finishes in a deadly point. The airmen drops them in lots of five hundred, and there is a special apparatus which spreads them out, so that they cover an area of 200 yards when dropped from a height of 500 yards. One of these 'arrows' will easily go right through a man and, as a matter of fact, they have already played great havoc among marching troops.

TS, 11-1914

These Flechettes or Lazy Dogs were also used by the Americans as recently as the Vietnam War.

Too Young at 55
Veteran warriors who are in the thick of the fight

At what age does a man cease to be of use? The question has been often asked, and various answers have been given. The late Professor Huxley, for instance, was of opinion that, after sixty, a man became more or less 'fossilised, ' and, acting up that theory, he resigned all his public appointments on his sixtieth birthday. Yet Huxley was a standing contradiction to his own theory, for much of his best work as a controversialist was done during the latter years of his life. Particularly is that true with regard to the great military leaders of history. In the United States – where they attempt to do things on scientific principals, and very often fail in consequence – they have passed a law enforcing the retirement from the army every officer who has attained the age of sixty-four.

Battle of old men

It will be sufficient to say that such a law would more than decimate the list of generals now fighting in Europe, whether on the side of England and her Allies, or of Germany and Austria. Of all the generals fighting with the enemy none has achieved a more brilliant military reputation than Von Kluck. He is nearly 69. General Julius von Moltke, who until quite recently was in command of the German forces, and who was primarily responsible for the rapid and effective mobilisation of the German Army, is 66. General von Hindenberg, who is in command of a force in Eastern Prussia, is 67. General von Hausen and General von Buelow, both of whom have distinguished themselves during the present campaign, are each 69. Nor can the armies of our French Allies be said to be remarkable for the youthfulness of its generals. General Joffre, the commander-in-chief, is rapidly approaching his seventieth year, while General Galliene, who is in supreme command in Paris, and Paul Pau, the one-armed hero, are of about the same age. In the English Army the most brilliant work has frequently been achieved by the veterans. It is long since Sir John French was a young man, and Sir Horace Smith-Dorrien passed the meridian of his days many years ago.

Kitchener is 66

It is difficult to think of Lord Kitchener as elderly, or even as middle aged. Ardent, tireless, indomitable, he has brought to bear upon his duties at the War Office an energy and resourcefulness that might well be envied by many a young man in the early 'twenties. Yet the Secretary for War is not less than 66 years of age. Then there is Lord Roberts – 'Bobs. ' It is only a few weeks ago since Lord Roberts celebrated his eighty-second birthday. Yet he seems to have discovered the secret of perpetual youth. Finally, the eyes of Western Europe are being turned, with interest and with hopefulness, upon the great Russian Army just now, Commander General

Soukomlinoff, the re-organiser of the Army of the Tsar, may be destined to play a very important part in the history of the war. And Soukomlinoff is a man of 88.

TS, 11-1914

Urlingford Private's Story

Private Cain, of Urlingford, who belongs to the 4th Battalion of the Royal Irish Regiment, told an interesting story of the fighting in France to an 'Irish Independent' representative. He was wounded on the shoulder by shrapnel, and is now in the Mater Hospital, Dublin. Having left the troop train the advance was ordered, and after about two miles of a march the Royal Irish were in close quarters with the Germans. The bayonets work he described as awful, and the shell-fire unceasing. While the shelling and rifle firing went on, people were running away from their homes and the crops were being destroyed. His regiment marched on a village called Lascines. The enemy advanced towards the village, and he got a piece of a shell on the arm. There were 900 of the Royal Irish advancing, and afterwards when the roll was called only 55 answered. The battle lasted from 10 o'clock in the morning to 10 at night. The scene was desperate. Captain Smithwick, Kilkenny, who was in charge of his company, was shot through the mouth. The Germans used both shell and rifle fire with terrible effect. His experience was that though some of the Germans might waver before the bayonet, the majority stood their ground and fought. Their rifle dire is generally accurate. 'We had to retire from the trenches, ' he continued, 'owing to re shell fire. It was Sunday evening, and the people who were reciting the Rosary in the village, were disturbed by the shells, which burst over them. Some of the church was taken away. About a mile away from the village the Germans posted a battery close to a church, and the British were obliged to shell it. A remarkable circumstance in connection with the demolition of the church was that not one of the sacred images were destroyed. ' As to the 'Jack Johnson, ' the name given to the German shell, he said its killing capacity extends over three hundred yards, and when it explodes the ground shakes like a moving bog. His wounded arm was bandaged by a comrade, and eventually he was taken to a hospital at the rere. 'The Germans, ' he added, are wonderful snipers, and take most accurate aim from trees. Sometimes the red Cross wagon they carry as a Maxim gun, which is twice as effective as the English Gun.

KP, 11-1914

Private Cain survived the war, however, Kilkennyman, Captain Smithwick died in November 1915, after a long time as a POW of complications from the wounds he received.

Warriors on Wheels

'A Horse! A Horse! A kingdom for a Horse,' No longer holds good. The modern soldier's cry is a bike! A Bike!

The Motor-car, the motor-cycle, and the common or garden bicycle are playing a prominent part in the present war, and there is no doubt that the use of these machines is doing much to assist the movements of the armies. The soldier-cyclist is regarded to-day as indispensable a part of an army as the commissariat and the engineers, and the influence they exercise on minor tactics is considerable. Owing to the fact that they can move about swiftly and silent they make excellent scouts, and as such they are proving themselves invaluable on the Continent. Thousands of soldier of both Germany and Austria are equipped with bicycles, and the men are chiefly engaged in making observations, carrying dispatches, an performing patrol duty. The Austrian soldier-cyclist is perhaps a little too well equipped. He carries a short sword, a rifle, a revolver, and a small folding tent. The French cycling corps is far superior to that of Germany, and a great number of the machines possessed by the soldiers are collapsible, and can be carried on the back when roads are too bad to be ridden. It is interesting to know that France has used the bicycle for military purposes since the year 1887. Cycles that can be used as ambulances and others that carry quick-firing guns are with the French forces on the field of battle to-day. Russia had not been behind in recognising the merits of the wheel on the battlefield, and a whole corps of soldier cyclists have been sent to the front by the Tsar. Many of the men have been supplied with folding cycles.

Perhaps the most expert bicycle-soldiers are those forming the cadet corps of the North Western Military Academy situated near Chicago. The young men of the corps are trick riders, and they can accomplish with comparative ease the difficult task of scaling a high wall with their bicycles and accoutrements strapped to their backs. Hundreds of motor-cars, armoured and otherwise, and motor-lorries are at the front, as well as motor buses which a few weeks back were carrying passengers through crowded streets. For purposes of transport on the field of battle the value of these vehicles cannot be overestimated. In a sense this is a war of speed, and consequently armies must have a quick means of moving their 'belongings'. The armies at war to-day possess motor bakeries. They are practically ordinary motor-cars, but at the rear of them are bolters and kneading troughs which are driven by the petrol engines which propel the cars. While a motor-bakery is skipping over the ground it can make fresh bread at almost lightening speed. Is wireless telegraphy being made use of at the seat of war? It is a question that we cannot answer offhand (but we do know that 'wireless' motor-cars are in existence. These vehicles carry apparatus for utilising the motors for either traction or for generating electric energy for radio-telegraphic transmission, and also for raising and lowering telegraph 'poles' which are attached to the roofs of cars.

TS, 11-1914

What Wireless Does For War

In the air, on the land, and under the sea

For the first time in history wireless telegraphy is playing a big part in a European War, and Marconi's invention is proving its military value in many interesting ways. For instance, during the combined sea and land battle off Ostend recently, when our monitor battleships combined with the land troops against the Germans, wireless proved invaluable. On a high building in the rear of the troops fighting on land an observer sat watching the effect of the shells from the British warships. When their direction was at fault he telephoned to the Allies wireless station near the fighting line. From here messages were sent out to sea, which were caught on the aerials of out battleships. In this way the Naval gunners were kept continually informed as to the direction of their shots, and they were enabled to alter their range when the wireless calls informed them that it was at fault. By means of wireless our warships can keep up 'conversation' with submarines even when they are running beneath the water. The smaller craft is, of course, not entirely submerged; it travels beneath the surface with its aerials above water. Owing to lengthy experiments conducted some time ago between the cruiser 'Bonaventure' and the submarine D1, both equipped with wireless, this form of signalling has been developed to a reliable stage. The manner in which wireless communication between submarine and cruiser is generally utilised for the underwater craft when scouting near the enemy's fleet to signal its movements to the larger vessels.

On land wireless is used almost every hour of the day amongst the field forces. Poratble Marconu telegraph stations are employed for the purpose of conveying messages from one military unit to another. This apparatus is so light that it can be carried by a motor-cyclist with a sidecar or a single pack horse. It can be erected in fifteen minutes and send messages and receive them over a distance of fifty miles. Scouts utilise these outfits for conveying information in code to headquarters. For hurried work the six-foot wireless mast is held upright and dynamo apparatus worked by a foot pedal, supplies the necessary power.

The large two-seater biplanes suitable for slow but steady cross-country work, are in several cases provided with wireless. The wires which catch the messages are stretched from the front plane of the machine to the tail, between the main planes. The passenger or pilot in the aeroplane has strapped to his knees a keyboard for transmitting messages. At a height of two thousand feet it has been found possible to send messages back to the headquarter wireless station twenty miles away. Wireless on aeroplanes, however is largely used for signalling messages to military aviators, which contain instructions.

A wireless invention has been discovered which enables lighthouses and other land stations to send messages to ships which tell them the exact positions of dangerous rocks pr mined vicinities. These signals, by means of a radio compass, tell the commander of a warship the exact locality from which they have emanated. Thus, knowing the position of the station which has sent out the warning, the vessel is able to shape its course so as the steer clear of mines or others menaces.   TS, 11-1914

Local Comforts for Our Defenders
To the Editor *King's County Chronicle*

Dear Sir,

May I ask you to kindly publish these letters to encourage the many working for our soldiers and sailors, and to see how our poor noble fellows are minded when they get home. I do not put in the lady's name but she has worked for years in the soldier's homes.—Yours,

A Small Worker

October, 28th, 1914
Dear Mrs Walker,

It may interest you to hear of a visit I paid yesterday to one of our six convalescent homes connected with the hospital—a beautiful park rich in autumn colouring, handsome mansion with grass terrace down to the lake, fountains, flowers, &c. The lady who owns it has it perfectly fitted for 70 patients. There they lie in picture gallery and recreation rooms, surrounded by beauty and comfort, lovingly tended by trained Red Cross ladies. Others strolling about the grounds, a group of Belgians by the fountain. I knew them all of course, they were delighted to see me, to tell of their splendid time. One lad started up in bed with very wild eyes at sight of me, sister thought he was suddenly ill, but was reassured when he in a good brogue called out 'There now, and is it alive I am at all and is this Miss----
I see.' A lad I had often played draughts with in Clonmel last winter. He came with the wounded from Lille on Friday and was sent straight on to the home.

Another day she writes:
So many thanks for these lovely fresh eggs, they will be a treat indeed. We got 130 Belgian wounded soldiers into the hospital, you would pity them, so lonely, not able to speak a word of English. Some very badly wounded.

I am just bringing some French-English dictionaries as a help to them.

October 3rd

How very kind of you, that 5s will bring two mothers to see their noble sons, just home from the front, next Sunday, and also supply stamps to relieve the anxiety of others. 120 men arrived in Cambridge Hospital today from the front. I have been writing letters and giving out stationary and stamps since 1 p.m., it's nearly 7.p.m. now. I have just come home; still many letters to write from hastily written notes. I wish friends could just see even one ward, its varied needs.

Shall I sketch one ward visited to-day. Bed 1—A warm greeting. 'Why Miss P—s it yourself I see, still going strong, its none years since I saw you last in Kilbride Camp.'

Bed 8—A patient some time in, eight cruel wounds, so gentle I read a few verses to him.

Every man gladly took a small Gospel. I saw about 90 altogether to-day and I gave out 64 testaments and Gospels. Besides many words of comfort, its most deeply interesting work. Do pray for us.

Here follow other instances. Now for our wants – they are many and varied – shirts, socks, cholera belts, mufflers, fresh eggs, stamps, pencils. A weekly *Irish Times* would be very welcome to Irish men, they long for home news. Bandages are very useful.

Yours sincerely.   H-P.KCC, 11-1914

Delvin Union

Mr E Dargan, JP, presided at the fortnightly meeting of the above Board on Friday week.

Delvin Soldiers dependents

Mr P Darby brought before the Board the case of Mrs Power, Delvin, whose son has recently been killed at the war, and who got no allowance from the War Office, although he was her only support. The Clerk said it was stated that she had an allowance of 6d per day.

Mr Beresford—There is no such thing as separation allowance at the rate of 6d per day.

Mr Darby—She is getting 6d per day, but it is not from the War Office. It was allowed to her voluntarily by her son, and it is part of his own wages.

Mr Beresford—That is the only way she could get it. She will get an allowance from the Soldier's Dependents Benefit Association, if there is a branch here.

Clerk—We have been looking that up, and cannot find it out.

Mr Beresford—If you communicate with the police sergeant he will tell you where the headquarters of the district are.

Mr Keegan—She will, no doubt, get something from that. She must be seen to in the meantime. She might be dead before that comes along.

Mr Darby—There was a circular read here after the war started, which stated that if the Guardians relieved any necessary case in the first instance, they would get a refund from the War Office. Is that so?

Clerk—Yes.

Mr Cully—Let that be done in this case and give the woman something.

Mr Darby—It can be claimed from the War Office afterwards. The case is a bad one, and the woman is nearly blind.

Mr Beresford—Where does she live?

Mr Darby—She lives in a labourer's cottage about a couple of hundred yards down from Delvin.

Mr Cully—I was told the other day that Mr Fetherstonhaugh was to take the case in hands.

Mr Keegan—Colonel Pollard-Urquhart took up a lot of cases around Castlepollard and got a very fair allowance for those dependents.

It was decided to give Mrs Power 5s per week relief, application to be made to the War Office to indemnify the Guardians.

The meeting then adjourned.

WE,11-1914

Private William Power, Leinster Regiment, was killed in action in October, 1914. He has no know grave and is listed on the Ploegsteert Memorial in Belgium, See Delvin Man Killed at the Front.

Feigning Death
Westmeath Man's Clever Ruse to Deceive the Germans

James Browne of Clougahan, who was recently invalided home from the Front, stated that what impressed him most in the war was the artillery fire of the Germans, which he described as terrible. He was four days in the trenches under a heavy fire all the time. At Lille he was supplied with one hundred and fifty rounds of ammunition, and had fire about one hundred and twenty five rounds when a comrade beside him was wounded in the arm. Brown took a piece of his coat to make a bandage for the man, and had just finished his work of mercy when he himself was wounded. He lay in the trenches until darkness set in. The Germans passed over the place, and he had to feign death fearing that they might dispatch him. When he found the 'coast clear' he went towards a farm house which had been turned into a temporary hospital. Here his wound was dressed by the Red Cross people.

WE,11-1914

James Browne survived the war.

From the Front
Interesting Letters from Mullingar Men

Vivid Description – Shelling in the Mangold Fields
The following has been addressed by the writer from the 'Front' to a Mullingar Friend – 7th 11-1914.

Dear Sir—I received your letter alright, and was glad to hear you are well, as this leaves me at present. Yes, we had two engagements, one on the 10th and the other on the 18rth of last month. We got a terrible shelling with shrapnel when advancing across the mangel(sic) fields. It Was Cruel.

My company was the first to advance, and the guns opened on us on the road. We got under a ditch at a graveyard for a few minutes rest, and then got out into the open again. A battery in front shelled blazes out of us, but we shifted their infantry men an took up their positions. We lost only one killed and eleven wounded out of the company.

It was a miracle we were not wiped out. I thought my number was up. We were sniping at each other all day, waiting for one other division to advance. Again they opened a terrible rifle fire on us, and never hit a man. But we cleared them out. We could not advance any further as the rest of the Brigade were not up, and out captain halted us and we dug trenches, and are here ever since. They give a shelling now and again, and our artillery give the same to them. The weather is bad and good. It is wet every second day. The trenches are not very good in the rain, but we are all in good spirits and have plenty to eat. No more at present.

I remain.
Yours faithfully,
Pat Doyle.

WE,11-1914

Private Patrick Doyle, Royal Dublin Fusiliers, died of wounds in October, 1917. He is buried in Dozinghem Military Cemetery in Belgium. His sister drowned on the *Lusitania*.

Two Sons For The Front

Mr William G Flood, eldest son of Mr Dan Flood, JP, Co C, Mullingar, a well known and prominent Westmeath auctioneer, has been appointed to the engineering department 16th Irish Army Division, the headquarters of which are at Mallow, under the command of Lieutenant General Sir Lawrence Parsons. Mr Ford was engaged as mechanical engineer in the firm of Messrs Campbell, Liverpool, previous to his volunteering for military service, and the head of the firm intimated to him that his position will be open for him again after the war. This in the second member of Mr Flood's family who has given his services for active duty in the present grave crisis, his other son, Daniel, joining at the outbreak of the war, and is now a Corporal in the Leinster Regiment.

WE,11-1914

Private Daniel Flood was killed in action in Egypt in April, 1918 and buried in Ramleh War Cemetery in Israel. There are many photographs and articles about him in the newspapers of the time and he is also listed in De Ruvigny's Roll of Honour. William Flood survived the war.

Gallant Irishman on French Battle

The Carrick-on-Suir correspondent of the Freeman writes:

The following are some extracts from a remarkable communication sent from the front by Corporal Michael O'Meara, of the Irish Guards, to his relatives at Ballinagrana, Carrick-on-Suir.

Corporal O'Meara has been at the front since the outbreak of the war.

After giving a description of the green flag carried by the Irish Guards, from which, after so much stress and strife, he says, the harp and shamrock and the words 'Erin-go-Bragh' have almost faded beyond recognition, he writes:

'While testifying our loyalty by discharging our duty faithfully and conscientiously, we never can and never will forget in this supreme struggle, when the mighty nations of Europe are engaged in deadly combat, that we are Irishmen, and as Irishmen we must live up to tradition. We are British soldiers, and proud of the name, and through all our battles our foremost consideration is to add more lustre to the fair name of Erin....

'But to return to out flag, which is now faded, though treasured far more than ever, I will endeavour to describe how onthis occasion a C----, when the fate of the day seemed to waver in the balance and the ruthless enemy by sheer weight of numbers were pressing onward at every point of vantage, this faded flag turned threatened defeat into decisive victory.

'On our left were the Munsters, and on our right were the Leinsters and Connaught Rangers. All were hard pressed and about to retire, when suddenly from the firing line rose the stalwart figure of an Irish Guardsman flourishing the old green flag and shouting, excitedly, "Erin-go-Bragh!"

'With the blood curdling fast through my veins I watched with pride and admiration the marvellous effect produced by those simple words.

'With a mighty cheer that rent the heavens—a cheer that rose and swelled above the din of battle and the roar of artillery—here sons of Erin charged down on the advancing enemy with bayonet fixed and every nerve tense with excitement.

'The enemy hesitated, staggered by such a turn of events when victory was almost within their grasp. But they were given little time for hesitation—for, to alter slightly the lines of a well known ballad,

Like lions leaping at the fold
When mad with hunger's gang.
Right up against the Germans lines
Those Irish heroes sprang.

The Germans turned and fled in all directions completely routed and disorganised.'

Such is only one of many incidents which have occurred in the present campaign, but it is sufficient to show that, though loving and fighting for the Empire to which he is proud to belong, the Irish soldier still cherishes his true nationality and glorifies in the name of Ireland.

WE,11-1914

See Carrickman's Experience in the Royal Engineers. Michael O'Meara survived the war.

Irish Soldier's Ghastly Find
Lady's Severed hand in German's haversack

An Ennis correspondent writes: A young gentleman in Ennis has handed me a letter that he has just received from his brother, who is with the Veterinary Corps at the front, from which I extract the following:

'The weather is getting very cold now, especially at night, but we are very well provided for as regards clothing and grub. I daresay one gathers from the papers at home a good idea of 'German kulture.' He is another sample. Some prisoners were brought in last week, and on being searched one was found to have in his knapsack, wrapped up in a handkerchief, a lady's hand, with five rings on the fingers. I'll have a lot to tell you when I see you, as I'm taking notes."

LC, 11-1914

An Urlingford Hero and His Dependents
Why Recruiting has Fallen Off

Mr Thomas Harrington, JP, County Councillor, Urlingford, has addressed the following letter to a Dublin newspaper: Sir—Under the heading of "Harvest of Death" you publish in this day's issue a graphic description of the fighting in France, taken from the lips of Private Cornelius Cane, of Urlingford, in the Mater Hospital, Dublin, who lies there wounded. This gallant soldier, with his brother Thomas, volunteered and went to the war with upwards of 40 others from this little town of less than 500 population. Many of these brave fellows are wounded in hospital; others are prisoners of war in Germany; others are at the front, while others are in training to go to the front at any moment. Will it be credited, although such, unfortunately, is only too true, the dependents of these brave soldiers are left to starve in Urlingford, and are compelled to seek outdoor relief from the Guardians of the Urlingford Union. Only on Thurdsay last the father of Private Cane and his brother, a poor man beyond his time to labour, and almost totally blind, was put out on the outdoor relief list. There are other parents of brave soldiers in the same position in Urlingford, who have not received one penny either from the War Office, Prince of Wales fund, or any other source since their sons joined the British Army three months ago. Is it any wonder recruiting should be falling away under these circumstances? How is the Prince of Wales fund administered, which is well over £3,000,000? Certainly those in charge are not attending to the needs of the poor fathers and mothers of the soldiers in Urlingford who are risking their lives fighting in France and Belgium.

No doubt the same neglect and want of sympathy is happening generally throughout Ireland. If so, it is no wonder Mr Redmond's appeal for recruits for the front is not meeting with the immediate and great response which the Irish leader had hoped. It is an extraordinary thing why any of the elected public bodies in Ireland, County Councils, District Councils, Urban Councils, Old Age Pension or Insurance Committees were not called on to administer the Prince of Wales fund and see after the immediate wants and requirements of the dependents of the brave fellows who are fighting for the Nation and Empire. Let me hope this deplorable and sad state of things will be speedily remedied.

Thomas Harrington,
Urlingford, County Kilkenny,
2 November 1914.

TS, 11-1914

This man appears under the spelling 'Cane' in the papers, 'Kean' in the papers and Census. He is unfindable in the databases.

British Battleship Blown Up
Terrible loss of life, London

Thursday
It was announced in the House of Commons this afternoon that the battleship *Bulwark* was blown up in Sheerness Harbour this morning. Only twelve lives were saved. HMS *Bulwark* was a battleship of fifteen thousand tons. She was completed in 1902 and re-commissioned at Chatham in June, 1912. She had a compliment of seven hundred and fifty men, and carried four twelve-inch guns. The *Bulwark* cost £997, 846. It is believed that the cause of the disaster was an internal magazine explosion, which rent the

ship asunder. There was no upheaval of water, and when the smoke cleared, the ship had entirely disappeared. An inquiry into the affair will be held tomorrow.

EG, 11-1914

HMS *Bulwark* sank with the loss of 798 lives.

Indians in Action
How the Gurkhas Charged With the Kukri

Lieutenant J A Gendre-Chardoux, now attached to the Army Service Corps in the north of France—before the war he was French coach to the officers and army candidates at the Wellington Staff College, Aldershot, writes a letter to a friend in East Kent about the daring fighting of the Indian troops.

'The Germans are well equipped and fight well,' he writes. 'They are very brave. They advance in thick formation, spurning death. If they lose a position they try to recapture it regardless of lives. That game cannot last long. We took lots of prisoners. They all say they are glad to be taken.

'Yesterday I saw and spoke to two German boys of 15 and 16 years – one was crying. They said that the Germans have sent to the front all their male population from 15 years up to 55 years old.

'The explosion of the German shells is terrible. The noise made during the flight of the projectile is like that of a diamond cutting glass, only more awful. Last week I was with the Indian Troops, and they were worth seeing. They are a fine body of men, chiefly the Bengal Lancers. They eat only goat meat and they have an enormous herd of goats. They are very generous.

'One of them came to me with a cup of rum, and, after saluting 'Salaam, Sahib,' begged me to drink the rum and accept some nuts and dried raisins. I did, and he salaamed again and went away, showing a row of beautiful white teeth. Those Indians have fought remarkably well. They had never heard the guns before, and at the first they showed some nervousness, but they soon grew accustomed to it.

The Gurkhas the other day gave it hot to some German regiments. They crawled in the field for two hours without being seen by the Germans. When they got quite close to the enemy they sprang up with their kukri in hand, and what was left of the Germans took to their heels. The Gurkhas are born fighters. They are very small men, well knit, with a Japanese face. They are as nimble as cats.'

LC, 11-1914

Lieutenant Gendre-Chardoux survived the war.

Thrilling Story

by Clare Seaman

Experiences on Hermes
How a Submarine did its work
Flotilla of destroyers at rescue
Interesting Narrative

On Wednesday last from the 11.30 train arriving at Ennis a fine stalwart young man, in sailor garb alighted, and on being questioned by a Pressman, he told a thrilling story of his escape from the ill-fated cruiser, HMS *Hermes*, which was recently destroyed by a German submarine in an attack off the Straits of Dover. The Tar gave his name as James Power, a native of Querrin, West Clare, to which place he was then on his way to visit his relatives. Asked what he first experienced after the fatal torpedo had come in contact with his cruiser, he said at 8. 15 on the morning he was enjoying a good breakfast in the messroom when with terrific unexpectedness there was a terrible explosion, which, he declared 'finished his breakfast for the day'. Leaving the messroom, he proceeded quickly to the deck, where he found the cruiser had been torpedoed. The crew at once lowered the boats, which was done in good time. The crew of the *Hermes*, he said, consisted of 367 hands, of whom forty were lost, four being drowned, while about forty who were engaged in the area affected were killed. Power said the fatality occurred about nine miles off the coast of Calais. They were doing patrol duty, were constantly at the guns, and kept diligent look out for the enemy, either by aeroplane or by sea. At the time they were bound from Dunkirk to Folkestone, and his vessel was specially fitted for sea plane carrying. Questioned if there was any possibility of their being able to observe the submarine before the fatal blow was inflicted. Power explained it was very difficult to discover the vicinity of the vessel, except when the water was very calm and the periscope could only be seen, an affair six inches square, which was so placed as to travel over the water. He explained how mirrors fixed in this periscope enabled those operating in the submarine to detect ships passing on any side. The submarine fired three projectiles from a distance of 1,000 yards, two of which inflicted the damage that subsequently sent the *Hermes* to the bottom. A terrific explosion rocked and shook the ship, and Power divested himself of his sea boots. Acting on the instructions of the Captain, all their guns were discharged, and this brought a flotilla of five destroyers to the aid of the rapidly sinking *Hermes*. Those destroyers travelled to their assistance at the rate of thirty seven miles an hour, but before they arrived he had got into a lifeboat and proceeded to the work of rescuing his comrades, of whom he helped to take 61 into his boat. All the floating material in the ship was ordered to be thrown off by the Captain to enable them to have something to cling to until they were picked up. He cruised with his 61 rescued until the destroyers arrived, and having set them on board, the boat proceeded in search of others. His further heroic efforts were rewarded by his picking up a further number of his comrades, whom he also safely placed on board a destroyer.

There was no confusion at all, all being cool and calm, and he declared that while he was carrying out the work of rescue he found comrades swimming about singing to the air of 'It's a Long Way to Tipperary... It's a long way to that cutter' – meaning the boat. The *Hermes* kept afloat for about two hours. He paid a tribute to the bravery and coolness of the Captain, who stood at his post until about half an hour before the *Hermes* disappeared. Power is determined to take his part in the 'game of war', as he stated that at the close of his short holidays he would volunteer for submarine service, in which he claims to be proficient.   LL, 11-1914

There were 22 from HMS *Hermes*, none were from County Clare.

Letter from a Limerick Nurse

A letter dated 30 October, received by her relatives, from a Limerick lady, one of the red Cross Nurses, in Calais, states: 'The Belgians are so keen to learn English, and delighted when they are signed up for an English Hospital. I am working on night duty with seven other nurses in the railway engine shed, a huge and grubby place. All the wounded Belgians are dressed here before going on the boat. It is called the clearing shed. I have seen numerous German prisoners, they come here for a night, and on to prison after. Some are very ill, and badly mauled. I just think the little Belgians are splendid. They are so jolly good Hardly ever say a word about the worst wound. I should love to have time to talk to them. Last night I gave a cigarette to some of the men I dressed. They loved it – one could do with plenty. Queen Mary sent some splendid hampers over yesterday, with clothes for the men – we were so delighted.' The writer observes further on that 'People in general are awfully good to us, the soldiers are always giving us something, regimental buttons, bullets, etc'.   LC, 11-1914

Limerick Soldier

His Thrilling Experiences
Hair-Breadth Escapes at the Front

Letter to his Father.

John Greeney, a private in the Royal Engineers, writing from the front to his father, Mr P. Greeney, Brennan's Row, Limerick, says: 'My Dearest

Father – This is about the tenth letter I have written home, and I never had an answer from anybody. Of course I am not blaming you; I suppose you wrote—if you did I never received a letter nor from anyone else. If you get this letter I hope you will answer it as soon as possible as I expect to be going back to the firing line in a week or two.

I had a narrow escape the last time I was up there; I hope I will come off as lucky this time. We were going along the road about 8 pm, I was hanging on to a motor car when a shell hit about two inches above my neck. Killing the driver. You bet I made myself scarce after that. Another night we were billeted in a village, and I was on night duty. When we would be billeted anywhere we used to take our turn on night duty, so I had a despatch for the Cavalry Brigade, a distance of about four miles. I had gone about two and a half miles when I heard horses footsteps behind me, so I jumped off the bike and hid in a ditch just in time to let a patrol of Uhlans pass. The same night the bell of my bike was blown off with a bullet. That was the narrowest escape I ever had. The night I hurt my leg we were going along the road, and I never saw a piece of a tree lying on the road, which formed part of a barricade which the Germans put up, so I did the trick cyclist over it, and just as I fell a petrol lorry passed over my foot, so I was shifted to the field hospital, and this is where I am now. No more to say. Hope all the boys are well and trusting to hear from you soon. Love to all. Your fond son, Jack.

LC, 11-1914

John Greeney survived the war.

'Looks Like Hell'
Limerick Soldier's Experiences of the Present War

Letter from the Front
Mr John Sheahan, 2 Gerald Griffin Street, Limerick, has received the following letter from his son, who is at present at the front:

My Dear Father—Your letters, cigarettes, etc, received. The fags were a Godsend, as I had not had a puff for some days. Since I wrote last my brigade was kept busy, and we had very little rest or sleep. I am now in the thick of the fight, and it looks like hell. I have been sent back to the base for a few days rest, and I avail; of the opportunity by sending this long letter. I have passed through a terrible time of it for the past few weeks having been in most of the engagements. The artillery have lost a huge number of officers and men. I had some narrow escapes of being knocked out. The weather now is bitter and cold, and looks like a bad winter. Well, did I ever think that there was such a horrible time before me. It would take up all the available space of the *Limerick Leader* to give a brief account of it. All I have to say is that I have gone through the 'mill' up to with a good heart, and not in the least down-hearted. Last week was a restless one for us all, but we bore it well right through. Our officers are a grand lot of fellows, and their conduct in the field and behind the trenches is both brave and edifying. I was watching the burial of some of the 'Leinsters' yesterday (Friday). It was a sad spectacle, moreover as I knew some of the chaps at home. I have met several Limerick men, amongst them being young Saunders, the farrier's son. I learn he has been promoted to Battery Sergeant. Poor Paddy Carr (Engineers) is a prisoner of war and safe from the 'coal boxes' of the Germans, but now enjoying their hospitality.

According to military experts it looks just now as if there is a favourable turning point for the Allies. The Germans are apparently getting disorganised at several points, and from the outward condition of the German prisoners passing through our lines they are in a pitiable state. They look like a lot of "plucked geese" being brought to the markets for Xmas. Their hair has been clipped into the bone, suggesting that they came out for a protracted stay, but I think they will be shifted at any rate very soon. It is always at night time that the Germans favour us with their 'Jack Johnson's,' but we sleep with one eye open and ready to receive them, and don't we respond nicely. We seldom miss our mark, as our shells and shrapnel take good effect on them. Now, we have been billeted in several towns where the Germans had already done great havoc, and all one could see around was burned down churches, convents, business houses, factories, and civic buildings.

The Germans looted hotels, stores, and banks to a terrible degree, and when I read in the *Leader* of the timely action of the citizens to raise funds and provide home for the noble-hearted Belgians, I was proud to be a Limerick man. My comrades are mostly all Englishmen, and when I pointed out to them in the paper what Garryowen was doing for the Belgians I got a great clap on the back from officers and men. No doubt, special credit is due to your friend, the mayor (Alderman P. O'Donovan), Sir Vincent and Lady Nash, and the other good ladies and gentleman who are associated with this noble work.

Father, how I did laugh when I got the medal and ribbon of my old Alma Mater (the Boy's Confraternity). It was lucky you kept it safe for me. Anyhow the war had made good boys of us out here. By the time that this letter reaches you I shall be again on the look out for the German 'coal boxes'. However, let them all come. Down with Germany and Kaiser must go. We expect a few hot engagements from end of November, and we shall give them plenty of lead, I assure you. Our Xmas will be a lonely one this year, but we all hope to see matters squared by then. I must now draw to a close, wishing you all, brothers and sisters, a happy Xmas, and many years of good health – From your fond son, Christie, 21st Field Battery, RFA.   LL, 11-1914

Driver Christopher Sheahan survived the war.

Royal Recognition
An Irish Widow's Mite

Mrs Norah Dunay, a qualified midwife in Clonakilty, County Cork, has a family of six children, of whom three sons are in the Navy, one of them is present invalided home, and two in the army. The other is a daughter, in a convent in Paris assisting to nurse the wounded.

His majesty having been informed of this, has sent her the following gracious message:

Privy Purse Office
Buckingham Palace
12th November, 1914.
Madam,

I have the honour to inform you that the King has heard with much interest that you have at present five sons in the army, and Navy. I am commanded to express to you the King's congratulations, and to assure you that his majesty much appreciates the spirit of patriotism which prompted this example in one family of loyalty and devotion to their Sovereign and Empire. – I have the honour to be, madam, your obedient servant.

(signed) F E G Ponsonby
Keeper of the Privy Purse.

LC, 11-1914

All of Mrs Norah Dunay's son survived the war.

The Brave Munsters

In the course of a letter to a friends, Private Hanley, of Tobertynan, County Meath, says—We had a great time of it swiping the Germans (swiping is a colloquialism meaning threshing). The company, I was in (he belongs to the Munster Fusiliers) were in some great engagements. Leave it there if we did not do some bayonet charges. There was one place after Mons, between Landresie and Supier, we had them out of a forest. The crosses a tillage field on top of a ridge about 1,000 yards away. They were at the rate of twelve to one. We did a bayonet charge. When they saw the wild Irish coming they held up their hands, and also six white flags. We went over to take them prisoners. When we got out on the left of them they picked up their arms and shot us down. They opened up on us with a lot of maxims. Very few of us got back. There were five of us got back without a wound. But we paid them for it. Our artillery kept it shelled night and day, and every rifle shot took down a German. When we got done they were as thick on the ground as grass—dead and wounded. They are awful savages. It would go to your heart to see the towns and villages after they pass through. It is awful the way the Germans treat the girls and children.

LC, 11-1914

There was only one soldier named Hanley to die from County Meath, he was Private Owen Hanley, Royal Dublin Fusiliers from Kilmessan.

Victims of the War

The Government on Monday night issued a memorandum of their scheme of new allowances and pensions in connection with the Navy and Army. Scales of pay to widows and orphans have been substantially improved. A widow of a man in the lowest grade in each service with four children will receive a minimum of £1 weekly, instead of 11s; a widow with three children, a minimum of 17s 6d, instead of 9s; a widow with two children, 15s, instead of 8s; a widow with one child, 12s 6d, instead of 5s, Allowances will be increased on pensions. In necessitous cases a widow's full separation allowance will be continued for 26 weeks after the death of her husband. The allotment previously made by a soldier for his children will now be paid by the Government, and provision will be made for assisting an unmarried man's dependants. Allowances for particl disablement will be from 3s 6d to 17s 6d weekly, and for total disablement 14s unmarried men to 23s married men with children. Apart from the National Insurance benefit, the actuary estimates that on the various assumption the new scheme will involve a total capitalised liability of from 99 millions to 202 millions.

LC, 11-1914

Work in Trenches

The following graphic description of life in the trenches has been forwarded to the *Morning Post* by the mother of the writer. It is from a British Infantry Officer, and dates October 31:

Thank you very much for all the parcels. Yesterday there arrived cigarettes, pillow, soap, etc. The soap amused us. The only water I have seen for the last four weeks is the precious water we get for drinking. I have not washed even my face and hands for three weeks. Nevertheless I have been completely soaked through several times, and no doubt that washes you a bit. I have a huge beard, ginger colour, and look exactly like 'Consul'. After a fortnight's scrapping we have 'been dug in' here for a month. The night before last was for two hours, and the trench then became a foot of so deep in mud. I got three hours sleep just before dawn. There were two night attacks that night, and during that time the sky cleared, and it froze. When I woke up I was covered with ice and frost.

"We can seldom get much rest, even at night, as there are continued alarms, and in the day the shells completely prevent one's sleeping. A huge shell burst near one of our officers, and it so affected him that although not wounded he had to go to the base. Yet he was a big, strong fellow, who had served fifteen years in the Natal Police. In one hour the flames and concussion of certain shells which came from the same spot in sixes and eights, six times hurled me against the wall of my 'dug-out' without hurting me, but it does shake one up terribly. In an attack two weeks ago the scabbard of my sword came off without my knowing it. I stumbled, and the point of my sword went clean through my foot, luckily at the outer edge, only. It is all right now, and I did not have to go sick. It was lucky I did stumble though, as otherwise a bullet which touched my hat would certainly have gone through my brain. During the attack I had the man on either side of me shot dead more than once. These German bullets when they hit a bone turn over and make the most awful hole, like a dum-dum. We shot four captured Germans found with dum-dum ammunition.

'All night the cries of the wounded and dying are very distressing to hear. Of course the man who groans most is the man who is unconscious and has hallucinations or something of the sort. We have hardly an officer left, but luckily only about six have been killed. The day after our attack the Germans attacked us, and we had to withdraw three miles at dusk. They lost 7,000 killed and wounded in front of our Division.

LC, 11-1914

With the 18th Royal Irish at the Front

Private Robert Walsh, of the 18th Royal Irish Regiment, who has returned to his home at Carrick-on-Suir from the front, suffering from a bullet wound in the leg, relates how the Royal Irish, after two days under a terrible fire of German shell and rifle bullets, advanced right up to the German trenches, near Lille, amidst the cries of their officers to 'Remember the gallantry of the Royal Irish in South Africa!' and took 600 German prisoners and captured near the trenches two heavy guns. The courage reckless daring, and utter disregard for death of the officers of the Royal Irish was, Private Walsh says, wonderful. In a village near where the fighting took place he saw a Catholic Church, the walls and roof of which had been demolished, but the altar and tabernacle, even to the flowers and candles, were quite intact. They found a wounded German officer in bed in a small farm house. He died of his wounds on the ship on which Private Walsh returned to England. The Royal Irish, both officers and men have, he says, suffered great losses both killed and wounded.

LC, 11-1914

Private Robert Walsh survived the war.

Delvin Man Killed at the Front

The sad news came to hand a few days ago that Private William Power, of Delvin, had been killed in action at the war. He was in the Leinster Regiment, and for some time before the war had been on the special reserve. Like so many other Irishmen, when war was declared, he had to re-join his regiment and proceed to the theatre of war. He was a stalwart young man, who left delving taking with him the best wishes of the whole community for his safe return. His brother, James, was also a reservist in the same regiment, and he it was who communicated the sad news of the death of his brother. It was a sad feature to convey such news to a poor aged widow. William was her only support for some time past, and words cannot express the grief of the poor old woman, when the sad news was made known to her. She received no compensation or allowance of any kind from the War Office from the date that her boys left, and she has to depend largely on the generosity of her neighbours. We pointed out the facts before, but nothing has since been done. It is really a case in which the Prince Of Wales Fund would apply, and it is to be hoped that those in delving district who have connection with that fund will have this most deserving case attended to.

At a meeting of the Delvin Volunteer Corps held on Sunday last, Mr P Kearney proposed and Mr P Darby seconded a vote of condolence with the bereaved mother of William Power. The deceased was drill instructor of the delving Corps before being called away. It was agreed that a subscription list be opened for the purpose of showing in some way the appreciation of the Volunteers for deceased and also to comfort his grief-stricken mother. A generous response has already been made.

MR, WN, 11-1914

Private William Power, Leinster Regiment, was killed in action in October, 1914. He has no know grave and is listed on the Ploegsteert Memorial in Belgium. See Dead Soldier Honoured.

Had Been Through Five Engagements
Wounded Soldier in Mullingar

Private Adams, of the Royal Fusiliers, has arrived in Mullingar from the front suffering from a bullet wound in the arm and also in the leg. Our representative visited Private Adams on Monday evening and had a chat with him concerning his experiences at the front. He was in excellent health and spirits, his progress toward recovery being very favourable. His wounds are being medically treated in the County Infirmary. Private Adams, who seemed most anxious to comply with out representative's wish to give and interesting narrative of the happenings at the Great War, was modestly reluctant to mention anything about the part he took in the fighting. We learned from him, however, that he passed through no fewer than five engagements, and it us not too much to presume he had many hair-breadth escapes. His regiment was out at the start of the war in August and was called into action as the first reinforcements in the memorable retreat from Mons. Questioned as to what hour in the morning fighting started, he replied about 2 o'clock. Fighting he said was practically continuous. The bursting shells he said make a terrific noise. They usually make an attack at dusk and at day break is another favourite time for the German offensive. He states he got wounded at the battle of the Aisne, and was lying eight hours on the battle field before he was picked up by the ambulance corps. The bullet which struck him in the arm, was extracted by a German doctor. It was of a brass colour and tapered to a point. He showed our representative the bullet which was bent where it came in contact with the bone. Private Michael visited them in the Hospital and Private Adams had a valuable amber pipe which he said the Prince gave him. They were very kindly treated. He produced some beautiful groups of photographs taken by the prince of the wounded soldiers in the hospital. He said the Germans were good fighters. When our representative suggested that they should be in constant fear of being struck by bullets or shells, he laughingly replied in the negative, "You become used to it all, " he added, "and you never mind them." Our representative then intimated that he was curious of the battle-line. Private Adams thereupon produced an ingeniously drawn map which he had sketched himself, showing the positions of the opposing armies, the trenches, the position of the artillery and the reserve forces.

MR, WN, 11-1914

No soldier named Adams died during WWI From County Westmeath.

Dead Soldier Honoured
Delvin Drill Instructor

The Delvin Volunteers paid a very fitting tribute to the memory of their late drill instructor, William Power, who was killed in action on the battlefield in France on the 18 October. On Sunday last a special Mass was offered at ten o'clock for the repose of deceased's soul. The Delvin, Clonmellon and Reynalla Volunteer Corps turned up in full numbers, all marching to the Church in processional order under the command of their respective officers. Emblems of mourning were worn by each of the Corps. When all had filed into the Church it was pretty well filled. Rev. P Conlon, CC, celebrated Mass. After Mass all the men lined up outside the Church and marched through the town, the Clonmellon men carrying a fine banner

....From the staffs of banners were floating streamers and bows of crepe. The whole affair was most impressive, and the behaviour of the men was most creditable. Each Volunteer fully observed the solemnity and movements were gone through in dead silence. The action of the Volunteers in showing their appreciation and sympathy in such a fitting way has received the highest praise of the whole community. William Power was known to all as a young man full of vigout and energy, and most winning and obliging. The people's sympathy at his tragic fate is all the more intensified by the fact that he was the only support of his invalid mother. For many years she depended in him for her maintenance, and he has never failed in that duty. It is little wonder that when he was called to arms that the unhappy mother collapsed and soon was one of the saddest sights one would wish to see. The mother got no allowance from the War Office, and a local collection was made to prevent the poor woman from starving. This, of course, could not continue, and at last the meeting of the Guardians Mrs Power was allowed 5s a week out-door relief. It is a hard case that when a stalwart young Irishman has to obey the call of "King and Country," that he must go regardless of his dependents. Surely this is a case in which some of the millions to the credit of the various funds could be usefully applied.

MR, WN, 11-1914

Private William Power, Leinster Regiment, was killed in action in October, 1914. He has no known grave and is listed on the Ploegsteert Memorial in Belgium, See Delvin Man Killed at the Front.

Delvin Union
Soldiers Dependants

The Local Government Board wrote relative to the proposal to grant relief to Mrs Power, tenant of a labourers Cottage who has two sons on active service, and stating that as intimated on recent circular letters, the duty of providing assistance to the dependants of men in service, pending the grant of Government allowances has been entrusted to the Soldiers and Sailors, Families Association. The Hon Sec. Of the County Westmeath Division of the Association is Mrs Tottenham, Tudenham, Mulligar, and the board here brought the case in question under her notice. In connection with the above the following letter was received from Mrs Fetherstonhaugh, Rockingham, Killucan,

Sir—I wish to inform you that I have been reading in the local paper, the discussion which arose at the Workhouse about Mrs Power's means of support. I should like to inform you that directly the war broke out I visited Mrs Power and ascertained that her son the late William Power, allowed her sixpence a day, this I augmented by a weekly allowance of four shillings from the Soldiers and Sailors Families Association, making in all seven and six a week from both sources immediately in hearing that William Power was killed I applied for her to the Royal Patriotic Fund. I am now all-owing Mrs Power eight and six a week. I have visited all the dependents of the soldiers belonging to Delvin, and have given allowances where it was necessary to do so. I should be obliged if you would read this letter at your next Board meeting.

Mr Daly, said that Mrs Power was getting 3s 6d. per week from her son before he was killed, and he did not know if that was now stopped.

Chairman: It will not be necessary for the Guardians to give her relief now.

Clerk: No. She was paid one week.

Chairman: I propose we thank Mrs Fetherstonhaugh for her kindly action in this matter.

This was agreed to, and the Clerk was directed to acknowledge Mrs Fetherstonhaugh's letter.

MR, WN, 11-1914

Private William Power, Leinster Regiment, was killed in action in October, 1914. He has no know grave and is listed on the Ploegsteert Memorial in Belgium, See Delvin Man Killed at the Front.

Another Westmeath Man's Exeriences

Private John Ward, of the Leinster Regiment, formerly in the employment of Captain Large, Mullingar, is home from the war invalided. He says at one time he was over 16 days in the trenches under rifle fire. One time his regiment was ordered to take a bridge. The Germans were quite close at the time, but lay low, and adopted an ingenious device to warn themselves of the approach of the British soldiers. They securely tied a terrier dog to the bridge in the hope that the animal would bark on the approach of a number of men. The terrier did bark and the Germans sallying forth opened a heavy fire on the Leinsters, who temporarily fell back and the sudden onslaught, and took shelter in sheds and other out offices on an adjoining farm, the bullets raining like hailstones on the roofs of these buildings. Later on Ward's regiment went forth and captured the bridge. He said he had seen a tree shattered and three men and an officer killed by one German shell.

MR, WN, 11-1914

Private John Ward aged 29 was killed in action in march, 1916, and buried in Menin Road South Military Cemetery in Belgium).

New York Irishmen
Volunteer for the Front
Arrival in Ireland

Letter from Athlone Man

Private P Crawford, of the 3rd Leinsters, stationed at Victoria Barracks, Cork, writing to his brother, Mr B Crawford, Burnbrook Mills, Athlone, says, 'I know you will be surprised to hear I am here soldiering again. I came over on the *Olympic*, leaving New York on October 21st. 162 of us (Irishmen) volunteered. We had a desperate voyage on account of mines. We were laid up in Lough Swilly for seven days…we should have landed in Glasgow, but we were sent to Belfast, then to Dublin, then to Birr, and now I am landed in Cork in the 3rd battalion Leinster Regiment. It is great sport to see the way we are all mixed up here – all waiting to go to the Front.'

Note.—The excision from this letter announces an important Naval fact, which has not been given out by the Press Bureau, and which we do not feel at liberty to publish. This is the first intimation of volunteering in New York among Irishmen to fight in the Allied lines.—Ed. W.I.

WI, 11-1914

Private Crawford survived the war.

In The Firing Line
Four Athlone Men From One Family
Three at The Front—One Wounded

Athlone has given many men to the service of the Empire since war broke out early in august, and many parents have given one, two, or three of their sons to the cause, but perhaps the proudest of all is Mrs Hickman, of Patrick Street, who has given four sons to the army. Three of them are at present in the firing line, while the fourth is at home invalided from wounds sustained in the trenches. The wounded man at home is Trooper John Hickman, regimental number 6840, of the Royal Horse Guards. Trooper Hickman has exactly ten years service, and considering the terrible experiences he has gone through, since the outbreak of the war, he is a remarkably young man, and his appearance would suggest that he is not long of his teens. Originally belonging to the eighth Hussars, on mobilisation Trooper Hickman was transferred to the Royal Horse Guards. Joining that famous corps soon after the outbreak of hostilities he proceeded to the front and was for nearly five weeks in the firing line. His term there would have been much longer were it not for the fact that every few days he and his squadron were relieved so that the horses might be taken back to the base to get refreshed and some other remounts obtained in place of those which were injured. Though having gone through many exciting experiences the injured man is rather inclined not to speak much of what he went through. Though wounded in the calf of the leg he appears to have had marvellous escapes from death, and he attributes his miraculous escapes to the bad shooting on the part of the Germans. On the day on which he was wounded his squadron were ordered to advance on the German trenches so as to draw the fire for the infantry, who were waiting behind to clear the trenches with the bayonet. When the word of command was given the squadron charged at full gallop and never cried halt until they came right on the enemy's trenches. During the charge of over a couple of hundred yards bullets were flying thick all round them, but thanks to the bad marksmanship of the enemy only about 20 of the Guards were knocked over. As soon as the desired object of the manoeuvre had been obtained the squadron returned to the friendly lines, carrying with them their killed and wounded. The Germans still continued to pour in a veritable hail of lead on the attacking party, from rifles, and machine guns, but as their aim was faulty not many more casualties were sustained. Trooper Hickman had had his horse shot underneath him, and while endeavouring to capture a riderless horse received a shrapnel bullet in the calf of the leg which out him out of action. After some time he was able to crawl along and eventually got back to the shelter of his own trenches.

Asked as to the shooting capabilities of the Germans with rifles, the injured trooper replied that they were by no means as good as the English or the French, for, had their aim been accurate or reasonably so, very few, if any, of the attacking squadron wound have lived to reach the friendly lines. The squadron consisted of 200 men, and of these only 20 men got knocked over in the charge and the retirement, though, as a matter of fact, they got right in the enemy's trenches. The particular action in which he was wounded took place in Zoonebeake, in Belgium, about 12 miles from Ypres. After the enemy's fire had been drawn, the infantry charged with the bayonet, and the Germans retreated all along the particular line, 'for', said Trooper Hickman, 'as far as we could see, they could never face the cold steel and the sight of the men charging from trench to trench was quite enough to set them on the run at any time'.

The artillery fire of the Germans was infinitely superior to the rifle fire, and the shrapnel shells seldom fell far from their objective. Indeed, the vast majority of the wounds were all shrapnel ones, and in his squadron rifle bullet wounds were by no means numerous.

Describing German tactics in the various towns and villages they marched through, Trooper Hickman said the favourite plan of the Germans was to put sharpshooters into houses and snipe all the columns as they passed through. Even when the troops were in action the enemy stationed parties of men in houses in which were friendly occupants, from which individual troops were fired at. In one place, about 3 miles from Rouolleers, a party of twenty German sharpshooters did a great deal of damage by sniping from a house When discovered they still kept sniping away, but the English very soon silenced them, with the result that nineteen were killed in the ruins of the house, and two more were shot while in the act of sniping at the rear.

Asked if he had seen any evidence of German brutality towards non-combatants, Trooper Hickman said, as far as he was personally concerned, he had seen but one such case. One day when they were advancing near a village vacated by the Germans after a bayonet charge by an infantry column, he saw a young woman lying dead by the roadside apparently killed a short time before. His squadron could not wait to give the hapless creature burial, but the rear guard, as is customary in all such cases, saw that the remains were interred in a Christian manner. How the woman met her end he did not know, but apparently her death was not a natural one, as appearances did not indicate that.

He had heard a number of stories of German atrocities from other persons, but during his five weeks stay at the front he was not an eye witness of any. After being brought down to the base the wounded trooper was sent across to Southmapton, and afterwards to the Rathcliffe Infirmary, Oxford, where he lay for some time. After his discharge he was granted furlough to recuperate, and though able to go about with the aid of a stick, it will be still some time before he is able to re-join his regiment.

Trooper Hickman had nothing but praise for the manner in which the wounded were cared for in the Rathcliffe Infirmary, and while being conveyed to the hospital from the firing line.

The following members of Trooper Hickman's family are in the firing line at the present time, but so far have had the good fortune to escape getting injured, viz., Trooper Patrick Hickman, Fourth Hussars; James, in the Connaught Rangers, who, with his regiment were sent from India direct to the front, and Patrick, who is attached to the Fifth Leinster Regiment.

WI, 11-1914

None of these brothers died during the war.

From a Paris Hospital

Private Patrick Connolly, of Irishtown, Athlone, who is with the 1st Connaughts, arrived with the Indian troops at the front and has been now wounded and is in hospital at Versailles. Writing on the 5th inst to his mother he says, 'I am very glad to be alive. I just had a very narrow shave, but got off with a bullet through my left arm. I am in hospital since the end of this month. Dear ones at home, you do not know what this war is like.

It is beyond human description. Our regiment is getting it very hard. The worst of all is lying out at night in the cold and rain with nothing to cover you; and the cold after leaving India is intense. You know we left India in the middle of summer. The first wash I had for the last two months was when I came into hospital on the 2nd of the month, and we were not allowed to take off our boots or equipment day or night, but for food we are as well looked after as we could ask. The people of France are very good to the English troops. They give is plenty of tobacco and fags so we have nothing to fear but our God from morning till night. You could hear nothing but shot and shell. This is a pitiful sight – this hospital. Young men with legs and arms blown off.

Don't mind what the people say. It was a horrible sight to see the four fine men that were shot by my side—one officer and three others. This is the second battle we have been in. I am the only one of the Athlone boys who got hit so far. Christy O'Brien, is going on very well, and is 'safe as houses'.

WI, 11-1914

Christopher O'Brien and Private Patrick Connolly survived the war.

The Battle Front
Soldiers Tell of What They Did
And What The Saw

Private William Galvin, Irish Guards, has been at his home Carricknaughten, Athlone, for some weeks past recruiting, after his trying experiences on the retreat from Mons to Paris, in which he was eventually wounded. He is not disposed to speak much of the trying ordeal, but he is a young man of the type who may be described as every inch a soldier. Between Mons and Paris he was in eight engagements and several bayonet charges. These were, of course, exciting, and for a first experience somewhat unnerving, but the first shock removed all traces of nerves, and the driving of the bayonet into human bodies and dragging it out again became part of the day's work. The ugliest feature of it came afterwards in the uniform or great coat stiffening and sticking with human blood.

He agrees with the general experience that German rifle fire is similar and does little harm. The greatest destruction is done by bursting shrapnel. His wound was caused by a shrapnel bullet, which cut through three bullets in his ammunition pouch, just over his hip, and glancing down, ripped his right thigh, knocking him out. The wound was never a serious one, but two days elapsed before it was attended to. After he had fallen he had to remain on the field a considerable time, and then he dragged himself to a cottage where he was taken in. Finally, he was picked up by an ambulance and taken to an hospital in Paris, where he was under treatment for a fortnight before he was sent home. His wound is now quite well, and he is practically restored to perfect health. He is returning to his regiment, in the coming week.

A Run for the Germans
Private Maguire, of the Connaught Rangers, who has been convalescing at his home in Berries [Derries?], was also at Mons and the retreat to Paris. Near Paris he was wounded – receiving a number of pellets from a shrapnel shell in the leg. These were all successfully extracted and the leg is now as well as ever. Maguire describes an exciting run from a number of Germans. He had got cut off from his regiment, and was making his way across country when he fell in with a few others, amongst them, Willie Galvin of the Irish Guards. With the exception of Galvin they had all discarded their great coats as a source of weight and trouble when passing through barbed wire. They found themselves pursued by Germans. Their ammunition was low. Coming to an iron gate they all scrambled over, Galvin, with his great coat and carrying two rifles, vaulted over the gate. Maguire was exhausted and failed to get over. Seeing his predicament, Galvin vaulted back and lifting him, threw him over the gate, following immediately by the same nimble process. This incident left them in the rear of their companions. Looking back they spied three Germans close on them, and Galvin, picking up his rifle, shot them, one after another. This ended the pursuit, and when night fell they were both able to rejoin their respective corps. Maguire, like Galvin, is rejoining his regiment in the coming week.

Both the Irish Guards and the Rangers suffered severely in the many rear-guard actions in which they took part in the memorable retreat from Mons.

WI, 11-1914

Athlone man Private William Galvin is mentioned in many articles in the newspapers of the time. He survived the war.

A Roscommon Interpreter
17th October, 1914

Dear D.—Many thanks for letters. I got the cigarettes sent off on October 2nd, also Mother's of October 8th, and a couple of parcels; and have sent of P.C. also today, so you will probably get it first. We have been co-operating with the French the last couple of days. I have been acting as interpreter between a French Commandant—which corresponds to one of our Lieutenant Colonels and the Major.

The French Brigade had the observing station on top of a great pyramid of coal near a coal mine, so I had to stay up there with a telephone running out to the Major's observation and send the Orders of the Commandant as to targets he was on etc. I certainly improved my French, as they were all anxious to talk, and know hardly a word of English. They all get fearfully excited and on one occasion when one of their 'groupes' i.e., 12 guns or 3 batteries and our six guns on to a village, the French Infantry were attacking, the shrieks and yells of delight of the Battery Commanders at the spectacle was quite funny. The night was rather impressive as the 16 guns turned the tap on for 10 minutes as hard as they could go and by the end the village was a blazing mass with her stacks, houses, etc., throwing out volumes of smoke and flame, so that one could hardy see the buildings at all. I don't think there could have been many Germans in the houses; they were mostly in trenches along the front of the villages and I don't suppose came to much harm, unfortunately.

By the way, we left the Aisne about 10 days ago, and went north by train, and are now working out close to the German right flank. The Battery got complimented the other day on its shooting by the French by General Le Mestre, to be exact commanding the 21st French Army Corps; so perhaps the Major will get the Legion of Honour or something of the sort, as they seem to be pretty free with them. Perhaps they'll give one for interpreting.

Its beginning to get a bit cold at night now, with a white sort of mist which wets everything. We have managed to billet every night now for a long time in various farms so we can keep dry. We have started the early rising again the last four days and start anything from 2.30 am to 5 am, in the morning. I'll give you a list of things I should like. I've plenty of socks for myself, also shirts:

List—pair of Shooting(sic), roomy to take 2 pairs of socks; 1 pair puttees. Sweater (sleeves fairly ling to turn back if necessary); pair leather Breeches, brown leather, if possible, like a chauffeur's, as they keep the wind out, or else a sort of doe skin like hunting breeches, only brown. Don't get them if too expensive; 1 pair long drawers (thick) and thick vest.

I don't want more than this, as I can't carry it if I do get it. We would like tins or glasses of Potted Meat, Anchovy or Ham and Tongue, Beef or Chicken. Can you send out preserved eggs in grease in a wooden or tin box? We have had them up to now, but we are about to Pass over the country occupied by the Germans, so don't expect to find much as they leave everything in a fearful state or disorder.

We are in action now, 4 pm, near a village, which they make beer in, and which was shelled by both our troops and the Germans, so the houses are pretty well knocked about; there is a church spire in front with only the bare walls standing. It was shelled by the 6 am [?] as it had a German Observing Station in it. (I hope they did it for them). We can see the German shells burst all along the front, but, nothing has come very close. We are dug in with embankments in front of the guns and pits to get into behind the wagon on either side of the gun. We heard what sounded like a shell close by just now, and in a second there was hardly a man to be seen, it was quite funny. It turned out to be only a head of a fuse from a burst in front and whizzed over our heads and buried itself in the ground behind. It was the only thing that had been near us at all. I have been stalking hens with a revolver, but can't kill them, only makes them jump. Some of the people think the German people will bring matters to a finish when they know the truth. Haven't seen John since about October 6th or 7th—Love to all. Hugh.

WI, 11-1914

December, 1914

A Roscrea Soldier's Experience at the Front

Sergeant Major Drought Jackson, South Irish Horse, the only soldier in his regiment, and one of the lucky few in the British army to gain the coveted Legion of Honour, paid a short visit last week to his brother, Mr Burton Jackson, Cover Hill, Roscrea. The visit of such a gallant soldier who was rewarded for bravery by a foreign power, created no little interest, but the chief feature was the trophies of war that he brought with him. These were on view in Mr Treanor's window, Roscrea, and consist of an Uhlan officer's tunic, an infantryman's helmet, and the covering used for the latter while in service. When questioned, the Sergeant Major was reticent as to how he won the legion of honour, but quite readily he told how he got the souvenirs. He stated that a detachment of the South Irish Horse stopped for refreshments in a village near Rebais, in Belgium. The assistant in the café hinted that she thought a German spy was in a shed close by. He went over and saw a man wearing ordinary civilian clothes. Soon he was under arrest, and Sergeant-Major Jackson searched under some hay where he found a tunic and in the pocket was a cipher dispatch. The man was tried by court-martial, but as there was not sufficient evidence against him he was let go. Two day's later a couple of the Munster Fusiliers recognised the same man in a tree signalling to the enemy, and he was at once shot. The helmet and cover were got at Ypres.   TS, 12-1914. SGT MAJOR JACKSON SURVIVED THE WAR

About the Trenches

The men at the front now more forward by several narrow end-on approaches, which are open to the air a foot or two below the surface of the ground. Where open these approaches are zig-zagged to avoid being enfiladed. In either case forward progress is made by excavating at one end, at what is considered a possible assaulting distance. These approaches or saps are joined up by a lateral trench, roughly parallel to that being attacked. Here the stormers collect for a fresh rush. The extent to which subterranean or semi-underground life is forced on the combatants in the neighbourhood of the firing line varies with the nature of the ground, and depends on the character of the enemy's activity in a particular locality in which they are. When sniping or rifle fire is alone to be expected the amount of excavations behind the front line is limited. When a bombardment is, or has been, severe, everyone within range of the enemy's guns, the Brigadier not excepted will be found ensconced underground in dug-outs or funk-holes, as they are familiarly called, in the zone under fire. Houses are no better than shell traps.

Luxurious Underground Quarters

Behind the firing-line-trenches are found the shelters for men holding the line and those for the supports. These are more elaborate and comfortable than the fire trenches, and usually are roofed over, and contain cooking places and many conveniences. Some of these underground quarters have now become almost luxurious, and contain windows. Communication between the firing line and the various shelters in the rear and with the headquarters of the units is kept up along the approach trenches, all zig-zagged to prevent being enfiladed, liberally partitioned into compartments by traverses, so as to neutralise the effect of shell fire. For some time the character of the artillery fire has been such as to force both combatants, even for some distance behind the firing line, to burrow into the earth in order to obtain shelter and to conceal their works, and, as far as possible to gain protection both from guns and aeroplanes.

The Modern Battlefield

This has been carried on to such an extent that behind the front fire the trenches of the British, the French, and the Germans are perfect labyrinths of burrows in various types. The principal feature of the battlefield, therefore, is the absence of any signs of human beings. Where resort is had to siege methods the earth-works of both sides become still more complicated, though there is a definite system underlying their apparent confusion.

The Enemy at Close Quarters

Here is how the enemy is carrying on the close attack at some points. From the last position attained they sap forward in the two ways already mentioned. The approaches are excavated by pioneers working at the head. The German pioneers are technically trained troops which correspond to the British sappers. Owing to the close range at which the fighting is conducted, and the fact that rifles fixed in rests and machine guns are kept permanently directed upon the crest of the trenches, observation is somewhat difficult, but the head or end of the approaching sap can be detected from the mound of earth which is thrown up. This cannot be done, however, where the advance is being conducted by a blinded sap. In executing this type of sap a horizontal hole about a foot in diameter, and some three or four feet below the ground, is bored by means of a special earth-borer worked by hand. It is then enlarged by pick and shovel into a small tunnel, whose roof is one or two feet below the surface.

How the attack is carried out

Several of these saps having been driven forward, their heads are connected by a lateral trench, which becomes the front line, and can be used for stormers to collect for an assault. In some cases, usually at night, a sap is driven right up to the parapet of a hostile trench, which is then blown in by a charge. Amidst the confusion caused and a shower of grenades, the stormers attempt to burst in through the opening, and work along the trench. They also assault it in front. As in their ordinary infantry attacks, machine guns are quickly brought up to any point gained in order to repel a counter-attack. Most of this fighting takes place at such close range that the guns of either side cannot fire at the enemy's infantry without great risk of hitting its own men.

Us, however, is well replaced by bombs of all description, which are used in prodigious quantities. The larger ones, projected by the 'Minenwerfer, ' of which the Germans employ three sizes, correspond to the heavy howitzer shell of distant combat, and have much the same effect. They have a distinctive nickname of their own, but they may be termed the 'Jack Johnsons' of the close attack of siege warfare. The smaller bombs or grenades are thrown by hand from a few yards distance, just lobbed over a parapet. They are charged with a high explosive, and detonate with great violence, and since their impetus does not cause them to bury themselves in the earth, before they detonate, their action, though level, is very important in the enclosed space between two traverses in a trench. These grenades of various types are being thrown continuously by both sides, every assault precluded(sic) and accompanied by showers of them.

Blind Fighting

In fact, the wholesale use of these murderous missiles is one of the most prominent features of the close attack now being carried on. ; As may be imagined, what with sharp-shooting, machine-guns, and bombs, this kind of fighting is very deadly and somewhat blind owing to the difficulty of observation. The latter, however, is somewhat decreased by the use of the hyperscope, which is much the same in principle as the periscope of the submarine, and allows a man to look over the top of a parapet without raising his head above it.

(TS, 12-1914)

Are Brave Soldiers Mad?
Truth about the truth

It has always seemed remarkable to me that the world should be so eager to applaud bravery and yet at the same time so ready to condemn a man for not doing that which would make him a hero. It would seem that either a man must run the risk of sacrificing himself or be dubbed a coward. But, rightly considered, courage is merely a splendid kind of hypocrisy, after all, For there can be no real courage where there is no fear. There may be a sort of mad recklessness due to ignorance or lack of imagination; there may be the fury that disregards pain and danger in a frenzy of hate and rage; or there may be the hopeless, desperate valour of the rat penned into a corner by a terrier. These, however, are not manifestations of true courage. True courage, the courage that is purely human and has nothing in common with the fighting instincts of the lower male animal of the material daring and self-devotion of the female defending her young, is a quality very much finer and more subtle, in which heart and brain, as well as the body, should have their part. Thus it is sometimes nobler to decline a certain risk than to accept it, especially if the choice has to be made in the presence of witnesses.

Heroism or Would-be Suicide?

An indifferent swimmer, for example, with wife and children depending upon him, has no sort of right to plunge into a boiling torrent to save a would-be suicide is really the braver man of the two. To my mind, the best kind of courage is not born of a wild impulse to rush into danger, regardless of consequences, and thus make an end of the nervous ordeal as quickly as possible, rather than wait, in a twittering agony of suspense, for an opportunity to render some real service. I believe, as a rule, that it is not until soldiers or sailors feel that they have been betrayed into unnecessary peril by some misadventure, or by some miscalculation of their officers, that they ever do throw aside their habitual caution, and maybe lose their heads a little, even become panic-stricken. But that is the valour of the cornered rat. It is death, anyway. So they make a last desperate fight of it and – it has happened! Maybe snatch a victory, after all, out of the very jaws of defeat.

Hypocrisies that are Second Nature

But true courage is not of this delirious pattern and frothy substance. It is a thing of the reason, of the will, of the heart also. It is so far removed from the raw savagery of the primitive man as the human intelligence is above animal instinct. For as civilisation tends more and more to soften our fibres and refine out sensibilities, so the soul of man tends more and more to encase itself in a shining armour of hypocrisies –splendid hypocrisies, many of them – even as the body clothes and disguises itself in strange or beautiful garments. And – we are all hypocrites now, thank Heaven! We could not tolerate one another otherwise. To pretend to be interested in something that does not interest us in the least, so as to avoid hurting someone's susceptibilities; to feign an emotion that we do not feel, so as not to appear unkind; such hypocrisies have become a sort of second nature to us. And they have a tremendous value. Some years ago I helped to edit a paper which rather exploited heroism and during that time I interviewed many brave men. They none of them knew – though some pretended they did – why they had done the noble things they had done. But they all agreed, without exception, that the fear came before and afterwards, never at the time they were actually fighting. Which clinched an old conviction of mine that the only courage, really worthy of the name, is that which comes after, or exists side by side, with fear; the courage which is just a kind of splendid hypocrisy.   TS, 12-1914

Birr Sergeant-Major's Adventures

After being in most of the fighting since the Battle of Mons without receiving a scratch Sergeant Major William Brerton, of the South Irish Horse, returned to Clonoghill, Birr, for a few days leave. The hottest corner he was in, he told the *King's County Chronicle* reporter, was at Landrecies. Along with Sergeant Major Jackson, a Roscrea man, he was firing through a window when a shell entered between them and burst in the room without hitting either. He has some fragments of the missile as a memento of his narrow escape. When they got the order to retire from the village the British left close to 900 Germans in the streets. The retreat then went through the Guise and Chateau Thierry to Meaux.

This was the 'turning of the tide', and the Britishers pressed forward to Soissons and St Omer and were ultimately located at Ypres. When they reached here Ypres was a splendid town with many historic buildings, but the high explosive shells of the Germans soon left practically nothing bur a mass of smouldering ruins. The weather then became very bad, and four inches of snow fell. The cold was intense, and numbers of men had to be carried out of the trenches in the morning suffering from frost bite. The Sergeant Major who was eager to be back in the thick of it again, said that so far they had not met with the Leinster Regiment. He brought home several trophies with him of German uniforms, swords, helmets, etc.

KCC, 12-1914

William Brerton survived the war.

Bullet Shot Into Enemy's Rifle

A German volunteer gives to a Cologne newspaper a remarkable account of a peculiar shot. He says:

'At a distance of about 70 metres (about 76 yards) the outlines of a cap offered a remarkably good aim. I pointed my rifle, and was just pulling the trigger when suddenly a shot came from the other side. I staggered back, and when I recovered I found my rifle damaged at the lock and the chamber. I had a very ugly wound at the forehead and in the eye from pieces of my own rifle. I examined my rifle, and found in the barrel a French and a German bullet, both flattened. No doubt the French bullet had entered my rifle at the muzzle, followed the course of the barrel, caused the explosion of my cartridge, and so wounded me through my own rifle.'   CS, 12-1914

Can Aircraft be Made Invisible?

An American gentleman has recently been experimenting with kites, and various other things to find a colour which will render aircraft indistinct while in the air. He discovered that if an aeroplane were painted a dark sky-blue colour, it would be practically invisible, even if it were flying at a low altitude. When flying rapidly it would be very indistinct, and even against a background of white or grey clouds it would be almost invisible. A aeroplane that was entirely covered with this blue paint would, if the engine were muffled, be capable of flying over an enemy's country and making any observations necessary without being detected.

TS, 12-1914

Can an Entrenching Tool be Used as a Shield for Riflemen?

An instrument that can be used either as an entrenching tool or as a protection from rifle bullets is carried by the Canadian soldiers. This instrument which weighs about 4lb looks like an ordinary entrenching spade, only it has a hole in the blade. It can be easily carried on the back. When fighting commences, the handle of the spade is removed and the shaft stuck into the ground, the barrel of the rifle being thrust through the hole. Enough space is left to enable the rifle to be sighted, and the 'armour' is so strong that at 300 yards range a modern rifle bullet merely glances off it.

TS, 12-1914

These entrenching tools, or MacAdam shovels as they were more commonly known, were made at a cost of $1. 35 each. There were useless for their purpose and the entire supply, 50 tons of them, was sold as scrap in 1917 for $1,400).

Captain Gibson and Mr Cyril Triscott, Solicitor, Alive and Well

Letter from Captain W. Gibson

Rev. R. C. Patten, Rector of Fethard, publishes the following letter received by him from Captain W. Gibson (of Brittas Cashel), former Hon. Sec. To the Clonmel Horse Show, who is at the front:

'2nd Durham Light Infantry, British Expeditionary Force, 28-11-14, --My dear Patten – What is all your news and how are you these strenuous times? At last I am going to have a bath. I found on coming out of trenches that my hair was golden, but it washed off and is now snow-white again! We have just finished a tour of 14 days in the trenches within (in places) 25 yards of the Germans, so no changing of clothes, and we lived underground and slept in all our clothes, wet or otherwise! I had to get a tin-opener to remove some of them, they were so crusted with yellow clay! We are now out for three days and living in a huge farmhouse, and I have a bed to sleep in and feel like a lord! We have been having quite a peaceful time lately, only snipers and an odd coal-box thrown at us. Things go on very well. The last Fethard Battery are about a mile off me, and I go and dine with them tonight. I met (first man I knew out here) Dr Wetterell in great form, and the same evening I stumbled on Cyril Triscott, who did very well out here, and has been given a commission in the Sherwood Foresters. H--- --- and J--- B--- are near here; they all live on the fat of the land in farmhouses, while we, wretched, half-drowned people live the life of mad rabbits in the trenches! Love to you all. Yours very sincerely – W. Gibson. '

TS, 12-1914

Cyril Triscott, Dr Wetterell and Captain Gibson survived the war.

Carlow Red Cross Aid Society
Letter from the front

At the recent meeting of the Carlow Branch of the red Cross Society, presided over by Mrs Bruen, the following letter was read from a private serving in the British Expeditionary Force:

'I received a parcel through you, from the ladies of Carlow, and would be very grateful if you would convey to them hearty thanks from me. I was delighted with the articles sent, and they are all of the most useful type that are needed in this rather rough climate. The weather is by far the worst enemy we have to contend with, and when one is provided with useful articles, we can afford to grin at whatever turns up. I suppose that you are fairly well aware of the business that out especial unit is engaged upon. We are a species of RAMC, but doctor wounded and sick horses, instead of men. It is the first time that the corps have had the opportunity of proving its worth on active service, and I can safely assure you that we are a success, and have come to stay. This one section alone, has dealt with thousands of horses; in fact, in one period of six weeks, 16,000 horses passed through our operation lines alone. The percentage of horses destroyed and died, was almost of a negligible quantity, and although I have spent a life amongst horses, some of our cures have bordered on the miraculous. The saving in horseflesh to the Government, has consequently been very great, and the saving of unnecessary suffering on the humane side has been still greater. We are all doing our best, and I suppose that as one wheel in a machine depends upon another, so does our Expeditionary Force act in a same manner; therefore, although I can give you no blood-thirsty yarns of what we have done, and what we have not done, I hope that you will pardon me, for we can each do only our own allotted little bit.

'Once more thanking you for the trouble you have taken, and the ladies of Carlow for their splendid generosity.

I remain, yours, obedient, P. May.'   CS, 12-1914

Died in Hospital
How the Fallen heroes are laid to Rest

December 20

For have they not died for country and kin? This morning they were laid to rest, brave fellows, in God's acre on the summit of the hill rising near the cathedral – a white-sepulchred pinnacle in the centre of an amphitheatre of rolling hills, with a segment of sea stretching away beyond.

The sun shining bright – the first time for many days – in a radiantly blue sky, lighted on a melancholy scene. No gun-carriage here, with Union Jack o'erlaid, and the measured tread of martial mourners following the bier to the graveside. Just two coffins side by side in a deep trench awaiting the burial place, a small bunch of white flowers resting on one side. One is a private of the Dublin Fusiliers, the other corporal of the 2nd Essex. A Catholic chaplain comes, his robes revealing as he walks the khaki beneath. Follows a firing party, who form up on each side of the trench, rifles reversed, heads down.

Quietly sobbing, there is the corporal's young widow, with her a motherly woman who has lost a soldier son. Behind stand reverently the grave-diggers, two or three French people, and the writer. Sonorously in the clear air rings out the priest's appeal to the Almighty. He finishes, and the soldiers present arms. At once his place is taken by a Church of England priest, not the Chief Chaplain, Dr Gwynn, Bishop of Kartum, for he has just left for the Front.

Never have the beautiful simple words of the burial service sounded more impressive, more poignantly in the writer's ears, 'The Lord gave and the Lord hath taken away'. Once more the poor widow was shaken with sobs, for these last rites were for her beloved husband.

A pause – and then the melancholy-sweet calenza of the 'Last Post' trumpeting the triumph of these fallen warriors gone to their Valhalla. The men in khaki again present arms, about turn, and depart. No salvo. It is out of place here. An orderly stifles the lugubrious howling of someone's little dog. The clergyman goes to comfort the weeping women. The clouds fell.

Day by day has this sad scene been enacted, sometimes 30 burials at a time. Over a thousand British soldiers brought back from the field to die in the base hospitals are interred here. One day, a tall obelisk will be erected giving the names of these victims. Twenty-seven officers leave their graves here, including a colonel of the 1st Middlesex. There are just small wooden crosses with numbers as an indication at present. Crude temporary crosses with names, have been put up in memory of two captains and a lieutenant. Here and there are a few wreaths of immortelles.

In the officers section lies a nurse of the Red Cross, named Ethel Fearney. She also was given the soldiers funeral described above.

Fifty yards away may be seen a small forest of little wooden crosses-only a small patch of ground – the Germans sepulchre. Thirty-three of them have died in the hospitals, including a captain and three lieutenants and they were given the same honours and rites as our own men.

In a day or two there will be a new grave in the British officers section – a young lieutenant who passed away yesterday before his mother could reach him. He died as a soldier would. Was it not Carlyle who asked, 'What better could a man than die in the service of his country. '

UNRN, 12-1914

With a bit of detective work it was possible to identify these two soldiers and the cemetery as they had died relatively early in the war, buried in a cemetery that had a section for officers and was also the resting place of a nurse named Ethel Fearnley who died in 1914 (the article lists her as Fearney) The Corporal was Herbert Jones of Barking in Essex who also died of wounds the day after Private Edward James Leahy, from Leggetsrath, Kilkenny.

Fight in The Trenches
Nenagh Guardsman's Thrilling Experiences

A Nenagh man serving at the front in the Irish Guards, writing home to his parents, says that only by lying down in a trench and feigning death after he had been wounded was he able to escape from the disaster which overtook his regiment. He relates a most remarkable adventure. During the night he had been unable to sleep owing to the cold and having no overcoat. At six o'clock in the morning they were served with rations.

'I opened a tin of bully beef, ' says he, 'and we said 'We'll have a bit of breakfast before they come, ' I knew the Germans were coming. We could hear their Maxims. I had just had a mouthful when I saw them approaching in our rear and on the right flank. Many of them were directly behind us, and we opened fire. I am certain that I knocked twelve down. As soon as I pulled the trigger I saw my man fall, they were so close – only a hundred yards away. But they came on, right up to our faces. The last I heard was our Lieutenant ordering us to fix bayonets. The Germans were then twenty yards off, when I was wounded above the left eye with a ricocheting bullet, which glanced off. I could see our Colonel, who was about one hundred yards away, in tears, and then I saw our two Lieutenants being made prisoners. After this my mate, Private Morgan, who had two South African ribbons on his breast, was shot through the head by a German officer. His brains were scattered over the trench. I said to myself, 'I'm the next one, ' so I lay down in the trench to take cover, and from there they kept firing. One of them picked a wounded German up, and put him across my body, resting his head on my back while he dressed his wounds. I was covered with blood. After that I lay in the trench for five hours.   TS, 12-1914

Tyrone man, Pte John Morgan above, was KIA on 23-10-1914 and has no known grave but he is listed on the Menin Gate Memorial on Panel 11.

Germany's Prisoners
Life in an Enemy's Compound

While the life of the British soldiers and sailors who have been captured by the Germans varies somewhat, according to the locality in which they happen to be interned, it may be stated as a general fact, judging from the reports, private and otherwise, which have reached us, that prisoners are being treated as well in Germany at the present time as we are treating German prisoners in this country. Stories have been told to the effect that the Germans have set British soldiers and sailors who have been captured to work in the fields for their board and lodging, paying them the miserable pittance of 10 pfennige ($1^1/2$d.) per hour, and that the German Press is now complaining that by so doing the authorities are depriving the Germans who are not fighting of the work they so badly need. From inquiries which have been made, however, it would appear that so far only a certain number of Russians and Belgians have been put to work in the fields, and that the British prisoners, particularly those at Doeberitz, where over 4, 000 have been interned, are having a fairly easy time.

'Doeberitz, it might be mentioned, is not far from Berlin, and is a favourite run for Berlin cyclists in summer. It is very healthily situated, and, indeed, is regarded as one of healthiest districts near Berlin, bearing a close resemblance to the regions of Caesar's Camp at Aldershot. Representatives who have visited Doeberitz give some interesting facts regarding the housing and treatment of the prisoners. Three thousand British soldiers sleep in large tents, the bulk of the men being supplied with a sleeping sack and two woollen blankets. There is splendid accommodation for washing, soap, being supplied free of charge, as also are boots. The prisoners are commanded by their non-commissioned officers, the German commander only interfering in cases of difference, but this till now has been unnecessary.

'With regard to the catering, that is described as fairly good and sufficient. The daily rations are half a loaf of bread, three pints of soup. In the morning coffee, at midday meat and two vegetables, and in the evening cocoa or tea, and the organisation is such that the distribution of food for 3,000 soldiers in what is known as the greater camp can be done in a few minutes. Other refreshments, except spirits and tobacco, can be obtained by the prisoners for payment. In a second camp are 1,000 men, chiefly members of the naval Brigade captured at Antwerp. The American Embassy is doing all it possibly can in the way of providing for the prisoners.'   TS, 12-1914

Ghosts in Khaki

In a letter from Pte G Trover, to his mother at Plumstead, he writes:

'There was one night when we were burying the dead that we got a proper hair raising fright. It was a fine moonlight night, and we could see ahead of us a great pile of German dead lying at a spot where our artillery fire had played havoc with them. As we got nearer we saw what we took to be two of the corpses rise from the ground and walk slowly towards us. It was enough to make any man's blood freeze. The two ghosts were in khaki, and they belonged to one of our infantry regiments. They had escaped from the German lines and had hidden among the dead until they saw a chance of getting away.   CS, 12-1914

There is no casualty named 'Trover' in the War Dead Databases, nor does there exist any medal Index Card for any soldier named Trover.

How Does the Soldier-Cyclist Carry his Bicycle?

France, which, next to England, has the best supply of military cyclists in the world, supplies her cycling soldiers with bicycles that are specially suited to the kind of work for which they are required. These machines are so constructed that they can be taken to pieces in an incredibly short time – two or three minutes, as a matter of fact – and put together again almost as quickly. When a French soldier-cyclist comes to a piece od ground over which he is unable to ride, he dismantles his machine and, with the aid of straps, fixes it to his back. Thus men with machines of this types can go almost anywhere and one of the chief advantages of cycles in war is done away with.   TS, 12-1914

How the Royal Irish made their Last Stand

Corporal S. Hayden, Worcester Regiment, now at home wounded, tells the following story of the stand made by the Royal Irish Regiment. The engagement probably took place at Mons, though the Corporal in his account has neglected to give the name of the battle:

'There was one night when we were supporting the Royal Irish Regiment that we came on as fine a deed of heroism as I want to hear of this side of the Kingdom of Heaven.'

'It was the night the Royal Irish got cut up and were forced to abandon some trenches they had held for a day against fearful odds. In the retreat about ten of that fine regiment got separated from the rest and they were surrounded by thousands and thousands of the enemy. They were called on to surrender, but they wouldn't hear of it, and then they were forced into a position where they had to choose between surrender and a fight to the death. They chose the latter, and with their backs to the wall received the German attack.

'The bullets were so thick all around that a daddy-long-legs could not have scraped through without having some of his legs shot away, and the poor Irish lads had no hope of relief. Still they fought gamely. One by one they were picked off, and all were wounded but three. A German officer came over and asked if they would surrender. Not they. They had made up their minds that this was going to be a fight to the death and they were as good as their word. The fight was renewed and those chaps lay behind a rampart of their dead comrades, picking off Germans as coolly as though they were picking blackberries in the country in September.

'They couldn't keep it up for ever, and at last they were surrounded by hundreds of Germans at such close quarters that their rifles weren't much use. So they up with their bayonets and received the last charge. They went down after a time, and when we came we only found ten dead Irishmen surrounded by heaps of dead Germans.

'Every man of us bowed his head and uncovered it in silent attribute to the memory of fruitless valour as we stood around the spot where those Irishmen had fought to the bitter end.'   WN, 12-1914

In The Engine Room
Mainly about the men who make the Navy's wheels go round

There is a man in the Navy who is too often forgotten, even by the authorities, when they are 'dishing out' rewards and praise for successful operations at sea, and that man is the man who makes the wheels go round inside the ship. If the wheels stop, then the modern warship lies on the water like an armed tin can, waiting for someone to sail round it, plug it full of holes, and sink it. A fighting ship, to put up any sort of battle at all, must be able to get on with it at the rate of knots, as the sailors say when they mean a high speed, and the men who make that possible are the engineers and the stokers.

Below the Waterline

The stoker, far below the waterline, shovels coal, and he gathers there is a battle on, when there is, by the fact that he has to work twice as hard as he thought he could, and by the infernal racket made by the guns, and by the projectiles of the enemy which have found a new home aboard the ship. He has none of the glory and the fine thrill of battle – only an increase in his ordinary work. He works by lamplight to keep steam up, and he knows there has been a victory when someone tells him, unless he happens to be working in his 'spare' time at the ammunition hoists near the roaring guns. Even now n many ships, and once in all, the engineer-officers and their men are shut down in their working place, and they cannot get up, for it is necessary for them to be so closed up. It is not, of course, necessary to keep them there to make them do their work, but because the ships engines run under forced draught, and the only way to get that is to batten down the stokeholds. They become, in fact, part of the pipe, if one call it that, along which the air is pumped to the fires to make them burn more fiercely, just as one bucks up the kitchen range with the bellows. If the hatches leading to the upper decks were open the air would be pumped out through them, and would not pass through the white-hot furnaces. If she is torpedoed, and sinks suddenly, down go the engineers, and the stokers without the chance of swimming for it, as the others have when the order 'each man for himself' is given by the executive officer in charge of the vessel. In the case of the oil-driven warships there is not, it need hardly be said, that added risk for the engine room staff. There is no need to shut them down, and, in case of sinking, they have no further risk that that entailed by the time, and for them to get up on deck. They are, however, the people most likely to go to fragments when a torpedo comes knocking on the ship's side, or, rather, down among her foundations.

Amid the Steam Pipes

And there are steam-pipes, filled with scalding and sudden death, flooding the engine room in an instant with biting, blinding, searing fog, somewhere above boiling point, for high pressure steam is hotter stuff than comes out of the spout of a kettle. A shell through the main steam-pipes, and good-bye to those who are near the damage. The engineer-officer knows all this, and often has seen some of the things that can happen taking place on a small, but significant scale. While the gunners get the glory he watches the wheels go round, listens not to the scream of the shells or the hammer-strokes of projectiles on armour-plate, but to the tell-tale songs of the complex mechanisms over which he presides with the coolness of a naval officer, the skill of a man of science, ad the tenderness of a red Cross nurse. Every moment may be the last moment the life in his body has, but he must not think of that. Down there in the bowels of the fighting ship, he must keep his mind clear to think of a thousand details, and he must do it without any of the exhilaration that comes from watching the effect of the guns on the enemy's ships. He never sees a shot go home; he never sees an enemy's flag pulled down in defeat. He sees only his engines, and the men tending them. Just as the heart pumping keeps the body going, so the engines keep the ship fighting. The engineer in charge corresponds to that nerve in the human body which I=unceasingly stimulates the heart to action. That nerve doesn't seem to matter, until something goes wrong with it, until the body develops engine-trouble. Then there is nothing too arduous if it will only make that nerve do its duty again. If all goes well, and the enemy runs or strikes, the engineer-commander hears all about it at mess. If things go wrong, he feels it – quite unmistakably – in his person. Get one unlucky shot into the engine-room, and it is up to him, so long as volition is left to him, to put that thing right, and he must not draw fires until there is another thing he can do first. In battle, so long as there is a dog's chance to do so, he must keep steam up, for steam is the breath of life to the ship, and he must take risks, when he is making repairs, that would give the landsman spasms.

Making Practical Politics Possible

It is not only the motive power of the ship that is in his care, either. There are all sorts of vital engines that he is responsible for. There are dynamos for the electricity that is so essential in the modern man-o-war. There are the mechanical ammunition hoists. There is the power-driven steering gear.   TS, 12-1914

King's Christmas Greeting!

On Christmas morning each British and Indian soldier at the front, each sailor on our warships in commission and each of our wounded men in hospital received a Royal Christmas card. It was in an envelope addressed to him personally, and contained portraits of their Majestys' on one side and on the other,

> With our best wishes for Christmas 1914.
> May God protect you and bring you home safe.
> – Mary R., George R. I.

It took twelve men and fifty girls nine days to pack the cards, and the despatch of three-quarters of a million of them was completed on 23rd December.   KCC, 12-1914

Letter from a Royal Irish Corporal

The following interesting letter, written by Lance-corporal George White (6138) serving with the British Expeditionary Force at the front has been received by his parents at Knockanvar, Cappawhite. Lance-Corporal White is now recuperating in France after being five weeks in the trenches, and he has so far escaped uninjured. Out of 120 only himself and four others remained; 2nd Battalion, Royal Irish Regiment, British Expeditionary Force:

'Dearest Parent, Just a few lines hoping you are quite well; as for myself I was never in better form in my life. I cannot say much regarding the fighting only it is very like a slaughter house, and unless there is another German army the enemy cannot possibly hold out much longer. Of course, we have suffered a bit, but battles cannot be won without sustaining some losses. You need not imagine because you see a long list of killed and wounded on the papers that we are being defeated, far from it. If you could only come out here, you would then see what those poor fellows who have fallen, did before that yielded up their lives. They were heroes every one of them, and I am sure if you come across the enemy's list of casualties you would be amazed, although it would cause no surprise at all to us.

'It is a great pity that the Irish army serving out here is so small. Yet, although numerically small, in deeds of valour it is great. The men are of the best material and every man faces the music cheerfully and is prepared for whatever fate has in store for him. We all hope for the best, but so long as we tumble a few Germans before going to the other world we are quite satisfied. A short time ago Irish soldiers were called traitors to their country by some people, but now these very people are the first to cheer the Irishmen who join the army. If those who talk and shout so much would only come out here and do their part; if it was only to give others who have been bearing the brunt of the struggle an opportunity of resting it would be much better. Fireside talk and cheering will not win this titanic struggle.

'We are tired of this cheering business. It seems that the people at home think that Ireland is safe, but should Germany (which is not very likely) by any chance triumph, then the fate of Belgium will also be the fate of Ireland.

'With regard to letters sent to me I understand that they were forwarded to the War Office as I was reported to be killed. However they are all right and I shall get them later on. Don't imagine that we are down-hearted. We, Irishmen, are never down-hearted, and it would take a lot to make us so. – Your affectionate son. George.'   TS, 12-1914

George White survived the war.

Preparing Young Soldiers for Active Service

Generally speaking, it takes four to six months to form a raw recruit into a fairly efficient fighting unit. The system of training now devised by the military authorities for the various branches of the service is such that a man becomes fit and capable in the shortest possible time without the danger of being overworked. Training for infantry recruits is divided into two periods. What is termed 'recruit training' is completed in three months, after which 'collective training' of the company commences. This extends to five or six weeks, the company training under its own officers and non-commissioned officers.

Steady Work

During the 'recruit training' eight hours a day are devoted to steady work – squad drill, with and without arms, occupying four of the eight hours. The other four are devoted to musketry, lectures, physical drill, and instruction in what is known as fitting marching order. After the first week, however, the training varies somewhat. In the second week, for instance, the total of forty eight hours is made up of six hours physical training, ten hours squad drill without arms, twelve hours musketry, eighteen hours squad drill with arms, and two hours fitting marching order. In the third week there is another variation, twelve hours extended order drill and three hours night work being fitted into the schedule. Route marching begins in the fourth week, while outpost duties are added to the training in the fifth and sixth weeks and entrenching in the seventh and eighth weeks. Platoon drill and bayonet fighting does not begin until the ninth and tenth weeks.

Artillery Training

In this way recruits steadily and gradually acquire knowledge of their fighting duties, and then they enter upon the collective training of the company, to which reference has already been made, although it should be mentioned that specialists, such as machine gunners and signallers, do not perform company training, battalion and brigade training is carried on, the division being finally brought together. The training of artillery engineers and mounted men, of course, varies. For gunners and drivers of artillery the schedule for the day is as follows; Two to two and three-quarter hours dismounted drill without arms, and one hour in the stables. In addition, gunners have to do two and a half hours every day standing gun drill, including technical lectures, and one to two and a half hours laying, fuse setting, and visual training, while drivers do one to one and a half hours riding, and one hour fitting and cleaning harness, and one hour stable management ad horse mastership, including lectures every day. As in the case of infantry, the work of artillery recruits varies as the weeks go by and they become gradually efficient. For instance, after the finish of recruit training they begin collective training and from the seventh to the twenty-sixth week officers are busy training their own sections and specialists, such as signallers, range-takers, sergeant-major, director man, and layers. The art of taking up positions, laying out lines pf fire, mounted parades drill and manoeuvres, and practice on miniature ranges ultimately follows.

Engineers and Mounted Men

Engineers have a vast amount of detail to learn, and during the first three months are expected to acquire a knowledge, which varies according to their rank and position in the regiment, of the care of arms and parts of a rifle, regimental musketry drill, visual training and ranging, bayonet fighting, sanitation, duties of sentries and patrol, physical training ad swimming. Field geometry and the use of field level knotting, lashing and splicing, hasty field defences and concealment of works, encampments, demolitions, making up charges, fixing and wiring, are among the other subjects of military training which the engineer is supposed to be conversant with. The training of mounted men extends from the care of arms and elementary musketry, stable management, and the care of horses during the first few weeks, to various degrees of riding and driving drill. During the remainder of the training subsequent to the first three months, they take part whenever possible in the training and exercises of the field company, undergoing combined training with infantry and artillery. The field companies generally march to a selected training ground by a river – the Thames, Medway, Christchurch, or Lusk, in Ireland – where the pontoons (training equipment) can be concentrated and mounted men can practice swimming horses, if the weather permits. Mention might also be made of the divisional signal companies, who, during the first three months, learn drill, musketry and riding, semaphore signalling, despatch-riding and the care and riding of a motor-cycle, while during the fourth and fifth months, they study telephone cable drill, practical schemes with infantry and artillery brigade and divisional artillery training.   TS, 12-1914

Tragedy and Comedy in the Trenches

There is small cause for wonder that Continental people have been in the habit of referring to us as 'the mad British'. An amazing characteristic of our troops is the real enjoyment they get out of the most sever hardships and perilous situations. This is constantly exampled in the letters written in the trenches. 'It is all very interesting and great fun, ' wrote an officer in describing how 'we get shelled daily with shrapnel, and for about two hours by high explosives'.

'We are having jolly good fun' is the expression used by a subaltern in the course of a description of the defeat of a German attack. The 'jolly good fun' consisted in holding a building under a fierce fire.

This officer describes how he 'made a hole in the roof and got a perfect view. Then there was a loud whiz, a resounding crash followed by a patter of shot and slates; we found half the roof had gone; and two shells had burst on our jolly little loft.

'A private considers it is joke to see our fellows dodging the 'coal boxes'. He says: 'They give you about six seconds warning, and when we hear them coming you should see the heads diving down. A 'coal box' burst on the side of a road just as a fellow was passing on horseback, and a piece of it took three-parts of the saddle away without touching horse or rider; the fellow was so excited, calling it a miracle. Another fellow I saw had his jacket ripped in six pieces from a maxim, and he was not even scratched; he had three across his chest, one in each sleeve and one across the back. '

The coolness of the officer is proverbial. After falling from the air in his aeroplane, severely wounded, one of our daring aviators calmly informed his German captors that their shooting was 'devilish good'. A Sergeant in the Engineers declares: ' We have one of the finest officers alive leading our Brigade, as cool as a cucumber all the time. He then gives the following description: 'I have watched him calmly smoking while shells have been dropping all over the place. I think that if the German Army were firing at him he would carry on as usual, smoking and giving his orders as if he were in his club ordering a drink. Yes; he is a very brave man is General Sir Philip Chetwode.'

As war is unable to shake the coolness of our troops, or destroy their sense of humour, so it fails to harden their warm hearts. One man recently described how he went out of his way to minister to an injured kitten. It is a driver in the Field Artillery who writes: 'It was pitch dark, while several drivers were waiting near a lonely French farm, and suddenly a shell from one of the German howitzers dropped right on the farm. We though some of our chaps might be sheltering there, so we ran into the wrecked house. The father lay on the hearth, with his wife's head resting on his chest, a little boy of four was under the remains of the table and a little girl across a broken chair. They had all been killed, except the little girl of about seven years. Both her legs had been blown away near the knees, and one of her arms was missing from below the elbow. The rain was coming down into the wreckage and I took off my great coat and wrapped the poor, moaning child in it. I sat down on the floor to hold her on my knee and she just opened her eyes and gave me a grateful look. Then she moved her sound arm and lifted something to my head. Her arm dropped. She was dead. She had given me her rosary. I thought I had a heart of stone, but I cried like a child that night.'

KCC, 12-1914

General Chetwode survived the war.

Tricky Shot and Shell
Some amazing performances played by cannon and rifle

Two Australian officers once fought a duel for a ludicrous reason. During a battle they were together on an observation post, when a bullet took off the nose of one of them. The sight of the noseless man so upset his comrade that he burst out laughing. When the injured man recovered he remembered that laugh, and challenged the other to a duel; which was fought, happily without serious results. But, indeed, bullets do play strange tricks. It was not so long ago since an English labourer was shot dead by a ball that came seemingly from nowhere. But next day the son of a local landowner informed the police that he had emptied his rifle into a tree a mile away from the scene of the accident just at the time it occurred. It was proved beyond all doubt that the bullet went into the tree, but it went out of the tree as well, and travelled at a speed which enabled it at the end of a mile to kill a man.

Cannon balls have been known to act strange tricks. A French staff officer said the other day that if all the German shells had exploded there would have been no allies left by now. But the strangest this a shell ever did was at the bombardment of Alexandria, when a projectile from a British naval gun went right into the muzzle of one of Arabi Pashs's double-tier batteries, split the lower gun in two, killing all the crew, and then turned through the floor of the other tier and split the breech of the gun here, again killing all the crew.

Two officers, famous shots both of them, were practising once at the butts, and both of them registered bull after bull. At last they fired one shot together at the same mark, and neither of the appeared to register anything. This was so strange that they made a careful search of the range, and at last found their two bullets on the ground; fused together. They had crossed and struck each other in their flight, a thing that could not be expected to happen once in a million times.   TS, 12-1914

Vultures in War
Carrion birds that hover above the terrible banquet of the dead

The war has a curious effect of bird life. In the vicinity of battlefields, smaller birds are driven away both by the incessant shell firing and by the destruction of their habitats in the trees. On the other hand, birds feeding on carrion, like crows, are attracted to the zone of battle by the terrible banquet in the shape of dead horses and cattle who have fallen to the guns.

It is quite possible that vultures may be found swooping down on the Russian battlefields, for although they have fled before the advance of civilisation they are in great numbers in many parts of Asia, and their unique gifts for sensing prey will probably send them, on the tracks of the vast numbers of carcases that have been left unburied.

In the South African war a strange manifestation of the remarkable sensing powers of the vulture was forthcoming. Before the war, so Mr. W. L. Sclater, who was the director of the South African Museum at the time and is now justly regarded as one of the greatest living authorities on bird life, told the writer there were practically no vultures left in parts of South

Africa. The Boer farmers had got rid of them all by poison as they were such a nuisance to their cattle. But hundreds of miles away in Central Africa, undisturbed by man's wiles, the vulture dwelt in peace in great flocks. By some means or other the fact that there was carrion waiting for them on the South African veldt became known to them, and South Africa, which had congratulated itself on being free of the vulture, again became plagued with this detestable bird. It is a debatable point amongst scientists whether the vulture works through its sense of smell or sight. Many scientists are inclined to believe that it sees its prey, and with this view Mr Sclater is disposed to believe. He explained to the writer that vultures organise their forces very much like an army does. Their patrols go forward to spy out the land, and when they discover carrion the others quickly follow.

The possibility of hostilities with Turkey on the Egyptian frontier fore-shadows an invasion by vultures either on the part of the Egyptian vulture, otherwise known as Pharaoh's hen, or the commoner vulture which inhabits the northern shores and many parts of India and Africa. The mere fact that the vulture is practically extinct in a country like Belgium is no guarantee that the lure of the battlefield will not bring it from its nearest haunts. The vulture has a habit of turning up when lest expected. It has been captured in England and in Norway, and as there appears to be no limit to the distance it can travel, he would be a rash prophet who would dare to predict that the experience of South Africa during the late war will not be repeated. TS, 12-1914

See 'In The Trenches' and 'The War and Wild Game'

What is a 'Chakkar'?

Around the 'point' of their turbans the Sikh warriors carry a steel weapon which looks very much like an ordinary quoit, but is called a 'chakkar. ' This quoit has an edge like a razor, and the Sikhs throw it by twirling it round the finger, and then suddenly releasing it. The weapon flies through the air revolving horizontally, and inflicts a horrible wound on anyone it strikes. At a distance of twelve yards, one of these 'chakkars, ' in the hands of an expert, has been known to cut a two-inch bamboo completely in two. Obviously, the safest place in which this weapon could possibly be carried is on the top of the turban, where it is out of the way. TS, 12-1914

What is a Court Martial?
All about Military and Naval Trials

The execution by shooting at the Tower of London by Carl Hans Lody. The German spy, who was convicted by court-martial of war treason against Great Britain, has naturally led to the question 'What really is a courts-martial?' Briefly, it is a court for the trial of people who commit offences against the military or naval law – temporary or otherwise – of the country. In times of peace, civilians cannot be tried by martial law, but when the country is at war, naval or military authorities may take what steps they like for the safety of the realm, and make fresh laws or substitute others for existing laws. Altogether there are five different kinds of courts-martial- general, district, regimental, field-general, and summary. The last three chiefly concern the men in the Service, who are subject always and everywhere, in time of peace as in war, to martial law. General and district courts-martial may be said, at a time like the present, to deal with the cases of civilians who commit offences against the Emergency Laws, and it was really by a general courts-martial that Lody was sentenced to be shot.

A general courts-martial must, in the United Kingdom, consist of nine officers, including the president, who must all have held a commission for three years. A district court-martial may comprise three to five officers of one year's service, and a field-general court of three officers of any rank, and a summary court of the same number, if available. Otherwise two is sufficient. But in that case it cannot pass sentence of death and with three members all must concur in such a sentence.

Naval courts-martial consist of admirals, captains, and commanders to try captains, and commanders to try offences against the Naval Discipline Act. The chief admiral of the fleet or squadron appoints the members, but all captains on the station have a right to sit if not implicated and the courts-martial is open to all the crew and others as spectators.

TS, 12-1914

Stories from the Trenches
Connaughts at Ypres

Private Patrick Sweeney, of the 3rd Battalion, Connaught Rangers, who has been invalided home to Ballyhaunis, says:

'The Mons battle has somehow been pronounced as the greatest of all, but it was nothing to the battle of Ypres. For four days he was squatting in a trench. There was something like 300 strong of the Connaughts, and on their left they and the Irish Guards. On the fourth day the enemy opened on the British trenches with a vengeance. The men beside Sweeney were mown down like rushes, but those of them who remained fought doggedly on. The Sweeney felt something pierce his left breast which seemed to sting him throughout the body, but he "stuck to his gun" until from complete exhaustion he had to let it drop and call the next man to is assistance.

On examination of Sweeney his comrades said: 'There's nothing on your body. Come on and let us get near enough to give those fellows across the way a taste of the steel.' Sweeney then motioned to his friend to open his clothes, and on doing so a clean bullet hole was revealed in Sweeney's breast. The bullet passed one-eight of an inch alongside the left lung, and right through the back. Sweeney was subsequently placed in a semi unconscious condition on a stretcher and borne out of firing range.

A Dear and Deserved Penalty

One day, he adds, he saw a wounded German come out into the open to a water pump in order to wet his parched throat. On occasion view of the English soldiers he put up his right hand, meaning that he would give himself up as a prisoner of war if allowed to do so. There was no response from the English side, and the German soldier proceeded to the pump to get the drink, but when he had raised the bottle to his mouth and had drank for some time a bullet from the rifle of a private next Sweeney in the trenches ended the fellow's life by passing right through his brain. The English officer in command had his subordinate suffer a dear yet deserved penalty.

WI, 12-1914

Private Patrick Sweeney survived the war.

Artillery Duels

Private Thomas Hoare, Connaught Rangers is at present at home with hios parents in Roscommon, having been wounded at Ypres with shrapnel while repulsing a desperate attack by the enemy. Private Hoare has two brothers in the same regiment. Sergeant B Hoare, and Lance Corporal Hoare. In the trenches with him at Ypres were a number of other Roscommon men. In the engagement in which he was wounded Private Hoare describes the fighting as one continuous artillery duel. The noise of the German guns was terrific and unceasing, and escape from shell fire was providential. From the trenches they could see the roads and fields being turned up and scattered in clouds of dust after the shrieking of a German shell. The Germans appeared to fight shy of the bayonet, and in several bayonet charges in which Private Hoare took part they had no difficulty in routing the enemy.

In a letter received from Lord Cavan, Commanding 4th (Guards) Brigade, he says that the safety of the right flank of the British section depended entirely on the staunchness of the Guards, after the disastrous day, November 1st. Those of them that were left made history and he could never thank them enough for the way in which they recovered themselves, and showed the enemy that Irish Guards must be reckoned with however hard hit.

WI, 12-1914)

An Eye Witness of Shocking Scenes

Private Patrick Fury, who has returned home to Loughrea, fought at Mons, Soissons, La Bassee, Armentieres, and at Ypres, where he was wounded. Describing a bayonet charge which took place in the trenches one night, Private Fury tells how in the darkness they could nor distinguish their own men and had to use the bayonet on everyone they came in contact with. He pays a glowing tribute to the bravery displayed by the Irish soldiers. At Armentieres he witnessed the Sacred Heart being taken away from a burning church and hidden away. Some men of his regiment rescued statues from the sacred edifice that had been set on fire by the enemy. He saw the aged being wheeled away from their homes in wheelbarrows, the soldiers bearing the children in their arms sooner than leave them behind to fall into the hands of the Germans. He was an eye witness to a woman who stood in a doorway with a baby in her arms being blown to pieces by a shell from the enemy's gun. Captain Carberry and six men of the Royal Irish Fusiliers were riddled with shot while endeavouring to vacate a house occupied by a number of German soldiers. A comrade of Fury's named Peter Kelly, of Bray, County Wicklow, was killed beside him at the battle of Ypres.

Private Fury has three brothers at the front, and one a prisoner of war in Berlin. He has almost one hundred other relations engaged in the present war.   WI, 12-191

37 year old Eastbourne man Captain Miles Bertie Cunninghame Carbery, is buried in Houplines Communal Cemetery Extension in France. 'Peter Kelly' is listed in all databases as Private Patrick Kelly who was killed in action 09/11/1914, and buried in Strand Military Cemetery in Belgium.

From the Front

Private Luke Gilligan, 2nd Battalion Connaught Rangers, who is at present at home in Ballaghadereen suffering from wounds in the legs, in an interview with our representative, stated that when he went into the firing line the Germans were advancing as thick as grass and even though they were shot down in hundreds, they still came on in their usual close formation all of them firing from the hip. He spent three weeks in the trenches, and during that time the bullets and shells were falling round him like hailstones. It was the shells that did most of the damage. He had to march 20 miles one night and remained in the trench for 10 hours of the day. At the battle of Ypres he got four bullet wounds in the legs and a piece of shrapnel in the back. He was forced to lie on the field for three days before the ambulance could get to him, and while he was being carried away the Germans commenced shelling them, and the Red Cross men had to retire leaving him on the field. While lying there, the Coal Boxes and Jack Johnsons were falling around him and he thought every minute would be his last.

Questioned as to the atrocities of the Germans, Private Gilligan said he saw several little boys with their fingers chopped off by the German soldiers, and in many places women were found bayoneted and in a .... condition. The worst thing which aroused the anger of the Connaughts was to see nuns driven before the German... naked when making an attack on the English trenches.

The Germans he said, shell the Red Cross when attending to the wounded. Private Gilligan said he had many narrow escapes in the retreat from Mons, but the nearest approach to death was when he was lying wounded on the field and was approached by a German disguised as a woman. The German gave Gilligan a slight prod of the bayonet and then the wounded Ranger turned over slightly and blew his head off with his rifle. Although a good deal knocked up, Private Gilligan says he hopes to be soon well, and will willingly go back to the firing line again.

WI, 12-1914

Private Luke Gilligan later transferred to the Liverpool Regiment and survived the war

Late Lieutenant Colonel Morris
A Brave and Brilliant Leader
How he met his Fate

It was with the deepest regret that the friends of Lieutenant Colonel the Honourable George Morris, of the Irish Guards, heard last week that there was no longer any doubt that he was killed in action neat Villiers Cotterets, on the 1st September. It had been hoped and hoped that since he had only been reported officially 'wounded and missing', he might yet be alive in some German hospital, and have been spared to render further services to his country in the profession in which he had already earned such marked distinction.

The engagement in which Colonel Morris, Major Hubert Crichton, and Captain Tudall of the Irish Guards lost their lives; and the Adjutant, Lord Desmond Fitzgerald, and Lord Castle, Lieutenants Blacker-Douglas, Ashray Herbert and Lord Robert Innes Kerr, of the same regiment, were wounded and in which officers of the Grenadiers and Coldstreams were also killed and wounded, was one of the most severe that has taken place in the war.

Stayed Behind with his Men
The action was a rear-guard action during the now famous retreat of the allied force from Mons to the Marne and occurred on the great forest of Villieres Cottrets, about forty miles north of Paris. It would appear that towards the end of the engagement Colonel Morris stayed behind with the

very last section of his men, which had suffered severely; officers in order to encourage and help them as they fought their way back through the dense forest, heavily pressed by great numbers of the enemy, and in a final charge, led by him, of some of his own Irish Guards and also of Grenadiers and Coldstreams, Colonel Morris was fatally shot and so he died a valiant and chivalrous soldier's death, in the thick of desperate fighting, facing fearful odds, standing by an leading his men to the last; but those who knew him know that this is a death he would not have faltered to choose.

> *I would hate that death bandaged my eyes forebore,*
> *And bade me creep past.*
> *No! let me taste the whole of it, for like my peers—*
> *The heroes of old.*
> *For sudden the worst turns the best to the brave.*
> *The black minutes at end.*
> *And the elements rage, the fiend voices that rave.*
> *Shall dwindle, shall blend,*
> *Shall change, shall overcome, first, a peace out of pain.*
> *Then a light, then they breast,*
> *O Thou soul of my soul! I shall clasp thee again.*
> *And with God be the rest!*

That evening the regiment and brigade were filled with special sorrow when they learnt that Colonel Morris was 'missing,' for they felt that they had lost a most able commanding officer, full of energy and spirit, of strong will and undaunted bravery, and devoted to his profession. Testimony is borne on all sides to the capacity which he had shown during the terrible trying experiences of the retreat from the North of France.

WI, 12-1914

Lieutenant Colonel the Hon. George Henry Morris, 42 year old Galway man, was killed in action in September, 1914, and buried in Guards Grave, Villers Cotterets Forest in France. Major Hubert Francis Crichton 39 year old Westminster man was killed in action in September, 1914, and buried in Montreuil-Aux-Lions British Cemetery in France. There is no record of a Captain Tudall dying in the Frist World War. Perhaps it is Major Tisdall who died with the Irish Guards on the same day and the men above, and buried in Guards Grave, Villers Cotterets Forest in France. Lord Desmond Fitzgerald died as the result of an accident at a base in France in 1916. Lieutenant R St John Blacker-Douglass, 22 year old Dublin man, won the Military Cross and was killed in action in May 1915 and is buried in Cuinchy Communal Cemetery in France.)

Back from the Front
Experiences of Waterfordmen

Private Thomas Clemens, of the 2nd Battalion Royal Irish Regiment, arrived here in Waterford this week after nearly three months at the front. He left 6 August with a batch of 150 to join his regiment and landed at St Nazaire. They were joined on leaving the latter place by men of the Devons, Lincolns, Middlesex, and the Gordons.

The marched, generally, about twenty-five miles a day and had several minor touches with the enemy at Blaine and Vailly. At Blaine Quartermaster Sergeant Thomas Croke, a Ballybricken man was wounded, and, Clemens thinks, was afterwards taken prisoner. Jeremiah Aspel, another Waterford man, was also wounded there and is now in a convalescent home outside Glasgow. From Blaine they marched to Nantes where the Royal Irish did good work, losing very heavily. The principal engagement Clemens took part in was at Bethune and there he received a wound in the arm. He lay wounded from four o'clock in the evening until two o'clock next morning when he managed to reach a field hospital. Clemens is an old soldier with over twenty years service. He fought in the South African Campaign with the 5th Hussars.

Curios from the Battlefield

Amongst a collection of curios which Clemens took home from the front are the epaulet of a Death's Head Hussar, and a good service medal and ribbon of the French Army. He had in his possession also a French journal in which the following description of the battle of Mons appeared: 'The Royal Irish Regiment had an awful smashing earlier on, and also had the Middlesex, and our company were ordered to go along the road as re-inforcements. The one and a half miles seemed a thousand. When we got to the Royal Irish Regiment's trenches the scene was terrible. They were having dinner when the Germans opened up on them and their dead and wounded were laying all around. We kept up this sort of game (fighting by day and retiring by night) until we go to Cambrai on Thursday night. I dare not mention that place and close my eyes. God, it was awful. Avalanche followed avalanche of fresh German troops, but the boys stuck to it, and we managed to retire to Ham without molestation. Cambrai was the biggest battle fought. Out of all the glorious regiment of 1,100 men only five officers and 170 of the men answered the roll-call next day.

WN, UNKNOWN MONTH, 1914

Thomas Clemens, unsinkable, perhaps the name is mis-spelt, Quartermaster Sergeant Thomas Croke survived the war. Private Jeremiah Aspell, died in Salonika in March, 1918 and buried in Salonika (Lembet Road) Military Cemetery in Greece.

Carrickman's Experience in the Royal Engineers

Mr James O'Donnell, Main Street, Carrick-on-Suir, who had been just ten months a Sapper in the Royal Engineers when the war broke out, and who was at the front from August 18th to September 14th, has just returned to Carrick suffering from the effects of a bullet in the arm and from rheumatism contracted in the course of his work in making trenches and constructing pontoon bridges, etc.

Mr O'Donnell is a very intelligent and modest and retiring young man. A couple of days ago he gave our Carrick-on-Suir correspondent some interesting details of the work of the Engineers in the war, and the dangers they had to encounter, although they are not actual combatants. Mr O'Donnell, left England for the front 15 August and arrived at Rouen, in France, on the 20th. From Rouen they marched to Wesseigne, and arrived before Mons on the 23rd. They were sent at midnight to make trenches for the regiments of the brigade to which the Engineers were attached – viz., the Highland Light Infantry, Connaught Rangers, Berkshires, and the Irish Guards. During the retreat from Mons they were constantly engaged blowing up bridges, digging trenches, and constructing pontoon bridges and they were repeatedly shelled by the Germans, and so fierce was the shelling at times that they were obliged to temporarily abandon their work.

Mr O'Donnell witnessed some fierce fighting by the regiments to which his company was attached. In spite of their bravery and disregard for danger, the German heavy artillery proved too much for them and wrought terrible havoc amongst them, especially among the Connaught Rangers and the Highland Light Infantry. The Irish Guards and the Berkshires also suffered heavy losses.

During the retreat from Mons Mr O'Donnell had several miraculous escapes from death by German shells, which fell around them like hailstones, now bursting and doing very little damage, and anon laying many a poor fellow low.

On 14 September, at Ventrileuil, his company and brigade with which they were working had a terrible time from the German shells. Few escaped injuries of some kind, and many a one had there his last glimpse of France. A shell exploded within a few feet of where he lay. The shrapnel bullets flew in all directions. One of them grazed Mr O'Donnell's cheek, passed through the collar of his coat, and through a pocket-book he carried in his breast pocket. A man who lay beside him had his leg shattered and his rifle smashed by the same shell. Very soon after this narrow escape, Mr O'Donnell received the bullet wound in the arm. He was removed to a temporary hospital, which, he was informed, was before the war the country residence of Madame Cailleux, who figured prominently in a recent sensational trial in Paris.

Whilst in hospital he and other wounded soldiers were visited by Sir John French, who chatted gaily with them on their adventures and expressed the hope that they would soon be quite fit and well.

When making trenches for the Irish Guards near Mons, Mr O'Donnell met a fellow Carrickman and school-fellow, Mr Michael O'Meara, of Ballynagrana, Carrick-on-Suir, who is in the Irish Guards and has been at the front almost since the war began.

Mr O'Donnell says the German heavy artillery is the most effective part of their war machine. They send their shells with deadly precision and without a minute's interval. The shelling usually follows the visit of a few German aeroplanes. Mr O'Donnell was most enthusiastic in his praise of the marvellous heroism of the French and Belgian Priests and also in their spiritual capacity on the battlefield. They exhibit an utter disregard for death or danger, and are to be seen everywhere that men fall – succouring the wounded and preparing the dying to face judgement, and uttering a prayer for the repose of the souls of those who have gone to be judged and who will never again be troubled by shrapnel or steel. Many of the priests wear their surplices and stoles on the battlefield.

The soldiers take great interest watching the German shells fired from a distance at night time. They present a weirdly beautiful sight as they pierce the darkness in a long red line. The working of the German searchlights at night is another very interesting sight.

Mr O'Donnell gave some interesting details of life in the trenches for several days and nights, sleeping and eating in them, and always in danger from shrapnel and rifle bullets. Officers and rank and file share the same comforts or discomforts in the trenches. The food supplied was on the whole very good, and, considering the difficulties to be encountered in preparing it, it was well and regularly served.

WN, UNKNOWN MONTH, 1914

There is a James O'Donnell, Royal Irish Regiment born in Templemore who was killed in action two weeks before the war ended, it may be him. Buried in Cross Roads Cemetery, Fontaine-Au-Bois in France. Michael O'Meara survived the war).

Home From The Front
Lieutenant James Lanigan, RAMC, in Kilkenny

Lieutenant James Lanigan, son of Mr Pierse Lanigan, JP, Patrick Street and brother of Mr John Lanigan, solicitor, who received a commission on the Royal Army Medical Corps shortly after the outbreak of the war, and who, after a brief stay at Aldershot, was ordered to the front, arrived in Kilkenny on Tuesday morning on a few days much needed leave. He looks fit and well, notwithstanding his awful experiences amongst the killed and wounded amidst scenes of terrible carnage in the fiercest region of the battle zone. It does not need more than the briefest references to the appalling list of casualties to convince anyone that the duties of army surgeon in the area of conflict are no sine-cure (sic). For the greater part of five weeks- except for briefest intervals at the base hospital – Lieutenant lanigan has been constantly practically in the firing line, content to snatch a few hours sleep, from which the thunder of shot and shell oftened than not rudely awakened him, in a 'dug-out', with its attenuated comforts. Military regulations, of course, preclude him from speaking in other than the most general terms of his experiences and of the particular area which claimed his assiduous and skilful services that have given surcease (sic) of pain to so many of the wounded soldiers. The spirit and morale of the troops, he says, are excellent, 'particularly', he adds, 'of the Irish lads- always merry and bright, even in the tightest corner.' Lieutenant Lanigan left Kilkenny on Friday, and expects to resume duty on the battlefield on Saturday night. He carries with him to the 'far flung battle line' the sincerest good wishes for his personal safety and success of the hosts of friends of himself and his respected family in Kilkenny.

KP, 12-1914.

Lieutenant James Lanigan survived the war.

Officer in a Matchbox

An extraordinary attempt to escape by a young German Lieutenant interned in England was accidentally frustrated at Tilbury on 12th Decemebr. He had been enclosed in a wooden box, equipped with food, drink, and oxygen, and was only discovered as he was being put on board a liner for Rotterdam. The box was an ordinary deal case, used for the packing of matches, and bore the usual inscription, "Non-poisonous— safety matches." The case was not more than three feet six inches in length and about the same depth. It was fastened with a small cheap padlock and a wooden pin attached to a piece of wire. A portion of the label on the top born the words "Via Hamvro." The case was placed with the rest of the luggage in the goods van of the train until Tilbury Station was reached, and was then sent down a six-foot chute to the ferry boat. An observer noticed that it turned over in its passage and fell rather heavily on the bottom of the level, but no sound betrayed that it contained a living occupant. On the ferry, piles of other luggage were placed on to of it. It was then taken along to the gangway by two members of the crew. On account of its weight and difficulty of handling it, these men rolled the case over and over. They had just reached the gangway with the box when to their astonishment, the lid at the side gave way, and head and arm protruded.

"Man inside," they shouted, and the captain and other members of the crew rushed up to find a man in the box. Owing to the doubled-up position in which he had been for so many hours, he was unable to stand, he was so weak and dazed, but, after a time, he recovered, and rubbed his head vigorously, as it had been severely knocked about. He stated his name was Otto Koehn, and sailed from America in the Potsdaur to return to his regiment in Germany. The ship was captured and taken to Southampton, and he was interned at Dorchester. He added he had been in the box nearly fifteen hours. The box contained two champagne bottles, filled, and a blanket, with a water bottle of meat extract, and bananas. The most interesting thing in the box, however, was a rubber pillow, filled with oxygen.   KCC, 12-1914

'Brain' of the Army

Eye-witness writes in that rather vague area known as 'the front', omitting the 'bases', 'advanced bases', and lines of communication lying behind, the first and most important point for consideration is General headquarters of the Army, where is located the directing brain and driving force of the Army as a whole. GHQ as it is usually called is generally in some centrally situated town which may be within sound of the enemy's guns, but not within their reach, and at it are installed the Commander in Chief and the General Staff of the Army. That a Commander can afford to be so far away from the Front is due to the fact that he no longer has to, or can, depend on personal observation for information upon which to base action. He relies entirely on second or third hand evidence of things seen or heard by others over a fron of many miles, and communicated back by the agency of telegraph, wireless telephones, motorcars, motorcycles, and aeroplanes are the daily food of the General Staff. The handling of this mass of material collected by others, its analysis and its application to the situation for the purpose of training plans, is the work of the Headquarters of the Army. As at those of corps divisions, and brigades, a great part of this work is done by maps. Here in certain offices may be seen large tables spread with maps upon which every movement of both sides is carefully recorded by flags or coloured chalks, as news is received from the various sources of information available. At this centre also are the heads of the administrative branches and departments of the Army which deal with discipline, supplies of all sorts, transport of every nature, the transmission of information, and the medical services. The General Headquarters is always maintained at such a distance from the fighting line that it is not disturbed by the operations or influenced by what is going on in one part of the front to the detriment of other parts. For the more immediate control of operations, the Commander has one or more central posts nearer the front, at which he can more conveniently meet his subordinate commanders for consultation and to which the latter can, more quickly send reports or their representative . Touch is maintained daily between General Headquarters, Corps Headquarters, and the general and Corps Headquarters of the Allies by means of special liason officers, who travel to and fro by motor.   KCC, 12-1914

Pocket Wireless

A Boston paper recently called attention to the wireless telegraphy plant invented by an Abruzzi priest, which was so small that it could be carried in the pocket, but which was capable of receiving messages from high-power stations at a distance of 1,230 miles. The claim of this reverend professor raised a storm of controversy in Italy and the greatest interest among scientists everywhere. He was called upon to prove his claims, and he has scored a triumph in the presence of a large gathering of public men and scientific experts, including Sir Kennell Road. He gave a series of astonishing experiments without bobbins, receiving poles, or the other stock in trade connected with radio telegraphy. A simple switch attached by an ordinary apparatus was what he used for interrupting wireless communications transmitted by the London Foreign Office.

KCC, 12-1914

Irish Doctors Interesting Communication

Dr Ormsby, late medical officer of Ballyleague Dispensary, in the Roscommon Union, who volunteered for the front early in the war, has been transferred from the ASC to 20 Infantry Brigade of the Border Regiment, at present operating in the neighbourhood of Ypres. This is the third step Dr Ormsby has received since joining. With his regiment he states in letters home to his brother, Mr G O'Malley Ormsby, Rathmoy, Ballina, County Mayo, he is under fire constantly day and night. He writes that the enemy's fire is so heavy that on some occasions the trenches were completely blown on top of the men.

In another letter he gives a vivid description of his experiences in the firing line at Ypres. Dr Ormsby describes the town of Ypres as a heap of ruins. Its ancient and beautiful buildings are now a shapeless mass of stones. The Town Hall of Ypres was a very beautiful building, prized for its antiquity as it was for its architecture. It is now so ransacked amongst the things of the past, another loss which the world, as a whole, must bear as a result of the German culture of which so much is written. Indeed, the town of Ypres is one of the most ancient and historical on the Continent. Within it were many buildings of much interest to the student of history. In particular did it possess many churches and convents, all of which have been destroyed by the ruthless invader. No amount of sympathy or money cane ever restore such treasures. Amongst these was a convent of

Benedictine Nuns. It was an old Irish Benedictine foundation, established by pious and zealous Irish women during the penal days in their own land. It was a quaint old world building, and though in the heart of town it was the very home of peace and repose. To the present time the community consisted entirely of Irish women, and at the outbreak of the war one of its members was a niece of Mr John Redmond, M.P. Within its walls were kept as one of the most treasured possessions the honoured flag of the Irish Brigade, carried triumphantly through many a bloody battle upon the Continent by the brave exiles of ----.

Though riddled with the shots of the enemy, Irish valour prevented these flags ever falling into the hands of the enemy. What has now happened them, it is not now possible to say, but it is pretty certain that the Irish Nuns of Ypres have spared no effort to save them from the wreck and havoc wrought by Germany upon the brave little Belgium which has sheltered and preserved them for c—r—d--.

Dr Ormsby is in splendid form and send his brother a number of interesting trophies of the war, picked up by him at the fighting line between the two armies when engaged in bringing in the wounded. Three fuzes of the shrapnel shells, some of the cartridges shot by French Germans and British, and fragments of the exploded shells.

It is interesting to note that the German cartridges bear date October 1914, which bears out a statement made by some soldiers, asserting that the Germans are running out of ammunition. We find further confirmation of this statement is the following paragraph taken from a printing trade publication, *Sales and Wants:*

Music Plates for Bullets

It appears that there is some fear in Germany regarding the supply of lead for bullets, and it is stated that in order to maintain the supply the German Government have commandeered the whole of the printing plates of lead and – lead in the production of music scores. Furthermore, it is stated that no discontinuation has been made in the commandeering of music plates, and that even the classical works of the great masters have been seized for the melting-pot, in order that bullets may be manufactured at Krupp's for the army, in consequence of which many of the great German music publishers are said to have been seized. It is said that this is pressing harshly on certain composers in this country, and the comment has been made that had they had their work carried out in this country they would have had a cause to bewail their fate.

WE,12-1914

In March 1915, Lieutenant William Ormsby, R.A.M.C., former Doctor of the Roscommon Union was mistakenly reported 'died of wounds'. He survived the war).

South Africa and the War

Letter From a Westmeath Man

The following is a copy of a letter sent by a young man Michael Cunningham (who is attached to the Army Veterinary Corps in South Africa) to his parents in Westmeath:

Army Veterinary Corps.

Section II.

Carnarvon, C.P.

26th October, '14.

My Dear Father and Mother—I sent you a postcard last week. I had been in Johannesburg for a week as veterinary Officer. I left Johannesburg on Tuesday last and came to here to establish a Veterinary field hospital. I am living in camp and knock out a pretty good time. I am afraid I won't see any fighting as they keep us away behind the fighting line. However, I expect to be pretty busy just now when the sick and wounded horses begin to come in. There has been an attempt at rebellion here as you have doubtless seen in the papers, and so far it has done an amount of good, as the Boers who hitherto were inclined to a neutral course, have now all come out on Commando and are determined not to rest till every Rebel and German in South Africa is under ground or driven from the country. I expect you saw how General Boths is determined to take the field. They has raised an Irish regiment in Johannesburg—first they raised a mounted corps of 500 men, and then they started a foot regiment of 750 men and got to the full strength in ten days. They are a wild reckless crowd and I am sure they will give a good account of themselves when they get to the fighting line. Every political section is represented amongst them, Nationalist, Unionist, etc, but they all have a common cause just now—that is, to shoot as many Germans as possible. The weather is getting pretty warm out here just now—we are getting into summer. I suppose you are beginning to shiver at home. Well I have no news. I hope father got a good price for his cattle, and that he gets a fresh lot without much trouble. I am sorry my mare has not been sold yet, but I expect it was best not to take her to Mullingar fair. I have not had a letter from Dick though I have been expecting a line. I am very glad to see he has been so successful this season and I hope his luck will continue. Is Tom Lennon improving? I hope he pulls through. How is Nicholas getting on with the motor—the roads must be getting bad by nowl What are the Volunteers doing? How many have you? Are they armed yet? Let me know all about them. I hope you are both keeping strong. I must conclude with best love to selves. Nicholas, Joe, Ciss, and Dan, also Josephine and her father.

Your fond Son.

Michael.

P.S—It is best to address all letters to Army Veterinary Corps, Booyscns

Camp, Johhanesburg, S.A, and they will be sent to me, as I may be moving from here any time. I am getting my letters sent on from Mafeking through Johannesburg, so have not got a letter since yours of September 10th, but they will come alright. I have the rank of Captain. The Boer Commandoes are singing—'It's a long way to Tipperary'. M.

WE,12-1914

Captain Michael Cunningham survived the war.

Kilkenny Prisoners of War
Letter to the *Kilkenny People*
Christmas Greetings to Their Friends in Kilkenny
Kilkenny Priest Ministers to Their Spiritual Wants

We have received the following interesting letter, which will be welcomed by the many relatives and friends of the gallant Irish soldiers:

Limburg (Lahn), Germany

To the Editor *Kilkenny People*,

Dear Sir,

I would be very thankful to you if you would allow me space in your valuable paper to let all our friends and relations in Callan know that there are seven of us from that town prisoners of war here in Limburg, German, and many from Kilkenny. Our names are: Sergeant N Walsh, Sergeant E Power, Sergeant W Woodgate, Private Roach, Private P Roach, Private Russell and Private Halloran. Wishing you and all our friends and relations a Happy Christmas and a Prosperous New Year—(Signed),

No 4392, Sergeant Nicholas Walsh.

4th Royal Irish Regiment.

PS Whilst writing this note our Holy Father the Pope sent down a priest from Rome by the name of Father Crotty, a native of Kilkenny, for our spiritual welfare. He received a cordial welcome from the men of Ye faire Citie and its surroundings.—N.W.

(Father Crotty is a distinguished member of the Dominican Order, and is one of the two Irish priests in Rome selected by His Holiness to proceed to Germany in order to attend to the spiritual wants of the Catholic prisoners of war, who, of course, are mostly Irish. He is a brother of Mr T Crotty, merchant, Parliament Street, and of Rev. M J Crotty, C.C., Glenmore, – Ed. KP.)

KP. 12-1914

All of the soldiers above survived the war except Private Patrick Roache, Royal Irish Regiment transferred to the Labour Corps, who died at home in December, 1918 and is buried in Mallardstown (Whitechurch) Cemetery, County Kilkenny).

From the Fighting Line

Mr James Poe, solicitor, has asked us to insert the enclosed letter of thanks from his son, Major John Poe, RAMC, for flannel and woollen comforts which are being sent to him if France for the wounded under his charge. 4th November, 1914.

Dear Father and Mother,

I have not had time to write to you since I wrote a month ago asking for some things. We have been hard at it ever since incessantly; no time to take off our clothes, except once or twice, much less to write letters. Will you please thank every man woman and child who is helping to send out the splendid warm things for the wounded, and which are all arriving safely by parcel post, and tell them how much good they have done. Colonel Jameson has already written to you his thanks. It will be a God-send if you can beat up some more of the same sort of thing for us. All ranks have been simply magnificent in this hell and bear their knocks without a grumble. Our ambulance convoy has 120 drivers, all splendid fellows, who don't mind sticking to their job day and night, with very little sleep now and then. We have carried some wounded Indians lately, they are doing great work and love the fight. They like talking away to me in their own languages. They say, 'It's a grand fight! Like thunder here, Sahib; but much death—it is their duty'. It is very galling to see the way the Germans destroy all the farms and everything they can lay hands on.

Your loving son,

Jack.

Mr and Mrs Poe have already sent out for the wounded under their son's charge over 8 cwt. of warm shirts, vests, pants, stockings, socks, and mufflers, etc, and they hope with continued kind help to make it up to half a ton before long.

KP, 12-1914

John Poe survived the war and was promoted to Assistant Director Medical Services Lieutenant Colonel Temporary Colonel.

Four Sons at the Front
Mother in Receipt of Outdoor Relief
No Government Allowance Made
Peculiar Caser at Castlecomer

At the meeting of the Castlecomer Board of Guardians on Tuesday last, Mr John P Fogarty, JP, Co.C., chairman, presiding.

Mr William Delgan, secretary to the Kilkenny County Committee formed to relieve distress consequent on the war, wrote asking to be supplied with a list of all persons who were afforded in-door or out-door relief in the union.

Mrs Wandesforde: 'I am on that committee and they only deal with distress caused by the war and not with the distress that we always have with us. I have been asked to form a local committee to find out any cases that arise in our district in connection with distress caused by the war. I have already done that and sent the names to the Co. Committee. Canon O'Halloran has promised to act; Canon Harpur, Mrs Laracy and myself constitute that committee. I thought that was enough, because I don't fancy we will have very much to do with distress caused by the war here.'

Clerk: 'I don't see what this has to do with the application unless that some people in receipt of out-door relief will be claiming compensation from this committee.'

Mr Rice drew attention to a case in his district where a woman (Mrs Pierce) a recipient of out-door relief, had four sons at the front and she never got a halfpenny.

Mr Mooney said he understood that Mr Abe Shirley had got some money for her. He gave her 10s in cash and gave £1 to Mr Copley to supply food, etc.

The Clerk said that according to a circular from the L.G.Board in August last, no dependants of men at the front should receive out-door relief.

Mr Rice: 'I don't think you should answer that letter.'

Mr Mooney: 'She should be crossed off the list and let the Government compensate her.'

Mr Rice: 'She has 3s a week, and she has three small children.'

Mr Mooney said it was not on account of the war that this woman was getting relief.

Chairman: 'It is only because she was entitled to weekly relief.'

Mr Mooney: 'She has three sons at the front, and one is home wounded.'

Mr Mooney: 'Leave her the out-door relief until she is refused a Government allowance, and then stop it. They will have to give it to her then.'

Mrs Wandesforde: 'The Kilkenny Co. Committee has nothing to do with the Government. They are only concerned with the Prince of Wales Fund for distress. If that woman has sons at the front they should sign a paper that their mother is to get so much per week of their pay.'

Mrs Laracy: 'Every soldier is obliged to make his will.'

Mrs Wandesforde: 'The Kilkenny Co. Committee look into cases like this and make inquiries.'

Mrs Rice: 'This woman asked me to see you about the matter a fortnight ago. Mr Shirley, of Coolculle, wrote to the War Office for her. I will make further inquiries into the matter.'

Mrs Wandesforde: 'I know they are not paying very regular at present. Mr O'Brennan said he knew a woman in Ballinakill whose husband was the the front and she got £1 every Sunday morning.

Mr Costigan: 'It doesn't look well to see a woman with four sons at the front getting relief.

Mr Somers: 'It is a shame.'

Chairman: 'This application has nothing to do with Mrs Pierce. They want information from you of the names of those getting in-door or out-door relief.'

Mrs Wandesforde: 'Don't you think you should send it if they ask you to do so?'

Chairman: 'It won't relieve you. After all, those in receipt of out-door relief are not getting much.'

Mrs Laracy: 'Would it not relief the rates if they got something from the War Office? I think the War Office insists on the payment of 6d per day from any soldier to his parents.'

Mrs Wandesforde thought they should supply the information requested.

It was decided to forward the necessary information, and Mr Joseph Tobin, RO, was directed to inquire into the cases of those people who were receiving compensation and out-door relief.

KP, 12-1914

All of Mrs Pierce's son survived the war.

Accident to a Waterford Volunteer

The Waterford and Tramore Volunteers travelled to Limerick on Sunday and took part in the great review by Mr John Redmond. An accident occurred in one of the carriages of the train in which the contingent travelled. It appears that the merits of a rifle belonging to one of the Volunteers was being discussed, and another Volunteer produced a service cartridge which he said had been give him by a soldier. He tried to force the cartridge into position, but it jammed, and then when he endeavoured to close the breech the gun went off and the bullet struck Mr William Hartery, another Volunteer, in the thigh, happily inflicting only a slight wound. The bullet, it is stated, went through the floor of the compartment. The accident happened at the check platform near Limerick, and Mr Hartery was attended to by the ambulance party attached to the Volunteers. On arrival at Limerick he was taken to the infirmary there to travel back to Waterford by the special train in the evening, being congratulated on his lucky escape. Mr Hartery is at present in the Waterford County Infirmary.

ME, 12-1914

Michael Hartery went on to join the 2nd Battalion, Royal Irish Regiment as a Lieutenant. He was killed in action in July, 1916 and is buried in Danzig Alley British Cemetery, Mametz in France. He was a son of Edward and Margaret Hartery, of 11, Convent Hill, Waterford.

County Limerick Soldier's Letter

A letter, passed by the Censor, has just been received by Mr John Hollet, Glin, from Private Thomas Looney, a native of Glin, 2nd Scots Guard, at the front. In this he says: 'We had a very busy time when we came out here first, but things are much quieter lately, as the Germans have their hands full at home (sic) to meet the Russians, who are giving them a hot time. I have not much to complain about. We get plenty to eat and plenty warm clothing. In future we spend four days in the trenches, and we have four days rest in some farmhouse or village, which we call a billet, in rear of our trenches. We have also got what we call dug-outs. They are little houses dug out of the earth, and roofed in with straw and wood and earth, to make them proof against shrapnel. You would be surprised how comfortable some of them are, with plenty of clean, dry straw, a blanket, and waterproof sheet. We also get plenty of tobacco and cigarettes free of charge.

LC, 12-1914

Thomas Looney penned many articles and survived the war.

Death of a Wounded Sergeant

One of the few remaining wounded soldiers in Barrington's hospital died last evening in that institution, where he had been lying since his arrival from the fighting around Armentieres, in which his left shoulder was seriously injured by shrapnel fire. The deceased was Sergeant Clarence Chantry, 1st Battalion, King's Shropshire Light Infantry, and he was interned at Barrington's on 26 October last, with the party of some forty officers and wounded men, who arrived on that date from the front, and nearly all of whom have since left convalescent. The deceased was but 23 years of age, and was, it is understood, a native of Birmingham, the mother od deceased journeying from the midland capital to see her son, of whose condition she had been kindly informed by the hospital authorities. The funeral of the deceased with military honours will take place to-morrow.

LC, 12-1914

Birmingham soldier, Lance Sergeant 22 year old Clarence John Chantry was buried in Kings Island Cemetery in Limerick. The Ordnance Barracks supplied a firing party of South Irish Horse. His mother and some relatives travelled from Birmingham for the funeral.

French Decorations for Irish Soldiers

The President of the French Republic has bestowed the decoration *Medaille Militarie* on the undermentioned warrant officers, non-commissioned officers and men serving in Irish Regiments of the Expeditionary Force, with the approval of his Majesty the King, in recognition of their gallantry during the operations between the 21st and 30 August, 1914:

2870, Sergeant Major, Blakeney, J, 2nd Battalion Royal Inniskilling Fusiliers.

4897, Sergeant Major Bruen, W, 2nd Battalion, Connaught Rangers.

590, Private Colquhoun, R.F, North Irish Horse.

5732, Drummer Corrigan, M, 1st Battalion, Royal Irish Fusiliers.

5637, Quartermaster Sergeant Fitzpatrick, T.W, 2nd Battalion, Royal Irish Regiment.

7127, Private Gray, W, 2nd Battalion, Royal Irish Rifles.

5039, Company Sergeant Major Hall, R.S, 2nd Battalion, Royal Dublin Fusiliers.

7, Squadron Sergeant Major Jackson, D, South Irish Horse.

164, Private McArrow, J North Irish Horse.

8333, Sergeant Neville, R, 1st Battalion, Royal Irish Fusiliers.

6704, Sergeant Ray, A W, 2nd Battalion, Royal Dublin Fusiliers.

1041, Corporal Roberts, W J, 5th Lancers.

1073, Company Sergeant Major Rodgers, J, 1st Battalion, Irish Guards.

5741, Company Sergeant Major, Sarsfield, E B, 1st Battalion, Royal Irish Fusiliers.

9676, Sergeant Wilson, H, 1st Battalion, Royal Irish Fusiliers.

LC, 12-1914

Sergeant Major John Blakeney, Sergeant Major William Bruen, Drummer Matthew Corrigan, Private Walter Gray, Company Sergeant Major Robert Hall, Private James McArrow, Sergeant Richard Neville, Sergeant Hugh A Wison, Company Sergeant Major John Rodgers, and Company Sergeant Major Sarsfield survived the war.

Regimental Quartermaster Sergeant Thomas William Fitzpatrick was promoted to Temporary Major of the West Yorkshire Regiment, and survived the war. Corporal Roberts, unfindable. Sergeant Arthur Washington Ray, born in Pietermaritzburg, Natal, was killed in action in October, 1916. He has no known grave and listed on the Menin Gate Memorial, in Belgium.

Limerick Men at The Front

The following members of the staff, or employees of Messrs J Bannatyne & Sons, Ltd, and Messrs J N Russell, Ltd, are serving with H M Forces:

John Adamson, W J Agar, Fred Barry, James Bell, Henry Bouchier, Edward Bourke, J Bourke, Patrick Bourke, Christopher Casey, Con Collins, Patrick Costello, Denis Cronin, Patrick Doyle, Michael Drew, David Dynan, Patrick Earls, Thomas Gloster, Robert Gabbett, Patrick Galvin, John Gibbons, John Harper, John Hassett, William Higgins, John Hogan, Daniel Hourigan, Joseph Hourigan, Michael Hurley, George Jenner, John Kavanagh, Edward Keane, Joseph Kelly, Patrick Keogh, Albert Kerr, Michael Long, John Lyddy, James Lysaght, Maurice Marshall, Daniel McCormack, Patrick McCormack, John Meany, William Metcalfe, Henry Moore, Thomas Nulty, John Nunan, Michael O'Brien, John O'Connell, Owen O'Keeffe, James O'Rourke, William Phillips, Michael Roche, Thomas Sheehan, Joseph Skinner, William Smith, Michael Stapleton, John Stockil, Alfred Wilson, William Wilson.

LC, 12-1914

John Adamson, W J Agar, Henry Bouchier, Edward Bourke, Patrick Bourke, Christopher Casey, Con Collins, Patrick Costello, Denis Cronin, Patrick Doyle, Michael Drew, David Dynan, Thomas Gloster, Patrick Galvin, John Gibbons, John Harper, John Hassett, William Higgins, Daniel Hourigan, Joseph Hourigan, Michael Hurley, George Jenner, John Kavanagh, Edward Keane, Patrick Keogh, Albert Kerr, Michael Long, James Lysaght, Maurice Marshall, Patrick McCormack, William Metcalfe, Henry Moore, Thomas Nulty, John Nunan, Owen O'Keeffe, James O'Rourke, William Phillips, Michael Roche, Joseph Skinner, William Smith, Michael Stapleton, John Stockil, Alfred Wilson, William Wilson, all survived the war.

Private Fred Barry, East Yorkshire Regiment was killed in action the month before this article was published. He is remembered on the Ploegsteert Memorial in Belgium. He has no known grave. Private James Bell, Royal Munster Fusiliers, died of wounds in Greek Macedonia in February 1916, he has no known grave but is remembered on the Doiran Memorial in Greece. Private Patrick Earls, Royal Munster Fusiliers, died on 23-12-1916 and is buried in St Lawrence's Catholic Cemetery, Limerick. Private Robert Gabbett, Royal Munster Fusiliers, died of wounds in September, 1916, and is buriend in Dartmoor Cemetery, Becordel-Becourt in France. Private Joseph Kelly, Royal Munster Fusiliers Died at the 66th General Hospital, Salonika in October-1917 and is buried in Kirechkoi-Hortakoi Military Cemetery in Greece. Private John Lyddy, Royal Munster Fusiliers, Died of wounds in Greek Macedonia, and buried in Struma Military Cemetery in Greece. Seaman John Meaney died on SS *Devonian*; he has no know grave and is listed on Plymouth Naval Memorial UK. Sergeant John O'Connell, Royal Munster Fusiliers was killed in action on 20-07-1916. He is buried in Cabaret-Rouge British Cemetery, Souchez in France. Private Thomas Sheehan, Royal Munster Fusiliers died in February-1917 and is buried in Niederzwehren Cemetery in Germany

(Most of the soldiers buried in this cemetery were POW's).

There are two J Bourkes, two John Hogan's, and four Michael O'Brien's listed as killed from Limerick.)

Letter to Croom Merchant

Mr John Cregg, merchant, Croom, has received the following letter from the front:

2nd Royal Munster Fusiliers,
British Expeditionary Force,
December 14th, 1914.

Dear Mr Cregg—I received with joy the splendid parcel yesterday, and, needless to say, it was the very thing—simply splendid. A better parcel could not be got together by anybody. The shirt, pants, and socks were the real thing, and the gloves were great. Then the cigarettes were ripping—it was the very best parcel of service comforts I have seen, and the few friends who were with me when it arrived say I am very lucky to get such a parcel of real comfort. And now, Mr Cregg, I must ask you to give my sincere thanks to your daughter and the other young ladies who so nobly gave their assistance to send out such needy articles. And I am sure any man who is lucky enough to get such a splendid parcel will be as thankful as I am. And I can assure you that we shall at all times do our best to add more fame to the traditions of the British Army, and always uphold and bring honour on the name 'Munster', for we know by so doing we are adding more lustre to the fair name of Erin. And when I come back to see you I shall be able to show how I have done, as you wished me to do, out here. But, in conclusion, let me say there is the same amount of honour due to the young ladies of Croom, who are doing their share as well as we are doing ours; and as I am unable to thank all the young ladies who so nobly assisted your daughter in her great work individually, I must ask you to thank them for me, and accept my best wishes for a Happy Christmas and bright New Year full of victories. From yours truly.

Christopher A. Reardon.

LL, 12-1914

Private Christopher Reardon was wounded in June 1916, transferred to the Royal Irish Regiment and finally to the Royal Engineers. He survived the war.

The Gallant Munsters

A letter from Boulogne

Private Michael McCarthy, of the Munsters, writing to his father at Youghal from Boulogne Hospital, says that in their last engagement they were up against the Prussian Guards, whom they scattered in wild disorder at the point of the bayonet. Their troops were doing splendid work. He had been at Ypres, where it was rather hot. The Germans made an effort to take it, and when they saw that was impossible they almost levelled it to the ground with their monstrous shells. The inhabitants scarcely got time to leave, and a great many perished under their own roofs. The Germans were driven back with great losses. The fighting was terrible. When the enemy retired they went for a rest, which was short lived, for a 'coal-box' came through the roof, killing seven of their comrades.

LC, 12-1914

Although there were seven soldiers from County Cork who died in the war named Michael McCarthy, none are listed from Youghal.

Trench Tragedy
Soldier Killed while Opening Christmas Parcel

'There was on pathetic sight in our trenches after a "Jack Johnson" had exploded,' writes a corporal from Bristol. 'In a corner we found a chap of the Highland Light Infantry lying dead, with all the nice presents that had been sent out from home round him. There was a plum pudding and a packet of chocolate, some matches, and cigarettes, with socks and woollen comforters and things. His head had fallen forward on top of the box with the pudding and his hands were resting on the box of cigarettes. On his lips was the smile that you would expect from any man who found himself remembered so well at this time of year.'

LC, 12-1914

Catholic Spirit at the Front
Mass in Barns and Lofts
The Statue of the Blessed Virgin
Miraculous Preservation

A Youghal Catholic clergyman has received the following from Private Thomas Barratt, RAMC:

'Hearing that you were inquiring about my welfare at the front, I now avail of the opportunity to let your reverence know that up to the present I am enjoying good and vigorous health, thanks be to God for it. As a new member attending the weekly meetings of the Confraternity before hostilities broke out, I was very much disappointed at being called away on the eve of consecration. Therefore, it occurred to me to write to you for the medal which you so kindly sent me. Of course, with God's help, when I come back you will consecrate me with the medal on my neck, as usual. I am proud to say that I am not the only member here. There are several men in different branches, and there are members of the Limerick Confraternity also. I am proud to be able to tell you that the majority of the men are Irishmen, and, still better, good Roman Catholics.

'Rev Father, we had the good luck of hearing the celebration of Mass while in this country – five in chapel. One Mass we had the great privilege of attending, in a farmer's hayloft, which the priest told us was of a very venerable old age, Mass being last celebrated there 540 years ago by monks called the Knight's Templars. The place was in very good condition, considering its great age. We had another Mass in a barn, said, I am proud and glad to say, by an Irish priest, the Rev John Evans. We had no priest for a long time, up to about a fortnight ago, when Father Evans was attached to our Ambulance Corps.

'I have had also the privilege of witnessing, in a chapel in the village we marched through, the sacred relics of the martyred St Ursula, in a casket shrine on the altar. I and others of my Ambulance Corps have to say that we witnesses nothing short of miracles in the preservation of houses where the image of the Mother of God was enshrined, embedded in the mason work of the gables.

'We were one day marching through a village that had been reduced almost to ashes by German shells. There was hardly a house that was not damaged, some being entirely destroyed.

'What struck us most of all was the gable end of houses with those statues standing, as if defiantly, after being shelled, and not a brick left standing of the rest of the houses. It was a most awe-inspiring. There we stood looking at one another, and talking the matter over, saying, indeed, it was a miracle worked through the medium of the Blessed Virgin. Nearly all the houses have their statues in a conspicuous place on front.

'When Monday evening comes I say my Rosary just about the same time you are reciting it at the Confraternity meeting. I try to be with you in spirit in order to gain the advantage of your prayer. Rev Father, I beg of you to remember me in your Masses and pray that I may come safely through this war. I am after having two very narrow escapes when doing my duty as a stretcher bearer on the field. Thanks be to God I have not sustained any injury up to the time of writing.

'As a member of the Confraternity of which you are the spiritual director, I wish you and all my fellow members all the spiritual and temporal joys attending the holy season of Christmas.

'Goodbye, and don't forget the Irish here in your prayers.'

WE,12-1914

Rev John Evans survived the war.

From The Front
Granard Soldier, Home
Three Months Of Fighting

Private Joseph Walker, R.I. Rifles, late of Castlerea, has returned to his home in Ballybrine, Granard, to enjoy a dearly won rest after three months hard fighting, and to recover from the effects of his wound received in the shoulder during an engagement in Flanders, a few weeks ago.

In an interview Private Walker tells some thrilling stories of his experiences in the fighting line. There were 1,800 comrades with him, last August, in his regiment, in the First Expeditionary Force, and he believes only 12 or 13 so far, came safe, and he thanks God for being one of the extremely lucky ones.

His escapes from death and arrest were in some cases hazardous.

The R.I. Rifles took part in the retreat from Mons, and it was here his most desperate experiences took place. Every inch of the way had to be fought, while the army was withdrawing. He related again the undying story when on Wednesday 26 August, when the armies of the Expeditionary Force had to bear the brunt of the huge German attack. The bursting of the shells and shrapnel, and the whistling of the bullets, made the air reek with fire, but his comrades, and in fact the whole forces never lost their nerve, and the foe were answered, with a calmer, better directed and deadlier fire. It was at this retreat that his only experience as to the scarcity of food was endured. The next engagement was at the Marne, when the tables were turned and the Germans were driven back to the Aisne. He fought at the Aisne during the entire engagement, afterwards in Flanders. For 14 days he fought in the trenches at Ypres, side by side with the Lancasters, Worcesters, and KOSB, but the other Irish regiments in his vicinity were the Royal Irish.

The troops have plenty of clothing, and the food is excellent, but plenty of fresh socks were, he said, very necessary, as the trenches were very wet.

Filthy Soldiers

The men he said are very particular as to their personal appearance, but in this matter it is not always possible to satisfy the inclination. After spending a few days in the trenches, the growing beard gets matted with the clay of the trenches, giving the soldiers the appearance of 'putty men'. At first he said it was the practice that soldiers should dig themselves into trenches but that order, owing to the danger of being buried by the shells, has been countermanded, and regular trenches have to be made.

Private Walker, was on one occasion buried for hours in a trench with only his head and shoulders free, until the arrival of reinforcements drove the enemy back and he was rescued from his perilous position. The Germans were no match in a 'square fight' with the British forces. He confirms the stories as to the ruthless treatment of the wounded by the Huns, and the little respect paid to their own dead.

'The sights to be seen on the battlefield,' continued Private Walker, 'are many and fearful, as they are varied and exciting. On one occasion when sent out with two other comrades on a reconnoitring party they came up to four Germans in a farm house, two of whom they killed and made prisoners of the other two. One of the prisoners was evidently a gentleman and spoke English proficiently.

In answer to their questions, this prisoner said 'I will answer none of your questions, I am a prisoner of war, and I will give no information, one thing I will tell you, Germany is going to win in this war, and now you can shoot me if you wish'. This prisoner was handed over later for safe keeping. Private Walker expects to return in the course of a week or so, to the fighting line and to take satisfaction [revenge?] for his many gallant comrades who have fallen in the fight.   WE,12-1914

Private Joseph Walker survived the war.

Can't Break Through

Private Patrick Dolan, Mullingar, (of 2nd Leinsters) writing from the front to his brother in Mullingar under date 16th December, reports himself as still on the lands of the living and thanks God and His Blessed Mother that it is so as the experiences and dangers that it is so as the experiences and dangers are very trying. He says: 'If you were out there, you would laugh at times. The other night our Company started singing—

'Come, come, come and drink wine with us'
'Down by the old Bull and Bush.'
And the Germans from their trenches replied with a verse which I understand is 'I would if I could but I can't as your machine guns won't let us'. We will be having a "half-set" with them at Christmas. They are trying hard to break through our lines but can't do it…

'You would certainly laugh if you were to see me at times disguised in mud and clay. Tell all the boys I am all right and was asking for them.'
                                                                          WE,12-1914

Private Patrick Dolan survived the war.

Miraculous Escape of Castlepollard Man
Bullet Strikes on Medal of Blessed Virgin
Interesting Details of Fighting

Private Tom Gibbons., 2nd Leinsters, who is home now for a short furlough, until 28th Dec, was wounded in the trenches in France. He gives the following interesting narrative:

'I have been in a number of battles. We have a hard time of it. The Allies trenches and the German trenches are usually about 500 yards apart. The Allies trenches are about 5 feet deep, with parapets, so that when firing we can step up and look across in order to make the best use of the bit of lead, and, I can tell you, we do give it to them, and, mind you they do to us in their turn. 'I got wounded at the battle of Val', continued Gibbons, 'but God Almighty and his Holy Mother saved me. Just look at this medal,' he said to our correspondent who interviewed him. 'I carry it with my scapular. It was sent to me by my wife. The shot struck it, and twisted it, and, no doubt, miraculously saved my life.'

Our correspondent, who has examined the medal, which has also been so utilised by many other Castlepollard folk, describes it as a round medal of white medal, bearing the image of the Blessed Virgin. It is quite bent up, almost in the shape of a thimble, by the bullet, and there is a little hole on it, where the bullet pierced a part of it. On it are some drops of the soldiers blood.

The medal is stated to have come from the Franciscan Friary at Multyfarnham and to have been given by Mrs Kennedy, Castlepollard, to Gibbons wife for him.

Gibbons further stated that he was wounded in the battle of Val 2nd December and dropped to his knees on receiving the wound. He was immediately taken to hospital and the bullet extracted. He then got leave to come home to his wife and large family till the 28th.

'But', continued Gibbons, 'I am going back on 28th, please God, and will have my share in holding up the old Kaiser, dead or alive, when the day come.'

Gibbons said a great part of the fighting was done at night, and no matter what day it was, they were sure to have fighting on Sundays, as that seemed to be the favourite day with the Germans.

WE,12-1914

Private Thomas Gibbons, survived the war.

From the Front
Fighting at Ypres
Germans Mown Down
Mullingar Man's Thrilling Narrative

Private McEnroe, Military Road, Mullingar, who belongs to the Irish Guards, is at home from a wound in the leg. At Ypres, he said, the Germans concentrated great forces, ad were determined to break through at any sacrifice. 'When they were coming' he continued, 'we opened our ranks as if to let them pass through. Some of them did pass through, but they ran into the mouth of the guns. The artillery opened on them with deadly effect, and mowed them down. They retired in disorder, and suffered dreadful losses in the retreat. The country is very wooded, and this favours the Germans, who delight in fighting in woods and under cover, but they hate to face the open.

'On one occasion the Irish Guards were ordered to clear a wood which was held by the Germans. In going across the open they were exposed to a heavy fire, but succeeded, nevertheless, in taking the wood and driving out the Germans, who fled to the crest of a hill, about 200 yards off, and there entrenched themselves.

WE,12-1914

Private John McEnroe Mullingar, Irish Guards, was killed in action on 30/09/1915. He has no known grave and is listed on the Loos Memorial in France.

South Irish Horse

No 860, B Squadron, 1st Expeditionary Force, C/o War Office, London.

Dear Mother—Just a few lines to let you know I am A1, and I hope all at home are the same. I got your parcels alright a few days ago, with boots, shirts, drawers, tobacco, cigarettes. I have enough tobacco to put me over the Christmas now. I also have got plenty of clothing to do me for a long time, and you need not send anymore unless I ask for them. Hogan and myself are together, and we are as happy as the King himself—at least we imagine we are, and that is just as good. We had the pleasure of carrying arms in his Majesty and the Prince of Wales on Tuesday last, also to the President of France. They were up looking at their troops that are fighting at the front. I suppose it is beginning to look like Christmas at home now, and you are fairly busy in the shop. The only sign of Christmas out here is when all the boys are going to doss every night, and they start talking about whose old hen we are going to kill for Christmas. Tess if you were here you would hear some yarns. I suppose you heard young Allerdice was wounded, but it was a very slight one. You can tell Willie Lowe he need not be put about over it. I had a letter from----the other day. She is going to send me some cigarettes for Christmas. I had seen her letter from jack, and he said he was going to send some to. I must now conclude as it is getting late, and I want to go to doss. Tell all the boys I was asking for them, and I wish them all a happy Christmas. I will write you again before then. Best love to all from

Jim Blackburn, (Of Moate).

Received Tony's card today. Glad to hear he is well.

WE,12-1914

Private James H Blackburn later transferred to the Royal Irish Regiment and survived the war.

The War
Interesting Letter From Catholic Chaplain
Experiences at the Front

In the course of a letter written from the front to the Right Rev Monsigneor Keller, P.P., V.G., Youghal, the Rev. W Forest, chaplain to the forces at the front, says he is alive, and with God's Providence on his side and the prayers of the faithful ones, he intends to remain so.

'I sometimes think," the writer states 'that the people at home suffer more anxiety than those out here. We are so much engaged, and so many strange things are crowded into almost every hour that there is neither time nor room for imagination. I have had a big field since 15 August. The great retreat was great indeed, but the close shave of the army in Belgium and France has yet to be written up, Our men were often dead beat, and I honestly think that no army in the world could equal the performance at the time. Even men on horseback were absolutely 'diddled', and while asleep in the saddle I saw visions which no one, I believe, even has seen yet nor shall see. I was not afraid, but I was four days and nights without a wink of sleep. Haystacks walked along with me – owners' cottages became a foggy castle in the moonlight; trees walked, and Uhlans closed in on every side.' Continuing his narrative, Father Forest, refers to the Marne and the Aisne encounter, and goes on to say there was plenty to do with only one priest for 25,000 men of the 4th Division.

'Now we have a fairly full staff,' the letter proceeds, 'one English Jesuit, and two Irish priests for the Irish regiments. We have had great cold, with a corresponding cost of ice, in spite of frost preparations with my horse I had a spill a few days ago; result, a synovitis knee, with no bones broken. I am billeted for the present with an Abbe, and in spite of his knowledge of wireless, of which he had two installations before the war. This Abbe is hospitality itself, and while I am with him nothing is good enough for me.'

WE,12-1914

Reverend Chaplain William Forrest survived the war.

Mullingar Man Home From The War
The Irish Guards At Home
Thrilling Account of the Fighting at Mons and Ypres

Private John Scally, Military Road, Mullingar, who belongs to the Irish Guards, is at present home from the front, having been wounded by shrapnel in the leg at the battle of Ypres. On Wednesday morning our representative had an interview with Private Scally relative to his experiences at the front. He got wounded in the leg by shrapnel on the second day of the battle of Ypres and he is making very favourable progress towards recovery. He stated that he went through several engagements at various places and took part in open fighting. His regiment went into action first in the retreat from Mons. To the Guards was assigned the heavy work of covering the retreat of the main army in the retirement from Mons. They were immensely outnumbered and exposed to a heavy fire from the enemy. Private Scally got safe through it and though several subsequent engagements and outpost fighting. The country he says is very wooded, and this favours the Germans who, he says delight in warfare in wood and under cover. They hate to come into the open. He described the trench fighting. He says they make the trenches as comfortable as possible by going to farm yards for straw at night and littering the bottom of the trenches with it. The weather was fairly good up to the first of October, when rain set in. The winter is severe, heavy falls of rain being followed by morning frost and then another teem. The fighting at Ypres he said was very heavy. Here the Germans concentrated dense masses and were determined to break through by sheer force of numbers. The battle proper of Ypres opened on Sunday. The Germans came on in great force. 'We opened our ranks,' continued Private Scally, 'as if to let them pass through. Some of them did pass through and beyond our line, but ran into the mouth of the artillery. The artillery opened on them with deadly effect and they were mowed down in great numbers.' Private Scally added that they suffered terribly in the repulse.

The Germans were in a wood, near Ypres, and the Guards were ordered to clear the wood. In doing so they had to run across the open, during which they were exposed to a heavy fire. They succeeded, however, in taking the wood, and the Germans retreated to a hill about two hundred yards away. Here they entrenched themselves. The Guards proceeded to take the trenches, but in going across the open they were exposed to a heavy fire. The Germans were in greater numbers than they expected, and the Guards took shelter behind a low hedge. When they found the range, they shelled them. He says the Germans do a great deal of sniping. Under cover of darkness they go out into turnip fields and remain in shelter of the turnip leaves. Immediately anyone appears above the trenches he is taken down by a sniper, and it is impossible to locate them. He says the German favourite time for attack is between ten and twelve o'clock at night. Our favourite time for attack,' he said, 'is about an hour before daybreak, when the Germans are drowsy and unprepared.' Asked when the fighting ceases at night and starts again, he said it varies very much. Usually it ceases a short time after nightfall and starts again at daybreak, but very often it continues all night. Then again it ceases at nightfall, and sometimes the enemy makes a sudden night attack with the object of surprising them, so they have to be constantly on the alert. Private Scally expects to be going back again when his wound is quite well.   MR, WN, 12-1914

Private Scally, survived the war.

Gallant Mayo Man
Decorated and promoted
How the Connaughts Fought and Suffered

To a representative of the *Herald*, Sergeant Major Bruen, 2nd Battalion Connaught Rangers, who has been promoted to the rank of lieutenant for distinguished gallantry on the field, has given an interesting account of experiences on the battlefield. Lieutenant Bruen has also been awarded the decoration *Medalie Militaire*, by the French President.

He bears marked evidence of the unerring aim of the German sniper, and is a living proof that not all Germans are bad shots, for, as he says, 'I saw the man take aim at me. He had the advantage over me for he was laid flat on the ground, and I was standing, I fired myself, but he eventually got there before me'.

The First Real Fight

It was impossible to get Lieutenant Bruen to speak of his own deeds. I was able to get from him a vivid description of what happened on that famous September 14th, which turned out for the Connaughts so disastrously, and et won for them so much renown and glory. September 14th is so impressed indelibly on his mind, and, as he told me the story, he seemed to live that day over again – and can one wonder.

He related how they were in the Fifth Infantry Brigade, which formed part of the second Division. They were early on the scene of fighting, and the subsequent advance march, the whole particulars of which we are all now conversant with.

'It was not until 14 September,' he said, 'we had what I call a real genuine fight.'

It was shortly after contesting the passage of a river, which they succeeded in crossing and entering a village, where they took up a position on a farm, that they were attacked by the 35th German Infantry Regiment.

Colonel Abercrombie, who was in command of the regiment at the start, had been captured in a rearguard action, when, to save the while regiment, he, with a few men, determined to stick it out and keep back the Germans who were attacking in overwhelming numbers. It can thus be said that he sacrificed himself for his regiment.

Sarsfield and Others

On this memorable day, 14 September at Soupres, however, Major Sarsfield, was in command, and was dangerously wounded. He afterwards died.

Lieutenant Lentaigue (son of Sir John Lentaigue, of Dublin), Lieutenant Frazer, Lieutenant Thomas (who had previously been mentioned in despatches), Lieutenant Spreckley (who had also been mentioned on despatches) were also killed.

Major Hutchinson, DSO; Captain C.L.O'Sullivan, and Lieutenant Swift were all wounded.

Lieutenant Bruen goes on to tell how Lieutenant Spreckley came in three times to have his wounds dressed. The last time he hopped out with the aid of an old stick that he picked up, and was killed, but he performed deeds of valour on that day that were never excelled on any battlefield.

Company Quartermaster Sergeant Galvin, who was a recognised crack shot, took up position within 30 yards of the gate, through which the Germans were pouring like sheep, and the Germans were kept too busy with the remainder of the Connaughts to spot him. He worked terrible havoc in that gateway, for it was piled up with dead. A stray bullet eventually found a billet in QMS Galvin's body and he has now returned wounded.

The Connaughts Losses
Captain C.J. O'Sullivan, was commanding on the left of the farm, using a rifle and giving his orders as if in the barrack square. Twice he was struck with a bullet, but still he kept his command and it was the third bullet, as in the case of Lieutenant Spreckley, that put him out of action. The Germans continued to receive reinforcements, but they had to eventually retire.

The Connaughts casualties were 270 killed and wounded (including officers), and a big number missing (taken prisoners).

They themselves took 260 German prisoners and treated in hospital over 300 wounded Germans. It was impossible to count the dead, for they were lying in heaps and the Connaughts amply avenged their comrades. The German prisoners could not realise how the Connaughts had escaped annihilation. They had known the strength of the regiment, and thought it was impossible for them to escape the terrible onslaught they made with the vast superiority in numbers. Major Sarsfield was fine type of a soldier and his death was felt keenly by every man in the regiment. He was a Cork man, and his wife now resides there.

Prize for Prisoners
Lieutenant Bruen, told me a story about Captain C.J. O'Sullivan that is worth repeating. It was in the early part of the war, and he was complaining that his company had not brought in a single prisoner while other companies were boasting of having done so. Very shortly after in came a couple of men, one leading a fine horse, the other in charge of a very fine specimen of a Uhlan. Both claimed to have captured the prisoner. They offered to fight for it but he settled the question amiably to the satisfaction of the disputers.

Lieutenant Bruen is a Castlebar (Mayo) man. He would not tell me anything about his deeds, but I had previously learned from one of his comrades how he was wounded at Soupier, but 'fought on', how on several occasions he received special mention by his officers for the manoeuvring of his men in action and keeping them together when their position seemed hopeless, and how at a place called Passchendale, in the vicinity north west of Ypres, he was severely wounded and left for dead (on the 26th October) in a beetroot field, and was afterward found by his comrades.

Many of the officers mentioned by Lieutenant Brown, notably Major Sarsfield, will be remembered in Athlone, Boyle and Galway, where they served for many years with the Connaughts.   WE, 12-1914

Sergeant Major William Bruen, Major Hugh Moore Hutchinson, Captain C J O'Sullivan, and Company Quartermaster Sergeant Galvin, survived the war. Lieutenant Colonel Alexander William Abercrombie was killed in action in November, 1914 and buried in Berlin South Western Cemetery, Germany. 48 years old Major William Stopford Sarsfield, a Cork man, died of wounds in September, 1914 and buried in Vailly British Cemetery in France. 48 year old Second Lieutenant Victor Aloysius Lentaigne, a Dublin man, was killed in action. He has no known grave and listed on the La Ferte-Sous-Jouarre-Memorial in France. 29 year old Roscommon officer, Lieutenant John Irwin Frazer (Fraser), was killed in action, he has no known grave and listed on Ploegsteert Memorial in Belgium. 21 year old Lieutenant Ralph Lessingham Spreckley, from Worcestershire won the Military Cross in the first 4 weeks of the war was killed in September, 1914. He has no known grave but is listed on the special memorial in Vailly British Cemetery in France. Corkman Second Lieutenant Henry Meade Swifte, survived the war. Captain C J O'Sullivan, was promoted to Major and survived the war.

Connaughts To The Rescue

The dawn just tinged the Estern sky
With a faint but roseate hue,
Lighting up that battlefield
Where dead lay thick as dew.
Peace, a moment, reigned around—
No warlike sounds arose
To point to where lay waiting
Those hosts of sworn foes.

The reign of Peace was brief, alas!
Up from their trenches came
Hosts of dusky warriors
Swarming o'er the plain.
To drive the foe by quick surprise
From the ground whereon he lay;
And make themselves the victors
Ere morn had passed away.

Before their journey was half sped.
The red artillery flashed;
And swarms of furious Germans
Down upon them crashed,
With rifle butt and bayonet
The deadly strife went on;
And soon remained a blood red field
To greet the rising dawn.

The fight raged fast and furious—
The Indians backward fell;
Huge rushes on their weakened ranks
At last began to tell.
Artillery raged around them
And rifle bullets flew
As downward in their trenches
The Indian fighters drew.

Dark was now the prospect
For the dusky warrior band.
Huge masses of the foemen
Swarmed up on ev'ry hand.
But rising over the all the din
Their broke upon the ears;
A ringing "fag-an-bealach"—
The Connaught Rangers cheers.

Down upon the enemy
The Irish bayonets bore
And many a gallant soldier
Fell to rise no more.
The German now rushed up his men
The Irishmen to meet,
And by sheer weight of numbers
Forced them to retreat.

It was only to reform
The Rangers backward drew-
To come again determined thento either die or do.
And o'er that field where bullets flew,
Thick as falling rain—
The gallant Connaught Rangers
Charged and charged again.

Yet still those close massed columns.
Stout as iron wall
Caused the hard-pressed Irishmen
Once more to rearward fall;
But not until in thousands
The enemy lay dead
And birds of prey, expectant
Were circling over head.

Tho' twice they failed to conquer
No fear was in their hearts—
Those soldiers true once more lined up
The Indians taking part.
And o'er that blood-stained field they rushed
A wave of bristling steel
That caused the stubborn enemy
At last to backward reel.

Three cheers the fearless Rangers gave;
At length they won the day,
Tho' many a well-loved comrade
Had fallen in the fray
But yet it was a victory
Which shall live in martial story—
How the Connaught Rangers fought and won
That fight for England's glory.

Here's to the Connaught Rangers
Who've fought with might and main!
May they keep their old flag flying
Free from dishonour's stain;
May each heart beat true to Ireland,
While sharing England's danger—
May Ireland's three leaved shamrock be
The badge of each Connaught Ranger.
J.G.

WI, 12-1914

Back from the Front
Experiences of Waterfordmen

Private Thomas Clemens, of the 2nd Royal Irish Regiment, arrived here in Waterford this week after nearly three months at the front. He left on August 6th with a batch of 150 to join his regiment and landed at St

Nazaire. Theye were joined on leaving the latter place by men of the Devons, Lincolns, Middlesex, and the Gordons.

The marched generally about twenty-five miles a day and had several minor touches with the enemy at Blaine and Vailly. At Blaine Quartermaster Sergeant Thomas Croke, a Ballybricken man was wounded, and, Clemens thinks, was afterwards taken prisoner. Jeremiah Aspel, another Waterford man, was also wounded there and is now in a convalescent home outside Glasgow. From Blaine they marched to Nantes where the Royal Irish did good work, losing very heavily. The principal engagement Clemens took part in was at Bethune and there he received a wound in the arm. He lay wounded from four o'clock in the evening until two o'clock next morning when he managed to reach a field hospital. Clemens is an old soldier with over twenty years service. He fought in the South African Campaign with the 5th Hussars.

Curios from the Battlefield

Amongst a collection of curios which Clemens took home from the front are the epaulet of a Death's Head Hussar, and a good service medal and ribbon of the French Army. He had in his possession also a French journal in which the following description of the battle of Mons appeared:

'The Royal Irish Regiment had an awful smashing earlier on, and also had the Middlesex, and our company were ordered to go along the road as re-inforcements. The one and a half miles seemed a thousand. When we got to the Royal Irish Regiment's trenches the scene was terrible. They were having dinner when the Germans opened up on them, and their dead and wounded were laying all around. We kept up this sort of game (fighting by day and retiring by night) until we got to Cambrai on Thursday night. I dare not mention that place and close my eyes. God, it was awful. Avalanche followed avalanche of fresh German troops, but the boys stuck to it, and we managed to retire to Ham without molestation. Cambrai was the biggest battle fought. Out of all the glorious regiment of 1,100 men only five officers and 170 of the men answered the roll-call next day.'   WN, UNKNOWN MONTH, 1914

Thomas Clemens, unfindable, perhaps the name is mis-spelt, Quartermaster Sergeant Thomas Croke survived the war. Private Jeremiah Aspell, died in Salonika in March, 1918 and buried in Salonika (Lembet Road) Military Cemetery in Greece.

Carrickman's Experience in the Royal Engineers

Mr James O'Donnell, Main Street, Carrick-on-Suir, who had been just ten months a Sapper in the Royal Engineers when the war broke out, and who was at the front from 18 August to 14 September, has just returned to Carrick suffering from the effects of a bullet in the arm and from rheumatism contracted in the course of his work in making trenches and constructing pontoon bridges, etc.

Mr O'Donnell is a very intelligent and modest and retiring young man. A couple of days ago he gave our Carrick-on-Suir correspondent some interesting details of the work of the Engineers in the war, and the dangers they had to encounter, although they are not actual combatants. Mr O'Donnell, left England for the front 15 August and arrived at Rouen, in France, on the 20th. From Rouen they marched to Wesseigne, and arrived before Mons on the 23rd. They were sent at midnight to make trenches for the regiments of the brigade to which the Engineers were attached—viz., the Highland Light Infantry, Connaught Rangers, Berkshires, and the Irish Guards. During the retreat from Mons they were constantly engaged blowing up bridges, digging trenches, and constructing pontoon bridges over their work ad they were repeatedly shelled by the Germans, and so fierce was the shelling at times that they were obliged to temporarily abandon their work.

Mr O'Donnell witnesses some fierce fighting by the regiments to which his company was attached. In spite of their bravery and disregard for danger, the German heavy artillery proved too much for them and wrought terrible havoc amongst them, especially among the Connaught Rangers and the Highland Light Infantry. The Irish Guards and the Berkshires also suffered heavy losses.

During the retreat from Mons Mr O'Donnell had several miraculous escapes from death by German shells, which fell around them like hailstones, now bursting and doing very little damage, and anon laying many a poor fellow low.

On 14 September at Ventrileuil, his company and brigade with which they were working had a terrible time from the German shells. Few escaped injuries of some kind, and many a one had there his last glimpse of France when one exploded within a few feet of where he lay. The shrapnel bullets flew in all directions. One of them grazed Mr O'Donnell's cheek, passed through the collar of his coat, and through a pocket-book he carried in his breast pocket. A man who lay beside him had his leg shattered and his rifle smashed by the same shell. Very soon after this narrow escape, Mr O'Donnell received the bullet wound in the arm. He was removed to a temporary hospital, which, he was informed, was before the war the country residence of Madame Cailleux, who figured prominently in a recent sensational trial in Paris.

Whilst in hospital he and other wounded soldiers were visited by Sir John French, who chatted gaily with them on their adventures and expressed the hope that they would soon be quite fit and well.

When making trenches for the Irish Guards near Mons, Mr O'Donnell met a fellow Carrickman and school-fellow – Mr Michael O'Meara, of Ballynagrana, Carrick-on-Suir, who is in the Irish Guards and has been at the front almost since the war began.

SCOTLAND AND HUDSON'S FOR EVER!!

 HUDSON'S Soap makes Linen as fresh and as fragrant as the breezes which blow from the hills. Its reputation for wholesome cleaning might even be said to be AS OLD AS THE HILLS. Certain is it that Hudson's Soap has been the daily maintainer of cleanliness for generations.

Hudson's Soap is universal in its uses. A little shaken into the wash tub makes the dirt slip away from the clothes—A little shaken on to the scrubbing brush ensures the whitest of white tables and floors—A little shaken into the "Washing Up" bowl makes an ever recurring task a sure and simple pleasure. Hudson's Soap gives lustre to Chinaware and Glassware, and destroys the greasiness often associated with Washing Up after meals.

IN PACKETS EVERYWHERE.

R. S. HUDSON LIMITED, LIVERPOOL, WEST BROMWICH AND LONDON.

Mr O'Donnell says the German heavy artillery is the most effective part of their war machine. They send their shells with deadly precision and without a minute's interval. The shelling usually follows the visit of a few German aeroplanes. Mr O'Donnell was most enthusiastic in his praise of the marvellous heroism of the French and Belgian Priests and also in their spiritual capacity on the battlefield. They exhibit an utter disregard for death or danger, and are to be seen everywhere that men fall – succouring the wounded and preparing the dying to face judgement, and uttering a prayer for the repose of the souls of those who have gone to be judged and who will never again be troubled by shrapnel or steel. Many of the priests wear their surplices and stoles on the battlefield.

The soldiers take great interest watching the German shells fired from a distance at night time. They present a weirdly beautiful sight as they pierce the darkness in a long red line. The working of the German searchlights at night is another very interesting sight.

Mr O'Donnell gave some interesting details of life in the trenches for several days and nights, sleeping and eating in them, and always in danger from shrapnel and rifle bullets. Officers and rank and file share the same comforts or discomforts in the trenches. The food supplied was on the whole very good, and, considering the difficulties to be encountered in preparing it, it was well and regularly served.

WN, UNKNOWN MONTH, 1914

There is a James O'Donnell, Royal Irish Regiment born in Templemore who was killed in action two weeks before the war ended, it may be him. Buried in Cross Roads Cemetery, Fontaine-Au-Bois in France. Michael O'Meara survived the war.

The Twenty-Seven
Newspapers
1914

The Saturday Record
and
Clare Journal

(CJ) *Clare Journal*, Microfiche, Clare Library, Ennis, County Clare. Excellent content and reportage of the war.Some references also to soldiers in neighbouring counties – Tipperary, Waterford, Limerick, Kerry and Galway. Like most of the Great War newspapers reporting on the war and recording local casualties dwindled dramatically after the rebellion in April, 1916.

(CS) *Carlow Sentinel*, Microfiche, Carlow Central Library, Tullow Street, County Carlow. Period newspaper covering the county for the war period. Some references also to soldiers in neighbouring counties – Kilkenny, Laois (Queen's County), Kildare, Wicklow and Wexford. Like most of the Great War newspapers reporting on the war and recording local casualties dwindled dramatically after the rebellion in April, 1916.

Dungarvan Observer
AND
MUNSTER INDUSTRIAL ADVOCATE

(DO) *Dungarvan Observer*, Dungarvan Central Library, County Waterford. Period newspaper covering Dungarvan and surrounds for the war period. Like most of the Great War newspapers reporting on the war and recording local casualties dwindled dramatically after the rebellion in April, 1916.

THE ENNISCORTHY GUARDIAN.

(EG) *Enniscorthy Guardian*. Wexford based newspaper, Microfiche. Wexford Library, Mallin Street, Wexrford Town. Some references also to soldiers in neighbouring counties- Wicklow, Waterford, and Carlow. Like most of the Great War newspapers reporting on the war and recording local casualties dwindled dramatically after the rebellion in April, 1916.

King's County Chronicle

(KCC) *King's County Chronicle*, (Ended publication in 1921 and is recorded as the 'The Offaly Chronicle' in 1924) Microfiche, Local Studies, Offaly Library, Cormac Street, Tullamore. Also available in the Library, Birr, County Offaly. Some references also to soldiers in neighbouring counties-Galway, Westmeath, Laois (Queen's County), Kildare, Tipperary, Waterford and Carlow. With The King's County Independent these two newspapers were the best for this project. They had many rolls of honour, casualty lists, short individual items on local casualties and the best selection of War-time general interest items. Like most of the Great War newspapers reporting on the war and recording local casualties dwindled dramatically after the rebellion in April, 1916.

KING'S CO. INDEPENDENT AUGUST 29, 1914—2

(KCI) *King's County Independent*. Became obsolete, unknown year. Microfiche, Local Studies, Offaly Library, Cormac Street, Tullamore. Also available in the Library, Birr, County Offaly. Some references also to soldiers in neighbouring counties – Galway, Westmeath, Laois (Queen's County), Kildare, Tipperary, Waterford and Carlow. With The King's County Chrinicle, these two newspapers were the best for this project. They had many rolls of honour, casualty lists, short individual items on local casualties and the best selection of War-time general interest items. Like most of the Great War newspapers reporting on the war and recording local casualties dwindled dramatically after the rebellion in April, 1916.

(KP) Kilkenny People, Microfiche, Local Studies, County Council Offices, John's Green, Kilkenny. Period newspaper covering the county for the war period. Some references also to soldiers in neighbouring counties – Tipperary, Waterford, Laois (Queen's County), Wexford and Carlow. Like most of the Great War newspapers reporting on the war and recording local casualties dwindled dramatically after the rebellion in April, 1916.

The Limerick Chronicle

ESTABLISHED 1766   148th YEAR OF PUBLICATION.

(LC) *Limerick Chronicle*, Microfiche. Established 1766. Local Studies, Limerick City Library, County Limerick. Excellent content and reportage of the war. Some references also to soldiers in neighbouring counties – Clare, Tipperary, Waterford, Kerry. Like most of the Great War newspapers reporting on the war and recording local casualties dwindled dramatically after the rebellion in April, 1916.

(LL) *Limerick Leader*, Microfiche, Local Studies, Limerick City Library, County Limerick. 'Circulating in the City and counties of Limerick, Clare, Tipperary, Cork, Kerry and Galway'. Some references also to soldiers in neighbouring counties – Clare, Tipperary, Waterford, Kerry. Excellent content and reportage of the war, and like most of the Great War newspapers reporting on the war and recording local casualties dwindled dramatically after the rebellion in April, 1916.

The Munster Express

And The Celt.

(ME) *Munster Express*, Microfiche, 1894-1920. Waterford City Library, Waterford. Excellent content and reportage of the war. Some references also to soldiers in neighbouring counties – Clare, Tipperary, Waterford, Kerry, Cork, Kilkenny and even Limerick. Like most of the Great War newspapers reporting on the war and recording local casualties dwindled dramatically after the rebellion in April, 1916.

(MR, WN) *Midland Reporter and Westmeath Nationalist*, Mullingar, Microfiche. Excellent content and reportage of the war. Some references also to soldiers in neighbouring counties – Roscommon, Longford, Meath, Kildare and Offaly. Like most of the Great War newspapers reporting on the war and recording local casualties dwindled dramatically after the rebellion in April, 1916.

The Midland Tribune

TIPPERARY SENTINEL AND KING'S COUNTY VINDICATOR.

(MT- TS-KCV) *Midland Tribune*, Tipperary Sentinel and King's County Vindicator. 1881 to date, Microfiche. Local Studies, Offaly Library, Cormac Street, Tullamore. Also available in the Library, Birr, County Offaly. Midlands newspaper covering most of Munster and Leinster. Like most of the Great War newspapers reporting on the war and recording local casualties dwindled dramatically after the rebellion in April, 1916.

The Nenagh Guardian

OR, TIPPERARY (NORTH RIDING) AND ORMOND ADVERTISER.

(NG) *Nenagh Guardian,* Microfiche. Local Studies, The Source Library and Arts Centre, Thurles, County Tipperary. Some references also to soldiers in neighbouring counties – Laois (Queen's County), Kilkenny, Clare, Limerick, Waterford and Carlow. Like most of the Great War newspapers reporting on the war and recording local casualties dwindled dramatically after the rebellion in April, 1916.

The Nationalist

AND LEINSTER TIMES.

(NLT) *Nationalist and Leinster Times*, 1885-Present, Microfiche. Carlow Central Library, Tullow Street, County Carlow. Carlow based newspaper covering the county. Some references also to soldiers in neighbouring counties – Kilkenny, Laois (Queen's County), Kildare, Wicklow and Wexford. Like most of the Great War newspapers reporting on the war and recording local casualties dwindled dramatically after the rebellion in April, 1916.

THE TIPPERARY STAR
AND MIDLAND ADVERTISER

(TS) Tipperary Star, 1909 to present, Microfiche and hard copy. Local Studies, The Source Library and Arts Centre, Thurles, County Tipperary. Some references also to soldiers in neighbouring counties- Laois (Queen's County), Kilkenny, Clare, Limerick, Waterford and Carlow. Like most of the Great War newspapers reporting on the war and recording local casualties dwindled dramatically after the rebellion in April, 1916.

(WE) *Westmeath Examiner*, Mullingar, Microfiche. Mullingar Library, County Buildings, Mount Street, Mullingar, County Westmeath. One of two major Westmeath newspapers, the other being The Westmeath Independent, printed in Athlone. Excellent content and reportage of the war. Some references also to soldiers in neighbouring counties – Roscommon, Longford, Meath, Kildare and Offaly. Like most of the Great War newspapers reporting on the war and recording local casualties dwindled dramatically after the rebellion in April, 1916.

(WI) *Westmeath Independent*, Athlone. Microfiche. Aiden Heavey Public Library, Athlone Civic Centre, Athlone, County Westmeath. One of two major Westmeath newspapers, the other being The Westmeath Examiner, printed in Mullingar. Excellent content and reportage of the war. Some references also to soldiers in neighbouring counties – Roscommon, Longford, Meath, Kildare and Offaly. Like most of the Great War newspapers reporting on the war and recording local casualties dwindled dramatically after the rebellion in April, 1916.

(WN) *Waterford News*, Microfiche, Waterford City Library, Waterford. Excellent content and reportage of the war. Some references also to soldiers in neighbouring counties – Clare, Tipperary, Waterford, Kerry, Cork, Kilkenny and even Limerick. Like most of the Great War newspapers reporting on the war and recording local casualties dwindled dramatically after the rebellion in April, 1916.

THE KILKENNY JOURNAL,

(KJ) *Kilkenny Journal*, 1915 only. Microfiche, Local Studies, County Council Offices, John's Green, Kilkenny. Period newspaper covering the county for the war period. Some references also to soldiers in neighbouring counties – Tipperary, Waterford, Laois (Queen's County), Wexford and Carlow. Like most of the Great War newspapers reporting on the war and recording local casualties dwindled dramatically after the rebellion in April, 1916.

(LE) *Leinster Express*, Laois County Library, Portlaoise. Excellent content and reportage of the war. Some references also to soldiers in neighbouring counties – Offaly, Kildare, Kilkenny, Tipperary and Carlow. Like most of the Great War newspapers reporting on the war and recording local casualties dwindled dramatically after the rebellion in April, 1916.

THE ECHO,

(TE) *The Echo*, Wexford based newspaper, Microfiche. Wexford Library, Mallin Street, Wexrford Town. Some references also to soldiers in neighbouring counties – Wicklow, Waterford, and Carlow. Like most of the Great War newspapers reporting on the war and recording local casualties dwindled dramatically after the rebellion in April, 1916.

THE FREE PRESS.

(FP) *The Free Press*. Wexford based newspaper, Microfiche. Wexford Library, Mallin Street, Wexrford Town. Some references also to soldiers in neighbouring counties – Wicklow, Waterford, and Carlow. Like most of the Great War newspapers reporting on the war and recording local casualties dwindled dramatically after the rebellion in April, 1916.

THE NATIONALIST

AND MUNSTER ADVERTISER

(TN) The Nationalist, based in Clonmel, County Tipperary.1899 to present, Microfiche and hard copy. Local Studies, The Source Library and Arts Centre, Thurles, County Tipperary. Covers 'Kildare, Queen's and King's Counties (Laois and Offaly), Wicklow, Dublin, and Midland Mercantile Agricultural counties'. It continues to be published and is most popular in South Tipperary. Like most of the Great War newspapers reporting on the war and recording local casualties dwindled dramatically after the rebellion in April, 1916.

THE PEOPLE.

(TP) *The People,* Wexford based newspaper, Microfiche. Wexford Library, Mallin Street, Wexford Town. Some references also to soldiers in neighbouring counties-Wicklow, Waterford, and Carlow. Like most of the Great War newspapers reporting on the war and recording local casualties dwindled dramatically after the rebellion in April, 1916.

THE WICKLOW PEOPLE

(WP) *The Wicklow People,* Hard copy only. Bray Public Library, Eglinton Road, Bray, County Wicklow. The hard copy of this newspaper is in a sad state. May disintegrate in the near future. Some references also to soldiers in neighbouring counties – Wexford, Dublin, Kildare and Carlow. Like most of the Great War newspapers reporting on the war and recording local casualties dwindled dramatically after the rebellion in April, 1916.

THE TIPPERARY PEOPLE, FRIDAY EVENING,

(TP) *Tipperary People,* 1906 to 1918, Only 1918 was available. Microfiche. Local Studies, The Source Library and Arts Centre, Thurles, County Tipperary. General war news and items on local Tipperary military personnel. Like most of the Great War newspapers reporting on the war and recording local casualties dwindled dramatically after the rebellion in April, 1916.

People and Places Index

238

A

B